NOPE, NOTHING WRONG HERE:
The Making of *Cujo*

Written and Edited
by Lee Gambin

BearManor
Media

Albany, Georgia

Published in the USA by
BearManor Media
P.O. Box 71426
Albany, GA 31708
www.BearManorMedia.com

Softcover Edition
ISBN-10: 1-62933-134-1
ISBN-13: 978-1-62933-134-8

Printed in the United States of America

To Buddy

...and to all dogs, be they ladies or tramps...or Cujos...

The following people have contributed to this book:

(and I wish to thank each and every one of them)...

CAST:

Dee Wallace – Donna Trenton
Danny Pintauro – Tad Trenton
Daniel Hugh Kelly –Vic Trenton (credited as Daniel Hugh-Kelly)
Arthur Rosenberg – Roger Breakstone
Jerry Hardin – Detective Masen
Terry Donovan-Smith – Harry
Robert Craighead – Joe MaGruder (uncredited – deleted scene)

CREW:

Lewis Teague – director
Don Carlos Dunaway – co-screenwriter
Marcia Ross – casting director (credited as Marcia S. Ross)
Alexander Witt – assistant camera
Vern Nobles – second assistant camera
Robin Luce – makeup (credited as Robin Neal)
Nancy G. Fox – costumes
Michael Hilkene – sound (supervising sound editor)
Mark Ulano – sound (sound mixer)
Patrushkha Mierzwa – sound (boom mic operator)
Ian Kincaid – lighting (lamp operator)
Charles Bernstein – composer
Robert Clark – SFX (prosthetic dogs)
Kathie Clark – SFX (prosthetic dogs and creator of dog suit)
Christopher Medak – production manager
Gary Morgan – stunt man (man in dog suit)
Jean Coulter – stunt woman (Dee Wallace double – credited as Jeannie Coulter)
Conrad E. Palmisano – stunt coordinator

ADDITIONAL INTERVIEWEES:

Teresa Ann Miller – daughter of animal trainer Karl Lewis Miller
Peter Medak – originally assigned director
Tony Richmond – originally assigned cinematographer
Mina Badie – daughter of Barbara Turner (screenwriter)
Margaret Pintauro – Danny Pintauro's mother
John Pintauro – Danny Pintauro's father
John Sayles – screenwriter of Lewis Teague's *Alligator* (1980)
Hope Alexander-Willis – star of *The Pack* (1977) (dogs trained by Karl Lewis Miller)

Thank you to "Fireball" Tim Lawrence, Aine Lecht, Alexandra Heller-Nicholas, Anthony Smith, Antony Botheras, Ariel Levy, Barry Pearl, Ben Ohmart, Camilla Jackson, Chris Alexander, Chris Hallock, the Cinemaniacs team, Craig Anderson, Darren Cotzabuyucas, Dean Brandum, Gale Adler, Jason Sechrest. Jay Fosgitt, Jennifer Jason Leigh, Jerry Grandey, Joe Zaso, Johanna Greenway, John Klyza, Judy Rich, Kelli Thompson, Kim Rebecca Gottlieb-Walker, Lisa Bartolomei, Mark Goldblatt, Marsha de Fillipo, Michael Broom, Mick Garris, Penney Riches, Richard Osborne, Robert Tanenbaum, Rob Taylor, Robin Salter, Sally Christie, Stephen King and Therese Martschinke.

A very special thank you to the wonderful Justine Ryan, who is a devoted fan and perpetual great help (so much time saved because of her devotion to film history), and a massive thank you to Adam Dallas, who offered his eyes – fresh and uninterrupted.

"Cujo" painting by Michael Broom and cover design by Darren Cotzabuyucas.

CONTENTS

Animal trainer Karl Lewis Miller and "Daddy", one of the St. Bernards that got to play the titular rabid canine.

DESMODONTINAE DAYS: Opening titles, Cujo chases a rabbit and is bitten by a rabid bat and a change in direction

Following the production company's credit and the first ever time star Dee Wallace would have her name feature before the title, we bear witness to a spiralling bloody vortex that seems to be concentrated blood forming the name "Cujo". The linguistic origin of the name of Cujo seems to not be in the Spanish-English dialect, however, there are pop-cultural links to the moniker and one that primarily stands out and supposedly drew inspiration. According to some sources, novelist Stephen King based the name "Cujo" on the *nom de guerre* of Willie Wolfe, one of the radical activists and members of the leftist terrorist group the Symbionese Army who orchestrated the kidnapping and indoctrination of Patty Hearst. Another circulating rumour about the name "Cujo" which did make an appearance on various VHS releases of the film during the eighties (such as the Australian Roadshow release) was that it was supposedly a Native American Indian term for "unstoppable force" – although, this is an untruth and in reality, King came up with the name whilst mapping out the plot which had connective narrative tissue to his recently published novel "The Dead Zone".

The bloody vortex taking shape as the film's title card helps set up the fact that this is most certainly a horror movie.

Along with the vortex of blood taking form comes composer Charles Bernstein's magnificent piece of music entitled "Cujo's Theme", which is a seven note menace fuelled trumpeting by French horns. Interestingly enough, this dark and foreboding opener swiftly makes way for a gradually delicate and serene composition that accompanies the opening credits which roll over an animal-centric curtain raiser. Here, the names of cast and crew fading in and out of the darkness of the entrance to a rabbit warren, through to a lush green field, to a bubbling brook and so forth, come to embody the notion of human artistry juxtaposed with animal interaction, play, chase, survival, descent and victimization. Much like Dee Wallace's credit emerging over the spinning vortex of blood, her fellow co-stars and crew bounce off the visual tapestry that surfaces and takes form – throughout the entire opening sequence where a happy, healthy and joyous St. Bernard races after a panicky rabbit, we are witness to a mini-three act play: beginning with chase, hanging off undisputed determination and finally ending in heartbreaking tragedy. With the threatening music making way for gentle piano and elegant distant strings that will eventually flourish and come to full majestic form, the image of a

2

wide-eyed rabbit waking to a new morning is pure animal-centric cinema at its most magnetic. Here, we are entering the secret world of beasts, and much like the voyeuristic impressions left by the young teenage girls showering in their locker room in a previous Stephen King adaptation *Carrie* (1976), the audience is invited to share the clandestine existence of woodland creatures. By the time Cujo has his head stuck in the entrance to a deep, dark bat cave, the credits would have ceased, making way for plot and dramatic animal action – they will recommence over an exterior night shot of the Trenton household opening with "Based on the novel by Stephen King".

The opening presented as idyllic animal-centric Disney-esque fare; here the loveable St. Bernard, Cujo enjoys chasing a rabbit in the early hours of a summer day.

The musicality of this sequence is outstanding. The entire scene is scored and from this dynamic, rich and complex orchestration, perfectly summarises mood, situation and the character of each of the animals working – the St. Bernard, the rabbit and the bats. Light piano is offered as we pull back from the warren hole to say "hello" to the rabbit, while strings whimsically play as the curious bunny explores the new dawn giving a palpable sense of early moments and the rationale of awakening to a new day. This brand new stretch of a new morning is what guides us through the sequence as frivolity becomes a living nightmare.

On Cujo's first appearance we hear the threatening theme from the title card, but once again that musical shift from monstrous to whimsical comes into play as the image of Cujo is revealed – and we are witness to a perfectly affable, sweet loveable big dog. St. Bernards (an extremely large breed of dog, originating from Switzerland) would forever be thought of as a heroic and valiant breed in the mind's eye of the public consciousness as they would be associated with assisting wayward humans in snow covered Alps. In popular culture, the St. Bernard would make an appearance in Disney's *Peter Pan* (1953) as Nana, the nanny dog to Wendy, Michael and John Darling. Although, the original J.M. Barrie story would feature a Newfoundland as the breed of the overly matronly dog, in the popular animated classic, the keeper of the children would be a senior St. Bernard committed to nursing and protecting her pintsize human companions. Jack London's 1903 novel "The Call of the Wild" (which would have six filmic adaptations) featured Buck, a St. Bernard cross who would be portrayed by a purebred St. Bernard in one of the cinematic interpretations. St. Bernards would go on to play buffoon (the comedy film *Beethoven* (1992) and its sequels) as well as the revered dedicated (the Swedish television series *Vi pa Saltkrakan* (1964)), but here in his novel "Cujo" (1981), horror author Stephen King deconstructs the pleasantries of the breed and turns the once loyal companion into a monstrous entity hell-bent on destruction. Similarly, what King does in "Cujo" is what he masters in his novels such as "Christine" (which would have its film adaptation released the same year as *Cujo*) in perverting America's long standing romance with the automobile.

The way cinematographer Jan de Bont's camera introduces Cujo (from underneath and through the gaze of his powerful legs) showcases his mass and his grandiose stature, towering over the rabbit and presented as a mammoth beast ready to lunge at a hapless victim. This kind of imagery

Nana, the loving St. Bernard who is the protector of the Darling children in Disney's *Peter Pan* (1953).

would be masterfully handled by director Lewis Teague who successfully and poetically composes electrifying images throughout the film that all serve the presence and omnipresence of this St. Bernard. Cujo is an incredibly well concocted character – he is an iconic cinematic dog that owns every single scene that he is in. Even here, in this Disney-esque curtain raiser, Cujo demands attention; it is a dynamic performance that captures the magic of bestial brilliance on screen. As the music flourishes into an elegant and melodic motif, Lewis Teague with the help of his maestros Jan de Bont and editor Neil Travis deliver an acute playfulness in the rabbit chase. Matching the soaring strings as helmed by Charles Bernstein, comes a breathtaking vision of the beautiful majesty of nature, this "paragon of animals" as Shakespeare once noted. *Cujo* is a film that comes from a long line of glorious dog-centric movies such as *The Biscuit Eater* (1940), *Banjo* (1947), *The Proud Rebel* (1958) and its most clear ancestor, *Old Yeller* (1957) which ultimately deals with a good dog who sadly falls victim to rabies. This heartbreaking element in both films enlisting the devastating tragedy of such a nasty physiological disease drives the dramatic pull straight to the heart strings and hammers an overwhelming sense of unfortunate happenings at the centre of the horror. *Cujo* is ultimately a tragedy of circumstance.

***The Biscuit Eater* (1940) - a charming story about color blind children and the dog they both love, would get a Disney remake in the seventies.**

As the film begins with a rabbit exploring the meadowlands, sniffing the fresh earth and searching the grounds, we are welcomed into an eighties variant of films about animals devoid of human interruption. A film such as *Benji* (1974) uses this as a structural force in that Higgins (the terrier cross who played Benji) would command sole screen time for lengthy periods without human co-stars. Joined with his female companion,

Banjo (1947) would celebrate the devotion and love shared between a young girl and her dog and is a perfect example of criminally underrated screenwriting legend Lillie Hayward's touching writing about girls/women and their relationship with dogs.

Screenwriter Lillie Hayward would present the frontier woman (here represented by Olivia de Havilland) as a stoic figure akin to the dutiful dog in *The Proud Rebel* (1958).

Possibly everybody's first fictional introduction to the disease of rabies was found in the heartbreaking *Old Yeller* (1957); one of the most gut-wrenching tales of a boy's love for his dog.

Animal trainer and activist Frank Inn with Higgins, the dog who would be known to the world as Benji.

Benjean (the daughter of Higgins) would go on to play Benji in multiple films and TV specials. Here she is with Maltese terrier Tiffany on location in Greece for *For the Love of Benji* (1977).

a Maltese terrier named Tiffany, the dogs would own most of the on-screen activity, while humans would pepper the film to evoke tangible and conventional plot. Here in *Cujo*, this opening sequence is essentially the solitary moment of the film where animals would dominate the construct of the film (bar a tiny scene where Cujo would stroll down a dusty path, slowly losing himself to the mania of rabies) and here it would showcase Cujo as a bouncy playful St. Bernard in his prime. The film presents the chase of the rabbit as play and as something highly energetic and joyous. As aforementioned, the beginning of the picture reads like an animal-centric Disney feature – and this is intentional. In many ways, *Cujo* strikes a tonal familiarity with a horror masterwork from over a decade ago when director Roman Polanski wanted the opening sequence of *Rosemary's Baby* (1968) to look and feel like a Rock Hudson/Doris Day romantic comedy. This is something that Lewis Teague intelligently brings to the film's mood and motive – essentially, what this prologue details is the fact that Cujo is a good dog, and that terrible things will happen to corrupt that, where his affability will transform from such gentility and sweetness into something almost demonic. Allowing the audience to have a moment of ease with such sunkissed outdoor earthy fun will fundamentally set up a dropping of the guard where terror and distress can weave within the emotional crevices to manipulate the emotions and comfort levels of the spectator – and this occurs as soon as the lovely picturesque chase ends and Cujo get his head stuck in the cave entrance, only to awaken rabid bats.

The musical shift when the rabbit descends into the vampire bat infested cave will let us know that, yes, this is in fact a horror film and horrific things are going to happen. Lyrically the film is essentially a parable, a play on the mythic, but grounded within a very stoic realism. If the rabbit leaps down a cave inhabited by very sick bats, then Cujo will follow, much like Alice in Lewis Carroll's classic children's story "Alice's Adventures in Wonderland" (1865), who will follow the White Rabbit only to discover a world of topsy-turvy nonsense. In essence, Cujo experiences much of the same distortion of reality and psychological imbalance as that literary "curious and curiouser" little girl obsessed with manners does, and later, Dee Wallace's character and her son will sing a recurring song that makes mention of Alice falling down the rabbit hole. With bats symbolically representing creatures of resurrection and reincarnation in many folkloric belief systems such as the ancient Mayans as well as in Mexican culture, it is an interesting allegorical purpose drilled with the contextual reality that Cujo will now go through some slow rebirth into something deadly, ferocious and devoid of any benevolence. Bats are also a major part of horror iconography, and Cujo's violent reaction to the bat bite is an honest depiction of animals in the throes of internal attacks and fights. In supernatural horror films dealing with bats as an extension of vampirism, bites are generally welcomed with heavy sexual overtones, however here in a film outwardly rejecting any mystical element, a bite from a bat is quintessentially an act of bestial violence and an introduction to something worse. Vampire bats are presented as plague carriers in *Cujo*, and rabies as a condition explored in numerous movies such as *Old Yeller*, essentially becomes the "vampirism" of the piece, or the "demonic possession" if you were to compare Cujo to previous horror movie "monsters" such as Regan MacNeil (Linda Blair) from *The Exorcist* (1973).

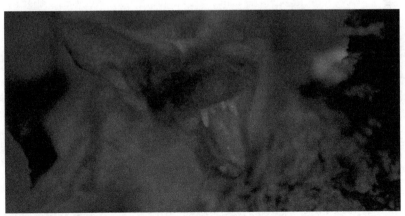

A rabid vampire bat; the cause of Cujo's descent.

Alice's fall down the rabbit hole in Disney's *Alice In Wonderland* (1951).

Visually the film uses light and dark as its obvious depictions of normalcy, complacency, the halcyon and the pleasant with decay, despair and malevolence. The countryside makes way for a dark cave devoid of any light – a descent into darkness and terror, and the scattered bones that the rabbit scurries across are distinct images of death, foreshadowing misery. Cujo is a dog wanting to play and to enjoy life; he is a hedonistic carefree animal, completely comfortable with his surroundings and soaking up the healthy environs. Here, animal trainer Karl Lewis Miller lets his dog run loose and have fun, while his trained rabbit and bats serve their purpose and do a fantastic job as well – this is animal cinema at its purist and most naturalistic; there is nothing seemingly forced in this entire sequence.

Wearing a collar, Cujo is clearly a dog owned by a nearby resident (later we learn he is the dog of mechanic Joe Camber played by Ed Lauter) and waking up the angry bats with his loud bellowing barking would gradually turn him from domesticity and push him into a nether region of carnal lust, bloodthirsty rage and psychological scarring. The image of the bats fluttering towards him and swooping onto his snout and biting is a vision of hellish torment and impending sorrow. The sequence ends with the bats hissing in extreme close-up, ushering in the world of horror – naturalistic yes, but monstrous nonetheless.

In Stephen King's draft of the screenplay, the opening would read incredibly different. His title sequence would involve the Trenton family watching family slides – an image of untroubled familial living. This ideal and typical family enjoying snapshots of their supposedly happy lives would emphasize the concocted made-up pleasantries of the domestic unit, however, the projector will freeze up making an assaultive suggestion of a glitch in the happy home; something that *Cujo* is fundamentally invested in: the breakdown of the American family. After this mundane and innocuous opening, King's script cuts to the action of Cujo chasing the rabbit, leading to him being bitten by the rabid bat. He then follows up on this with a further cut to yet another Maine household where a little girl would throw up red food colouring which would send her mother into a hysterical fit. This plot point will be underplayed in the final draft of the script by Don Carlos Dunaway, but essential in character development and story. Screenwriter Barbara Turner, who would pen the core script in between King's dismissed version and Dunaway's rewrite, would have the film open completely different again, with original director on the project Peter Medak taking cue from her writing and filming the first two scenarios. Opening with a lingering shot of Castle Rock, Maine's most busy freeway at night, Barbara Turner's screenplay had the course of action opening at a small rural cemetery where the grave of a serial killer (possibly Frank Dodd, the psychotic police officer from King's novel "The Dead Zone" which would also get its cinematic adaptation the same year) would be a focal point and bear a spiritual connection to a little boy's bedroom in a comfortable neighbourhood nearby.

Author Stephen King.

Author Stephen King signs copies of "Christine" and "Cujo" – these two horror classics would have film adaptations made the same year.

```
FADE IN ON BLACK:

BLACK

SOUND: A faint, whirring HUM -- the SOUND of the fan in
a slide projector.

                        VOICE (V.O)
              Now this first one --

A BRILLIANT SQUARE OF WHITE FILLS THE CENTER OF THE SCREEN.

SOUND: GIGGLES. A young woman and a small boy - DONNA
and TAD TRENTON.

                        VIC (V.O.)
              Whoops.

The WHITE SQUARE disappears. Blackness. Then:

                        VIC (V.O.)
              Now!

A slide of Donna APPEARS -- upside down. More giggles
from Donna and Tad.

                        VIC (V.O.)
              Damn, Donna, who loaded these?

                        TAD (V.O.)
                   (gleeful)
              Mommy! Daddy said a Bad Habit Word!

The upside down slide is removed. BLACK.

                        DONNA (V.O.)
              Sometimes daddies do say Bad Habit
              Words, Tad.
                   (to Vic)
              You loaded them!

More giggles from Tad at this. A new slide APPEARS.
Right side up this time. Vic, Donna and Tad are standing
in front of their house. To the right, in the driveway
is a small blue car -- probably a Pinto.

                        VIC (V.O.)
              There!

CREDITS ROLL as slides continue to show in a MONTAGE.
There's no other background dialogue, as if the Trentons
are watching these little freeze-frames of their life
in rapt silence. The MONTAGE shows us:
```

The original draft of Stephen King's screenplay had the film opening with the Trenton family looking over some slides – evoking the idea of a happy and functional domestic life.

a) Vic playing tennis with bearded man of about 30 --
STEVE KEMP. We see Donna and Tad in the b.g. Tad
is on the ground, playing with a toy. Donna is watching the match -- but it's Steve she's looking at, not
her husband.

b) Vic standing before a store-front in the city - "AD
WORK," the sign over the door behind him reads. He
shows great pride.

c) Vic pushing Tad (who is about four) on a backyard
swing, while Donna looks on, smiling.

d) A backyard barbecue scene. Vic in a barbecue chef's
hat and apron, turning hot dogs on the grille. Friends
with drinks standing around. Donna is looking at her
husband from a distance...and not smiling.

e) Donna and Tad running through a backyard spray in
bathing suits.

Now they come faster, half a dozen or more we just get
glimpses of: Donna in her slip, waving the picture-taker
(Vic, we presume) impatiently away; Tad in his bedroom,
lining up toy cars; Vic washing an old Jaguar -- he's
wearing a bathing suit and sunglasses. Etc.

We now seen all but the director's credit.

SCREEN GOES TO BLACK. SOUND OF THE FAN.

                    TAD (V.O.)
          I want to see my special picture,
          okay, Daddy?

                    VIC (V.O.)
          I was just lookin' for it, Tadder --
          there's so many...I hope I didn't
          lose it...

                    TAD (V.O.)
                 (agonized)
          Daddy -- !

                    DONNA (V.O.)
                 (sharp)
          Don't tease him, Vic!

                    VIC (V.O.)
          I'm not...oh yeah, here it is.

SOUND of the new slide being loaded.

                    TAD (V.O.)
          The special picture! Me and the
          doggy! All right! All right!

INT.   BAT'S FACE - EXTREME CLOSEUP - DAY

Horrid, evil, rat-like countenance. The mouth yawns,
showing those sharp teeth. Saliva courses out of its
mouth. It HISSES.

EXT.   CUJO ON THE BANK OF THE CREEK - DAY

WHINES, paws at his nose. Starts away. CAMERA HOLDS ON
HIM for a moment.

EXT.   A TRACT HOUSE AMONG OTHER TRACT HOUSES - DAY

A few toys on the lawn. Two sprinklers twirl. It's early
morning; as we watch, a newsboy rides by and a paper thumps
against the door.

TITLE CARD: SALT LAKE CITY, JUNE 27

                    WOMAN (V.O.)
          -- so I said I'd go to the meeting
          if she could show me how these cuts
          are going to cripple the day care
          center. And she said --

                    GIRL (V.O.)
          Oh, Mamma, I don't feel so good.
          I think I'm going to be sick.

                    WOMAN (V.O.)
          Hold on a second, Steff.

INT.   A KITCHEN - DAY

A bright, cheery room. Breakfast has not yet been cleared
away on the table in the b.g. We see milk, cereal bowls,
and prominently displayed, a box of Red Razberry Zingers
breakfast cereal.

The WOMAN is standing at the wall phone, holding the receiver
in one hand as she bends over the GIRL, who is about five.
The Girl looks woeful and very sick.

                    GIRL
          Oh, I'm gonna throw up...

She turns and runs down the hall. The Woman looks after
her.

INT.   THE HALLWAY - DAY

The Girl, holding her stomach, runs into the bathroom and
shuts the door.

In Stephen King's original draft for the screenplay, right after Cujo is
bitten by the rabbit bat, we cut to a family dealing with a poison scare
which would motivate the actions of the character of Vic Trenton.

Almost immediately (discreetly muted), we HEAR the
sound of vomiting.

INT. AT THE PHONE IN THE KITCHEN - DAY

The Woman rolls her eyes wearily and leans against the
wall as she puts the phone back to her ear.

> WOMAN
> I'll call you back, Steff. Marcy's
> got the crud. Billy had it last week,
> now she's got it. The only thing the
> little creep will share with her is
> his damn stomach flu.

> GIRL (V.O.)
> (faint)
> Mommy...I'm <u>sick</u>!

> WOMAN
> Coming!
> (into phone)
> Bye, Steff.

She hangs up the phone. Starts down the hall.

> WOMAN
> It's okay, Marcy, don't worry --

INT. THE BATHROOM DOOR - DAY

The Girl is breathing hard. Almost panting. Crying a
little.

> GIRL (V.O.)
> Oh, Mamma, I feel <u>sick</u> --

> WOMAN (Vo.)
> It's just the old upchuck express --

The door opens and the Woman comes in.

> WOMAN
> (continuing)
> -- and it happens to the best of --

Her expression, which says "I don't like this, but I understand it and I have the situation under control," suddenly
freezes -- and becomes one of horror.

> WOMAN
> What -- God, <u>what</u> --

INT. THE LITTLE GIRL - DAY

We see her on her knees before the opened toilet. Her
back is to the CAMERA. The rim of the bowl, the inside
of the lid, and the white tile wall all appear to be
splattered with blood.

She turns. Blood seems to be running down her mouth and
chin. It mats her dress.

                    GIRL
          I feel really <u>sick</u>, Mommy --

INT. THE BATHROOM DOOR - WITH THE WOMAN - DAY

She claps her hand to her mouth and screams...screams...
screams.

DARKNESS

TITLE CARD: CASTLE ROCK, JULY 3

TITLE CARD FADES. We hear NIGHT SOUNDS: crickets, chirring
cicadas. A new SOUND: GROWLING. Low, at first, then getting
louder.

TAD TRENTON sits up IN THE FRAME. He's wearing pj's. He
just work up. He looks around for that sound. His eyes
fix on:

INT. THE CLOSET DOOR - NIGHT

The GROWLING gets LOUDER.

INT. TAD IN BED - NIGHT

Scared. Looking at the closet door as if hypnotized. The
GROWLING gets LOUDER.

INT. THE CLOSET DOOR - NIGHT

The latch pops, and it swings open two or three inches.
The GROWLING gets still LOUDER...and then STOPS COMPLETELY.

INT. TAD IN BED - NIGHT

Stiff. Alert. All wires. Then he begins to relax.

However, director Lewis Teague's final choice for the opener would remove any suggestion of supernatural activity and ground the horror in a sturdy commonplace realism. It is also an astounding technical achievement and as previously stated, a beautifully condensed three act mini-feature. The rabbit chase is shot with broad strokes and sharply pieced together by precise and dedicated editing, and the animal action is mesmerizing and chipper: Cujo seems to let the rabbit escape at times, and the tone is completely playful. When the film turns to horror terrain and we follow the rabbit and then Cujo into the bat infested cave, we find ourselves in man-made construction designed on a sound stage. This is an incredibly convincing and beautifully styled bat cave, decked out with art direction by Guy J. Comtois consisting of skeletons of dead beasts, crooked branches, dense mud, flat faced stones and more. Intercutting the real St. Bernard with a puppet head created by effects team of married couple Robert and Kathie Clarke, the scene plays out with effortless tension and shocking pragmatism in terms of nature taking its course and falling into attack mode. When Cujo is bitten it is a startling moment made all the more upsetting when his yelp is echoed through the desolate cave. The sound design during this entire sequence from the chase of the rabbit through to Cujo being bitten is a melting pot of subtle naturalistic ambience (the bubbling brook, the nibbling sounds of the rabbit, the soft whistling of faraway birds and so forth), the driving musical score from Charles Bernstein and the highly dramatic war between Cujo's barking and the screeching of sick bats. Although the film was shot in Northern California, this sequence boasts some lovely big pine trees that look as though it is in fact Maine (the home of most of Stephen King's works), and into this Stephen King universe we catch a glimpse of the film's featured "monster" before he descends into a vortex of suffrage and fury.

Cujo is a major player in the history of the cinematic dog, and his place in film history as a dog that wanted to be good but who was caught in an unfortunate circumstance is a tale of reckoning, torment, relentless torture, harrowing desperation and oppressive isolation.

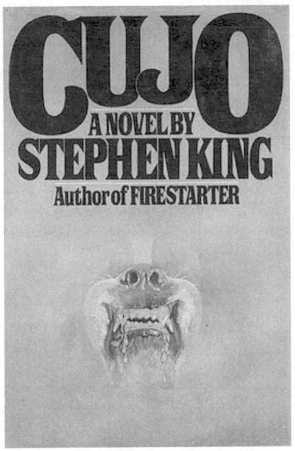

The first edition of Stephen King's novel from Viking Press.

LEWIS TEAGUE (director): I read the novel. Yes. As soon as the producer Dan Blatt set up a meeting I read the book before I went in and I did see immediately what I liked about the story and what would be the threat in my mind. I generally saw clearly what the major problem would be, or the major challenge would be and that was to trim it down to film length, which would entail getting rid of a lot of subplots and characters. I had a general attack plan in my head when I went and met with the producer for the first time.

DEE WALLACE ("Donna Trenton"): It's important in the business of Hollywood to have your name above the title, and it does, believe it or not, and as silly as it may seem, have something to do with how much you get paid. So back then it was more important than it is right now, and it did say a lot about your stature and your financial grade and how much clout you have in the business. Do I think it makes much difference in the kind of actress I am? Of course not! It's a business, so it's all a business thing. Nothing more.

LEWIS TEAGUE: There was this kind of optical thing that was created by a company who was hired to do the main title, and they came up with several ideas and the swirling letters forming was one of them and it sounded great; so we said "Go ahead and do it!"

ALEXANDER WITT (assistant camera): I worked with the producer, Dan Blatt, in Europe on a movie, and I told him that I was hoping to go to the U.S.A. to live there and work there. So I went in and I saw that the film started off with Peter Medak as the director and Tony Richmond as the director of photography. This was going to be my first American film, and I had no papers and I was working without papers. I went up to Santa Rosa and Dan Blatt told me to not say anything as the film was a non-union film and it was easy back then to work on movies without papers. I knew Tony Richmond and he asked me to be the camera operator on it and [within] three days of shooting the studio fired Peter Medak and then Tony. And that's when Lewis Teague and Jan de Bont came in. This is how I met Jan. I never got to meet Peter really, I had come three or four days before shooting and then not long after, he was sent home. I never had a connection with Peter at all. We broke down for two weeks and then Lewis Teague took over.

CHRISTOPHER MEDAK (production manager): There was a lot of cocaine and a lot of MDMA which was a precursor to Ecstasy around those days. We would sprinkle it all on our donuts. The costume designer Jack Buehler who we called "Uncle Jack" would love his amyl nitrate and mix it with his Coke. The drugs were always there. And there was a lot of drinking. It was the whole crew who partook in all that. I know that Lewis was not drinking in those days, and I don't think Jan was either. There wasn't a film during that period that I didn't take drugs or drink on, but we always, always made it work! Tony Richmond had to drink up on that fucking crane, it was the only way for him to keep warm! I was so grateful I had that girl I was sleeping with so I had that room with her and could be naked with her and keep warm! It was fucking freezing.

MARCIA ROSS (casting director): We cast the whole movie with Peter Medak. By like week two, they were replacing Peter, and Lewis came in. I don't remember casting any of the movie with Lewis at all. I didn't know him until way later on. It was exciting to work with Peter because he had directed *The Ruling Class* (1972) starring Peter O'Toole, which is a great movie.

ALEXANDER WITT: I do however remember we shot a sequence in a cemetery at night. It's not in the movie. And it was a bad start because Tony Richmond caught one of the dogs pissing on one of the tombstones. There was the Santa Rosa newspaper that reported this. There was a little town south near Santa Rosa, Mendocino, and there was an article in their local paper where they showed a big St. Bernard pissing on one of the tombstones! I can't remember what the scene was about; all I know is that we shot there at night. I think it was before the dog was bitten and got rabies.

TONY RICHMOND (original cinematographer): The night shot that was the preproduction shot was the graveyard shot that would end up at the house. My recollection is that when we were shooting the huge crane shot which came right through into the village of where the story takes place, we got rained out and that was when we wrapped and headed back to the hotel. This is where we found a very stressed out Dan Blatt, and I just thought he was fucking crazy to fire Peter. I tried to convince him to change his mind but Dan told me that he couldn't change plans because he had another director on the way, and that was Lewis Teague. And I was so angry, I said "That guy that did *Alligator*?! (1980)" And we had a very bad crew as well, because it was a non-union picture, and they were all from Salt Lake City and they were completely useless. They just did not gel. I don't remember who the production manager was, but he hired this crew from Salt Lake City who were all non-union guys and being so far out of Los Angeles and so way up north that the unions just couldn't get involved. They all stuck around when Lewis took over.

CHRISTOPHER MEDAK: I was very tight with Tony Richmond. We were shooting in Mendocino which I loved. Tony lit that town for about two days or two nights and I was the liaison between Tony and Ariel Levy. This opening shot was going to start on the freeway and close in on the town and go all the way to the cemetery using a crane. Tony was sitting up on the top of the crane, and the nights were incredibly cold, so he would keep himself warm with a little booze. We did whatever it took to keep warm. I can't account for the artistic intention of this opening, I mean that was Dad's world. I wasn't on the project as a filmmaker, for me, the main thing I thoroughly remember is trying to stay warm in the graveyard. The aesthetic of what was being done was brilliant however, and the fact that they had the time to do it, and have two nights lighting it was incredibly great, there is no way you could get away with that. Tony was a drinker and there were times when he was up on that crane and he was drunk and a little "south". Also, a girl I was sleeping with was the only punk in Mendocino, because Mendocino was a hippie town, and here was this blonde haired bombshell who kind of looked like Marilyn Monroe, walking towards me through the graveyard, and Tony saw her. It was pitch black and I remember Tony screaming "I saw a ghost!" and I

24

The crew (director Lewis Teague at the bottom) "fool around" during production.

was like "Where? What are you talking about?" and here comes this girl I was sleeping with, walking towards us through the cemetery, dressed all in black and with her extremely pale, un-sunburnt face and peroxide blonde hair bobbing through the graveyard. Tony was there shitting bricks screaming "Get me out of here!"

DANIEL HUGH KELLY ("Vic Trenton"): I really liked Dan Blatt. I had no idea that he passed away until doing this book. I'm not really in the business of catching up with people I worked with, and when I find out that people have died it really upsets me, that happens a lot. I remember Dan Blatt coming up to me after the first night of shooting and he was re-enacting the first shot Peter had done. A shot that didn't involve any actors. He was moving around and everything and had his hands over his face with the ole' square lens, to show me what Peter had done, and he is telling me how the camera was going up and down and around this way and that, and he was like "Oh Danny it's the greatest shot!". It was the opening scene that went down the street and into the town and I remember Dan Blatt being very excited about that shot. Dan and I were both very excited that Peter was directing the movie.

CHRISTOPHER MEDAK: Ariel Levy was a Buddhist and Dan Blatt and his Mormon producers had a problem with that. They were completely baffled by Ariel's religious choice.

ALEXANDER WITT: Because it was a non-union shoot we had a lot of people from San Valley in Utah because they were the non-union crew, and that's why it was cheapest in those days. If it was a union shoot then a couple more million dollars would have to be added to the budget. Why they picked Santa Rosa is because it was outside the union jurisdiction and most of the people weren't from Los Angeles, and the crew from *Cujo* were known to do non-union jobs. I remember we went back to Mendocino county after Tony and Peter left.

DANIEL HUGH KELLY: I really liked Peter. He had directed *The Ruling Class* with Peter O'Toole, which is one of my favourite movies of all time. And I liked him a lot because he kind of reminded me of Leonard Melfi, the playwright who was a great friend of mine, may he rest in peace. And every time I was around Peter I was like "Geez, I'm with Leonard here!" and everyone spoke very highly of Peter. I remember he had his son on the set, and gave him a job and I liked him too.

ROBIN LUCE (makeup): *Cujo* was my first department head job. I was only twenty years old and because I was so young I actually fibbed about my age and said I was older than I was when I talked with the producer Dan Blatt. I started my career with Ve Neill on *The Sword and the Sorcerer* (1982) and then she took me along for another movie starring Jerry Lewis and Madeline Kahn called *Slapstick (Of Another Kind)* (1982) and the director of photography on that was Tony Richmond who was originally assigned to be the DOP on *Cujo*, and he suggested me for *Cujo*. He told Dan Blatt and I was interviewed and my biggest fear was that I was very young and that I had never had a department head job. But I really wanted this job and after I interviewed I found out that I got it! And that's how *Cujo* came about for me.

DON CARLOS DUNAWAY (co-screenwriter): I never met Peter Medak, and I never knew why he was fired. I came aboard with Lewis who was already in production and I rarely got out of my motel room. I was often writing for later today or tomorrow, which meant being locked into events and sequences without being able to track them from end to end. It was exciting.

DANIEL HUGH KELLY: The firing of Peter went down in Mendocino before the company moved to Santa Rosa. I remember being in the Hill House, which was a nice little hotel and I was with Tony Richmond, the director of photography and he was the one that told me that Peter was fired and that he was also let go. It was a case of "Well if he's not doing it, then I'm not doing it." There were several other crew guys in the room and people were very upset. I didn't know anybody that well at all, I mean us actors had just recently arrived, but I met Tony and got to know him and I was upset. I never got to see Peter to say goodbye. It wasn't long after that that I met Lewis.

TONY RICHMOND: We never got into any artistic intention for the opening shots, we had no time. I don't really have a distinct style to my cinematography, I was taught by two masters Nicholas Roeg and Freddie Young, and I always thought that cinematographers shouldn't have a style, instead, the style should come from the script. It was a mishmash. It's very hard to remember much on *Cujo*, all I know is that I really loved the beauty of Mendocino. What I liked about it was the fact that I was going to be working on this strange horror picture set in this beautiful idyllic town. I mean the coastline and the little village – it was just stunning. One thing that I found funny about Mendocino is that there was a lack of young people, I think once they all turned eighteen or nineteen they all moved out of town. It's in the middle of nowhere and there is nothing to do there, but it is incredibly beautiful.

LEWIS TEAGUE: I thought that it was so important to film the opening as a picturesque and idyllic scene. Also, it was the beginning of the film and I did not want to farm it out to second unit, I wanted to shoot it. So I talked Dan into shooting the second unit myself, which meant we finished production on the film. We spent several weeks editing everything together, then I went out with a small crew, including Jan de Bont to shoot all the stuff with the dog. I had worked with animals, and I also wanted to have an idea how to shoot it. I didn't really trust the second unit director to accomplice. I came up with some ideas that I thought worked out great. For example, to chase the rabbit around the fields with the camera I came up with the idea to get a lawnmower handle and attaching it to a hub cap and mount the camera on the hub cap. The hub cap being a hemisphere that would slide across the grass! And so Jan put the camera on the hub cap, we would chase the rabbits across the fields, and that worked out really well. I have to mention the animal trainer, Karl Lewis Miller, did a great job! He was incredible. He did a great job. I brought him back to work on *Cat's Eye* (1985). The idea was to create the feeling of this St. Bernard who is this big, loveable, floppy dog, so we feel some compassion for him as he became sicker and sicker. I don't remember if Karl brought in somebody special to handle the bats. He probably did. The rabbit too! He probably had a rabbit guy helping him out on that. The bat cave was shot on a set. That was here in L.A. I don't remember where, but it was here in L.A. and we built the cave set so that we could control it and light it.

CHRISTOPHER MEDAK: I got hired as a production assistant while my father was on board. Even though the hands changed, the assistant director Jerry Grandey asked me to stay on and I agreed. By then it had become a kind of family unit, it was all very close and even though there was that upheaval. Lewis I have come to know over the years, but I didn't know him them. My dad's firing almost seemed like a joke at the time, even though it wasn't. I mean it was so stupid and so out of left field, but at the same time I was eighteen years old and I was having a great time on the film.

PETER MEDAK (originally assigned director): I never saw the movie for thirty five years or so, but then I thought, if I am doing this book than I should get over it and go and watch the fucking movie. And I liked it. I never talked to Lewis Teague about it, but I was most impressed with the film, I thought Lewis did a fantastic job. And this is the thing, I went on for years not liking him without even knowing him only because he was

Lewis Teague and team film the idyllic opening out in the woodlands of
Mendocino, CA. (photo courtesy of Gale A. Adler).

the guy who took over from my movie. And I just had to talk to him and tell him what I thought of it, and I want to ask him how it all came about progressively.

CHARLES BERNSTEIN (composer): When I first saw the film it was the first work print that I was working with. The movie opened on the fade in on the rabbit hole and the rabbit popping out; that was how the movie began. The titles were arranged in such a way that everything started at that point. When I saw it I said to Dan Blatt, the producer, that I was a little concerned because it was so idyllic, and so kind of family and Disney-like, and that there was really nothing significantly scary going on. Even when the dog gets bitten by the rabid bat, and even when the boy is frightened of his closet – that whole opening sequence is pretty kind of family-friendly; it doesn't feel like a horror movie. I explained to Dan Blatt that there would be music I would be establishing for that very long opening segment – all the way up until the parents come and turn the lights on in the boy's room. I wanted that entire sequence to set the tone for what will be following later in the movie. I asked Dan if there was any way that we could precede the rabbit coming out in the opening with maybe a darker graphic that establishes that this is a very dark movie and that there is some very dark material coming. Then go to the rabbit and kind of go light. So they did do that. I don't know if it was on my suggestion or whether they had been thinking about something like that, but in any case, my wish was granted! I was able then to establish Cujo's theme that would be Cujo post-rabies; right from the beginning so everyone understands that Cujo, the dog, will be represented by low French horns at the very opening, and that kind of horror-like music lets the audience know what they're in for. Then it is kind of a lovely transition when the rabbit comes out and the dog chases it around and it's all very upbeat and light. There are two aspects to Cujo's theme: one are the actual notes which you can play on the piano or you can whistle "Ba Ba Ba Baaaa," and those are sort of the notes that you would expect to hear on a hunting horn or at least it's reminiscent of a hunting horn. However, I play it very low which is not where a normal hunting horn would be sounded. So the first thing that transmutes the theme from a normal hunting tone to an idiosyncratic one and then to Cujo's character theme is that it is too low for a normal hunting horn. The second thing is that the instrument itself is the same instrument that I played in the higher registry. So when you play that same thing on a French horn and you play it low, it's harder to play in parts and that creates a sort of unease rather than the jolly hunting horn – it's more of a dark, low register befitting of the size of the dog and the menacing quality that it begins to take on. So those are my thoughts to the actual theme. I wasn't working directly with the sound people, but I was working with Lewis Teague, the director and Dan Blatt, the producer and they coordinated through the directorial process. If you notice, the music does respect the sound effects. A lot of times I was not working from a finished product; like for instance – and this is referring back to the main title – when I was working with that opening graphic, there was no visual there – it was a black slug of film, and it was described to me: "What we're working on here, Charles, is a graphic where it will start here and it's going to swirl and the name will emerge here". So I could kind of set the music up to do what was being described to me. But I think I never actually saw that graphic until maybe after we recorded the music. I'm not sure. I might have been working from a timing sheet that told me when the swirl began and when the title came. But by the same token all of the sound effects were not in, but it was described to me that when we cut to the bats shrieking, just before we cut to the external shot of going to the house on a crane shot after the bat cave, that the bats would be shrieking, and so I just went out for that moment knowing that the sound design sound effects would be all the sound necessary and I would just take a breath there musically and just let that shrieking happen. By the same token, when we go into the bat cave and there are bat noises, I went into the very low register because the bats are in the very high notes, the very top of the spectrum. So I went down into the very low notes so that the music could be played at a reasonably decent level and not have to be turned down so that the bats could be heard. In other words, the bats were taking up the high register of the south spectrum and I let the music bring Cujo's dark tones into the low when he pokes his head in. So those were a few ways in which I worked with the sound, even though the sound wasn't completed, it was described to me so I could work around it. It does give us the opportunity to pretty much plant all the seeds of the thematic musicality in all ways: the stylistic horror motif, the family theme, the brighter sounds, just all of the elements that unfold throughout the movie are in that whole opening sequence, so it gives the movie the opportunity to plant all of those seeds upfront and then harvest them later.

Composer Charles Bernstein's composition for "Cujo's Theme" (courtesy of Charles Bernstein).

DON CARLOS DUNAWAY: In my shooting script, the lovely Cujo and rabbit sequence is numbered page 29. What came before, I have no clue. Don't remember. But I'm a believer in *in medias res*.

GARY MORGAN (stunt man/man in dog suit): I gotta tell you, the animal trainer who had the bats had these special rabies shots, and special permits to handle bats from animal rank. The bats were fine, but it was interesting because they don't usually use vampire bats like that in a movie, I mean those are real bats that worked on that sequence to bite the dog. That was a puppet head with a puppet snout for the bite, but they were all real bats! I don't remember Karl Lewis Miller handling the bats, I am certain it was a woman animal trainer and she also doubled for Dee. I remember that she also had the rabbit that Cujo chases in the beginning.

PETER MEDAK: I wish I could find Barbara's script. I am sure she kept it. She has two daughters, Jennifer Jason Leigh and Mina Badie. Jennifer, who I adore and did a film with her called *The Men's Club* (1986). I was with Barbara a few months before she died, and I last saw her at Jennifer's house – because Jennifer took her there with a carer – and I knew Barbara was going to die. I thought, "Oh no I'm not going to see her again". When we reunited, we just held each other's hands and I brought her a dozen red roses and I told her that I would be back and we would go for a big walk, and I was there for hours. When she died, there was a big memorial at her house where she lived and where the kids grew up for most of their lives, it was five minutes from my place in Hollywood, and Jennifer organised the whole thing. I spent a lot of time with Barbara on *Cujo* and later she was determined to write a film all about my life, about my escape out of Hungary and she started writing it, but never finished it needless to say. I really loved Barbara so much. I was there for her when her ex-husband Vic Morrow was killed and not long after that we started work together on a film about the artist Jackson Pollock. She was a fantastic person. Barbara's house was a six thousand square house, and I had a tremendous

34

amount of books there and a lot of them were about anti-Semitism while we were working on the script of my life, and I am certain the *Cujo* script is there also.

MINA BADIE (daughter of screenwriter Barbara Turner): I love Peter Medak and he remained a good friend of the family ever since. What a dear, dear man, not to mention talented. My mother loved him. I'm sure I read my mother's screenplay for *Cujo*, and I remember it being scarier than the film ended up being. I wish Peter wasn't fired from the project, because then my mother's script would be the final result you see on screen. I'm sure him being let go greatly displeased her. I remember the whole concept she had with the bat being an evil entity that infects the dog, so it goes beyond rabies and adds a supernatural element. Peter loved this idea.

Cujo **screenwriter Barbara Turner would later use the pseudonym of Lauren Currier after her dear friend Peter Medak was fired from the production.**

PETER MEDAK: I was fired by Dan Blatt. And that is the only movie that I have ever been fired from in my career of fifty years. The reason I was fired is interesting and it all has to do with my British director of photography Tony Richmond. My whole career started in England and from growing up in England I watched movies and learnt about the industry in that country, I then started directing there, I mean my whole past life is there in the United Kingdom. So Tony and I met each other in 1956, when I escaped from Hungary and we happened to work at the same company. Tony became a very close friend. He would work as a clapper boy on Nicolas Roeg's movies and then I would be a clapper boy on Nicolas Roeg's movies and we would both work for Nicolas, Tony of course working on the wonderful *Don't Look Now* (1973) and all those films. We were all great friends. Fast forward and we're in Hollywood and producer Dan Blatt came along and had this project *Cujo*, and he wanted to hire Tony for it, along with me as director. At that time, Tony had a very difficult reputation, but he is absolutely brilliant, and if I were to do another movie in America I would do it with Tony. But at that time, Tony drank a lot, he was a heavy alcoholic and because of that, I was reluctant to use him. But Dan kept insisting and so he hired him. Dan Blatt in his great wisdom after our first two days of shooting – which mind you, were massive shots, these were outdoor shots that took a lot of time and energy – which were the shots establishing the film, being the opening of the movie. I will never forget shooting those for the rest of my life. We were driving into Mendocino at night and Tony had to light up the entire town at night, and the first shot was going into Mendocino with a crane going up and down, moving. But it started on the cat's eyes of the motorway, so that all the cars driving down the road would have their headlights flashing towards us. It was very close and that is how the credits were going to start! After thirty something years, I will never forget one single frame from that sequence. The whole idea was that there was this ghost of a serial killer that would be returning to the small town. It would start with the cat's eyes and then go up and down and fly into a village at night, and before it gets there, it stops over at a cemetery with a church – which are still very common in Mendocino – then flies over to the little boy's house and lands in his closet, and the door creaks open and that's how the movie begins. So we did these two shots with just two nights to do them, and then I started shooting the main unit. I was in a crane shot in front of the house and it started raining. Dan comes up to me and says "Can I talk to you?" I told him that I couldn't get off the crane, so Dan sat next to me and whispered to me "We've got to fire Tony Richmond." And I said to him "Have you gone out of your mind?!" and he said to me "The only reason he is on the film is because he's your friend" and I reminded Dan that Dan himself pushed for Tony. Also, Tony did an incredible job. Nobody had seen the two day's worth of dailies, which Tony did great. So I got very angry and said "You can't fire him! I refuse to accept that! You can't fire him!" So Dan turned around to me and said "Well, in that case, you're fired as well!" I said "Dan, you're out of your fucking mind. We haven't even started the movie!" I told Dan to take a big walk and come back in five minutes, just to cool off and reconsider. He came back from a walk in five minutes and told me that Tony and I were both fired from the film. I then went to find Tony who was at a pub having a drink, you see, there was so much rain that it delayed the shoot. So Tony was there having his drink, and he asked me what Dan wanted and I told him that he fired both of us. We then charted a plane and flew back home, drinking champagne, all the way back to Los Angeles. And that was the end of it.

TERESA ANN MILLER (daughter of animal trainer Karl Lewis Miller): I believe we had four dogs. Daddy was the lead dog. He was Big Daddy. They lived with us; they lived in our household and in our backyard. I was in school and I would still work with my father but not so much, I would just help with what he needed to do. He always had had his work scheduled and things going on and it wasn't until I saw the movie that it really put into question what are we doing with this dog in my backyard! I had no idea up until that point that after I saw the movie you looked at this dog in a whole different manner! Of course you know what kind of movie it is, but you would still see some of those common looks that the dog would give, because that is the St. Bernard. They don't smile like other dogs. Some dogs just smile with their eyes and look happy and crazy. You don't see it so much in a St. Bernard. So they really make you think twice. It was just so impressive and remains so impressive today with the amount of emotion that we were able to instil in that character. The dogs were around two to three years old when he got them. I know he had a younger dog that did most of the physical running and such, you know, because there was so much physical stuff for the dogs to do and that's just not their speciality. I don't remember if the dogs were from breeders or shelters. I really couldn't tell you, because they were usually between breeders or rescues or what have you. I couldn't tell you where those four dogs came from. The rabbits were also ours. They are taught to go from A to B for noise and for some food. What they would do is just follow a lead. In this case they were trained to go into that log. So what happens is you would have a little buzzer or something inside the log and he would buzz the noise and the rabbit will run and follow it into the log and that's when he will get his reward. I really don't know what we used for training the bats. I remember us having the box and the bats in it, and we had the dummy head inside it. Then I believe they put a little nectar or suckle or something sweet on the nose that attracts the bats. At that point the bat would go and land on the nose to get his food. I don't remember what it was exactly that he put on the nose, but it did the job!

The rabbit that inadvertently leads Cujo to danger.

"TOO MUCH OF THE TUBE, GUYS": Tad sees monsters in his closet, so it's mom and dad to the rescue

Opening with Stephen King's credit firmly secured over an image of a suburban house at night enveloped by oppressive darkness, this provocative visual is a sublime condensation of what the prolific and incredibly talented writer was at the point his novel "Cujo" was turned into a film: a master storyteller who got inside the homes of his readers to scare the living daylights out of them. By 1983, Stephen King would have written over ten best sellers starting with "Carrie" and had a number of filmic and TV adaptations come from them including *Salem's Lot* (1979), *The Shining* (1980) and two released the same year as *Cujo*, being *Christine*, directed by John Carpenter and *The Dead Zone*, directed by David Cronenberg. Carpenter and Cronenberg were already at that point in their careers staple directors in the horror genre, and their cinematic interpretations of King's work were box office draw cards and very well-received by critics.

Impressed with director Lewis Teague's socially aware eco-horror hit *Alligator*, Stephen King would suggest the Roger Corman affiliate to take the reins of his story about a rabid St. Bernard who traps a mother and her son inside a busted up Pinto and take on the job of writing the screenplay himself. However, the studio green lighting the project being Warner Bros. signed on Hungarian director Peter Medak, who had left an impression with his incredibly impressive ghost chiller *The Changeling* (1980) and eventually King's script would be rejected in favour of Barbara Turner's who would end up being trimmed and reworked by follow up screenwriter Don Carlos Dunaway. More changes would eschew when Peter Medak would be fired from the project, ushering in King's first choice for the film Lewis Teague as director. With this, Medak's long-time friend and collaborator Barbara Turner would remove her credit from the film and use the pseudonym Lauren Currier.

Lewis Teague's credit will scroll from behind the house in the opening titles, suggesting a playful graphic gesture departing from the standard fade in and out from the rest of the credit reel as the camera closes in on a set of two windows on the top floor of this large, white weatherboard two story. This is the home of the Trentons – a middle class family of three who will fall into a horror of circumstance. Zooming in on the Trenton house is atypical of masterfully concocted horror cinema, in that a lot of personal and character-driven horror movies hone in on the place of terror from the get-go, and also isolate the people or locales in question, closing in on the place of horror or the person it will most affect; much like the zoom in on Chris MacNeil's (Ellen Burstyn) Georgetown house in *The Exorcist* or the dingy apartment used for lunchbreak rendezvous for Marion Crane (Janet Leigh) and her lover in *Psycho* (1960).

Here, we are introduced to the first human character of the film; six year old, golden haired Tad Trenton (Danny Pintauro). Tiny in stature, already incredibly vulnerable and with delicate cherubic features, the little boy is weary eyed in the bathroom, wiping his face as he finishes up at the toilet. The room glows with a warmth from interior lighting, framing Tad with a bronze hue – a color scheme that will become commonplace throughout the film. When he switches the light off, the scene is dominated with blues and blacks which make a striking contrast against the orange tint. The art direction suggests this lovely Maine abode is a brand new home, with

42

characters yet to settle in, and Tad's bedroom is decorated with stuffed parrots and teddy bears, giving a sense of passivity and childlike frailty. Although there is a funny aside of a stuffed St. Bernard thrown in the mix, Tad's bedroom is a pastel place of innocence with its walls painted up with a blue summer sky theme, floor boards polished and new and a large rocking horse set next to a closet packed with clothing and toys.

Within his comfortable surroundings however, Tad has distrust for something hidden away in his closet, and when he sees the door creak open, his eyes flare up with fear. There is an undisputed paranoia here, a little boy terrified of the lurking monsters that hide in the closet. This is an age old childhood fear, and something that director Lewis Teague taps into from personal memory – as a child he would imagine a wolf in his closet and under his bed and would have to race to the safety of his quilt and covers when the lights went out. In this sequence, the entire set up is just that: a child lost in the throes of an active imagination that jeopardises his safety.

The Barbara Turner screenplay with dramaturgical input from initially assigned director Peter Medak, uses Tad's closet as a place where the ghost of a deceased serial killer (possibly Frank Dodd from "The Dead Zone") haunts, but in the final draft of the script and eventual outcome of the film, the monster lurking in the closet would be a manifestation of the fears and anxieties Tad concocts from his overt sensitivity and awareness of his parents' crumbling marriage. In *Poltergeist* (1982) released a year earlier, a child's closet will also be the place of horror where little Carol Anne (Heather O'Rourke) is kidnapped by vengeful "TV People" and in horror outings such as *Cameron's Closet* (1988) this horror embedded within a child's wardrobe is exploited even further. Childhood delusions and the making of monsters is all part of the unique terror of the unknown, and monsters birthed from hypersensitivity and burrowed sadness is an extension of internalising social anxieties – something that Tad is most definitely susceptible to. Fear inside the comfort of the middle class household is a palpable pain for little Tad as he tries to navigate his control of his overwhelming and very personal terror.

The serial killer Frank Dodd (Nicholas Campbell) in David Cronenberg's adaptation of Stephen King's *The Dead Zone*. Dodd would be considered the evil inhabiting the St. Bernard in Barbara Turner's original concept for the screenplay, which is a theme explored in King's source novel.

If the Trentons have just moved in to this large Maine house, they are determined to begin a new life away from the big city, and the small town of Castle Rock (a fictional coastal town that is the locale for many Stephen King stories) seems to be an ideal place to raise a child; a healthier alternative to the "big smoke". However, protecting their son from invading entities that haunt his closet is something that a sea change cannot fix – this is subjective and all about Tad's personal demons and personal battles.

Monsters in Stephen King's universe include the telekinetic Carrie who is pushed too far by her peers and oppressive mother, vampires who infest the entire town of Jerusalem's Lot, zombie cats and newly resurrected dead children struck down by trucks, killer cars with obsessive desires and psychotic nurses such as Annie Wilkes from his book "Misery" (1987) who is the most earthy of the monsters on par with Cujo – however, the fears unlocked in a child's mind play against those very tangible horror stories, and in this film, Tad's dreaded anxiety comes to full realization when he is eventually faced with a blood stained, frothing two hundred pound rabid dog snarling at him.

The first word heard in the film is screamed out in absolute terror – Tad hollers "Mommy!" beckoning for his mother to come to his aid. A thematic condensation and precursor as to what is to come, Tad calling out for the comfort of his mother and ultimately being rescued by her will be the fundamental surface core to the motion picture. The final act of the feature will be summarized by the simplistic notion that a mother must do everything she can to protect and save the life of her child, and the film sets this up straight away with this scene. When Donna Trenton (Dee Wallace) enters Tad's bedroom, she is followed by her husband Vic (Daniel Hugh Kelly) and the duo come to the "rescue".

Tad Trenton (Danny Pintauro) is reassured by his parents Donna (Dee Wallace) and Vic (Daniel Hugh Kelly) that "real monsters" do not exist.

Donna is a beautiful young woman with stylish short blonde hair and a slender dancer's body and Vic matches her beauty with a lean athletic musculature and handsome features. Where Vic comes to represent the quintessential eighties urban professional (he is in advertising and a campaign runner for television commercials), Donna is a woman trapped by stifling repression – cornered into being somebody's wife and somebody's mother. As she shuffles over to her son and lovingly takes him into her arms, she asks "Bad dreams?" then scolds the role of television in her household with "Too much of the tube, guys". The idea of television as a source of nightmares is something that horror films and other genres examine with upmost honest sensibilities, and in films such as Tobe Hooper's *Poltergeist* this is exploited in extreme measures where the invention itself swallows up little Carol Anne. However, in *Cujo*, Donna's comment is double loaded – here she is attacking the role of television as not only a nightmare inducer for her sensitive little boy, but also as the cause of distraction for her husband who works in churning out commercials that are wedged in between narrative based programming. As the film progresses and we learn of Donna's infidelity, Vic's career is scrutinized as something that is a constant disruption from his wife's affections and his connection to her psychologically, emotionally and, most explicitly, sexually.

Vic goes through the contents of the closet and retrieves an "over the hill" teddy bear which is a comforting crutch that seems to be discarded by Tad. Or at least forgotten. Complacency and taking safety for granted is a theme that runs through the construct of *Cujo*, and even here in this tiny "slice of life" melodrama it is made profound. Tad describes the monster in the closet to Donna and Vic (the monster's eyes, its sounds etc) and in doing this, the image of the fearful wide-eyed boy sitting in the arms of his loving parents represents the child bringing his parents together through his paranoia and fear. When he is assured that "there are no such thing as real monsters", Tad is put back into bed. This is the first time the film introduces this solid principle at its foundation and its base centre

– the concept of monsters existing in reality. It also revels in examining what makes a monster a monster, the evolution of monsters, the face of the monster and what one must undertake in order to confront and vanquish monsters. Donna comforts Tad with "Over, done with, gone" – another repeated mantra that bonds parent and child and is used to treat dark situations ushering in fast and much needed light. In *Cujo*, there is most certainly the impenetrable world of darkness and monsters exist in the dark, however, what will eventually result and become a crashing reality for young Tad is that monsters will most definitely appear in broad daylight and lit by the flaring summer sun.

One of the most vividly inventive moments during this sequence draws its inspiration from the Russian film *The Cranes Are Flying* (1957). Directed by Mikhail Kalatozov, this film about the effects of World War II features a scene where a young boy is being chased by a German tank. During this moment, the camera turns upside down to evoke the feeling of this boy's world being turned upside down. Lewis Teague and his cinematographer Jan de Bont, very much influenced by Kalatozov's choice of camera angle to comment on character displacement, turmoil and upheaval, use this incredibly innovative technique when young Tad races towards his bed to escape the deadly grip of his closet monster, and dives into bed. When he throws himself into bed, the camera has completely flipped and it is as if little Tad has fallen into space – a refuge from the monsters that lurk on the ground. This moment adds a certain dreamlike quality to an otherwise very realist film; it is also one of three moments in the picture to use slow motion (the next time this occurs it will be inserted to emphasize pure unadulterated cathartic primal screaming and finally to transition from relief to the resurrection of the eternal monster). Besides lending itself to dream logic and artistic expression that comments on character (namely Tad's extreme attempts to avoid hungry beasts lurking in the darkness), the flipping of the camera is a masterfully executed technical achievement and turns Tad's falling into space into something that cements the film as one devoted to a stylish and unique vision. *Cujo* is most definitely a stylized film, and although it lives and breathes in melodramatic realism, it is ultimately a fairy tale and allegorical tale of fear (personal, imagined, real, tangible, familial, marital, economical, social et al) and therefore utilizes an aesthetic that passes comment on this.

The scene ends with Donna and Vic retreating back to bed. The lingering image of Vic standing at the doorway with the moonlight spilling onto him leaves a comforting reassurance that there are in fact "no such thing as monsters". Here Vic stands shirtless and open, vulnerable and readily available to his wife and son; however, his wife Donna is dressed in a full bodied nightgown – her manner is sombre and downbeat, she is also "covering up" and concealing hidden truths. Costume designer Jack Buehler and his wardrobe assistant Nancy G. Fox would consciously bring this to the project, feeding character and subliminally suggesting acute insight into the very personal.

When Vic reassures Tad about the non-existence of monsters, Tad fearfully whispers

"Except for the one in my closet…" and the scene closes with an extreme close-up of Tad's face, peering from under his covers, begging "Please… please…" He is desperate not to be traumatized by the monster lurking in his closet, and from a child's psychological point of view, what he fundamentally wishes for is safety, sanctity, wholeness, togetherness and to not harbour feelings of unease about his surroundings. His "monster" is the fear imagined and concocted by a child fretful of his parents who may in fact not be in love. There is a fade to black here (the only one in the film) and when the time lapse to morning ushers in the following jump cut to the interior of Tad's bedroom, we follow Jan de Bont's camera to discover a closet door barricade. In a slight moment of comic relief (something that is decidedly very much unused in *Cujo*) the visual of everything in Tad's bedroom used to keep the closet door shut closes the sequence and acts as a narrative launch pad for the following scene.

HER
NAME
IS
VERONICA...
SHE'S
17
YEARS
OLD...
SHE'S
IN
LOVE...
AND
SHE
LIVES IN
MOSCOW!

THE
CRANES
ARE
FLYING

Filmed
in the
Soviet
Union!

The Cranes Are Flying **(1957) becomes the core inspiration for the camera flip for Tad's bedroom run.**

LEWIS TEAGUE: Tad's fear of monsters in his closet and running to bed was all based on my recollections of me as a child when I had to go to the bathroom in the middle of the night. I used to have to turn out the light and in my mind I had to race to the safety of my bed before I hit the light switch, or else the wolves would come out from underneath my bed and kill me. It was a game I played with myself. I knew it wasn't true, but it was fun to do that as a kid – to make sure I could hit the bed before the lights went entirely out. I told Danny about that and he understood all that right away. He was a smart kid. I then discussed it with Jan de Bont and how to make it scary and the drama came from the time period from where he is in a blacked out room to him reaching the bed. So I thought we should stretch out the room when he hits the light switch. So we built a set for the extended room. Before he hits the light switch

49

we were shooting from a real life location bedroom, and once the lights are out we built the room. The distance between the light switch and the bed was more than five metres away and to make it more fun I suggested to Jan that we do a flying shot and Jan was very well versed in films and understood what I was asking for. We wanted the camera to go upside down so that when we shot it in slow motion and he jumps into bed, it looks as though he is falling into an abyss. So Jan built a little contraption in the room that he could get up on and get that shot. The production designer was Guy J. Comtois who had already designed Tad's bedroom before I arrived on set. This was all designed while Peter Medak was on

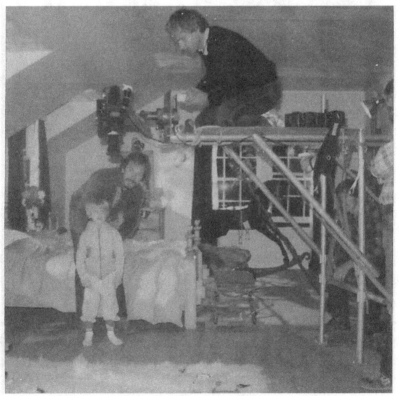

Preparing the camera flip: Director Lewis Teague preps young Danny Pintauro, while cinematographer Jan de Bont works on the shot. (Courtesy of Lewis Teague).

the film. I thought it was great and I loved Guy's work so much I hired him again on *Navy Seals* (1990). As much as he had designed everything before I had got there, Guy would discuss everything with me, and he was one of the hardest working people I had ever met. It was a wonderful relationship. He had great taste and an amazing eye for detail.

MARGARET PINTAURO (Danny Pintauro's mother): The whole monsters in the closet scenario in the film was pretty funny, because Danny never experienced monsters under his bed or in his closet when he was a little boy. That was all acting!

DEE WALLACE: In the interim between *The Howling* (1981) and *Cujo*, I had done *E.T. the Extra-Terrestrial* (1982) which was a huge blockbuster and the producer of *Cujo*, who also worked on *The Howling*, Dan Blatt asked me to come in and star in it. He also said that he wanted my husband Christopher Stone to play my lover. Dan knew how tight we were, so he offered us both the film. So I thought about it and asked to see the script and it was a huge *tour de force* for a woman, so how could I say no to a script like that! So we were off and running.

The crew sets up, while Danny Pintauro makes use of the large rocking horse while his stand in smiles for the camera. (courtesy of Danny and Margaret Pintauro).

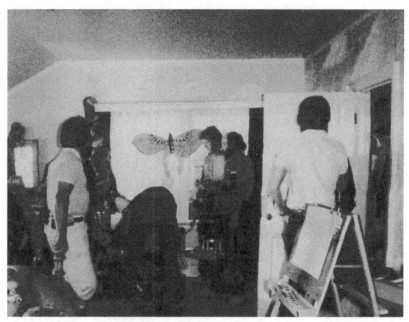

The crew assemble on the Tad Trenton bedroom set. (courtesy of Danny and Margaret Pintauro).

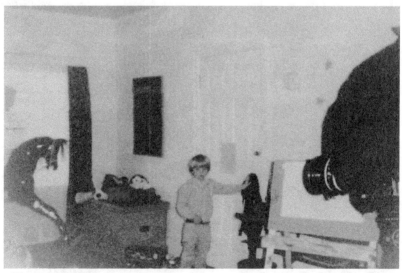

Danny Pintauro gets a feel for the elongated set designed by Guy J. Comtois. (courtesy of Danny and Margaret Pintauro).

Danny Pintauro gets to "know the set". (courtesy of Danny and Margaret Pintauro).

DANNY PINTAURO ("Tad Trenton"): I don't remember anything about the audition. The only thing I remember, and again, this is hearsay, this comes from my mom telling me the story, and I do remember doing this; after every audition that I did, she and I had created this idea that, you know – bless my mom and her heart – she really is the one who made things so much easier for me overall as a child actor. I would leave every audition, whatever it was for, whether it was for something important, or a commercial or print ad, and she would say "Alright, what do we say?" and I'd say "If I get it, I get it. If I don't, I don't." And what she said was that we were going up the stairs, in a hallway like in a stairwell and one of the producers, I think Dan Blatt was walking down the stairs and he heard me say that and that was what persuaded him to give me the job, that I was very simple and to the point of saying "Yeah, I get it! If it works, it works. If it doesn't, it doesn't! I'm good with that." That's all I know. Yeah, that's all I know. Again, that's my mom! I'm curious to actually hear what they say!

The Futura edition of the novel from the United Kingdom features artwork depicting young Tad Trenton outwardly terrorised by the rabid Cujo on the cover.

DANIEL HUGH KELLY: I was in Chicago and I just finished up on a series for NBC and returned to New York, so I had gone back home and I was doing a play and my agent called, and I am sure that was David Guc. He talked about it and I don't recall if I had to audition. I may have had to, but I don't recall. But I do however remember most significantly going out and getting a copy of the book "Cujo", and I read the book and I had never read any Stephen King stuff before, because I'm not a big fan of horror, but I genuinely enjoyed the book a lot. After I got hired I re-read it and that was just me doing my homework and working on the backstory for this character, getting to know him and what he was about. But that can be a double edge sword because you see what Stephen King was doing and I thought that that was very good – some people may dismiss his writing these days – but certainly at the time, I thought that that book was very good and very well written, but when they started changing things once the screenplay was written it was incredibly upsetting to me. But that is naiveté on my part because books are always changed, I mean they even changed Tennessee Williams's work when they did films such as *A Streetcar Named Desire* (1951). So I remember that and I remember casting director Judith Holstra was around, and I had to meet with her. Marcia Ross may have been in the room as well, but Judith was definitely involved and I really loved her. I also met with the original director on the film Peter Medak and I really liked him, and I remember I was sent a script while I was doing the play and I couldn't get to the script as soon as I wanted. So, I read it just before we started shooting and I remember thinking "Hang on a minute! This is not the book!" It was very upsetting to read this script and see how different it was from the novel. I thought, "Wait a minute, you could have so much more in it than what you have here". Then when we got on set it was changed several times more.

LEWIS TEAGUE: Well, there were two things I wanted to do: one was have a few very scary set pieces in it, and I spent a long time setting out to achieve that. And the other thing I wanted to do was make it as expressive and stylistic as possible. So I would ride out to that set when I wasn't riding with the makeup girl which only happened once. I would usually ride with the cinematographer, Jan de Bont, and talk about upcoming scenes, but try to talk about them at least in two weeks advance, to give him opportunities to prepare for them. I wanted to do half cinematic flourishes and scenes. For example, in the opening when Tad turns off the lights in the very beginning of the film and he is coming back from the bathroom and he turns off the light in his bedroom and has to get from the light switch into bed before all the light disappears, well that was all based on my childhood fears. I would have to flick off the lights and get into bed as quickly as possible – so I discussed with Jan how to do it. I said "Okay, we'll have a couple of different bedrooms, so that when the light goes off the bedroom can expand in size, so the distance to the bed will be magnified". And then also, Jan was well-grounded also in film history too, so, I said it would be a lot of fun to do the amazing shot from the film *The Cranes Are Flying* and he knew what I was referring to. *The Cranes Are Flying* is a Russian film from the fifties which has a shot at the end of the movie where the camera goes upside down when a kid is running off across a field, trying to escape a German tank and so that gave Jan the idea to build a set and build a superstructure to hang the camera from so it could go upside down. It went into slow motion when the kid is running across the room. The kid runs underneath the camera and the camera follows him upside down as he is jumping onto the bed, it almost looks like he is falling into space. I was looking for those kinds of shots and things. There is another shot in the film later inside the car where I wanted a three hundred and sixty degree spin. Dee Wallace has been bitten by the dog and she manages to fend him off and get back into the car and slam the door shut and she feels like she is passing out from shock and the pain of being bitten, and Tad is in the back screaming. The camera pans to her and never stops moving, and then pans off her and moves around to Tad screaming and then completes a three sixty back to Dee telling him not to open the door no matter what, and then back to the kid screaming. And the continuous motion it speeds up to a blur. I would pose these problems and challenges to Jan and then he would figure out a way to do it. In that particular case, he gave it some thought, he went out and bought another car and he built a superstructure on top of the car, so the camera could be above the car shooting down into it with a periscopic lens and the whole thing mounted on a gimbal that could spin around. So he was very cleaver. Jan wasn't afraid of work. One thing Jan was not afraid of was work! If he had a challenge, he'd get his teeth into it, he'd figure out a way to achieve it!

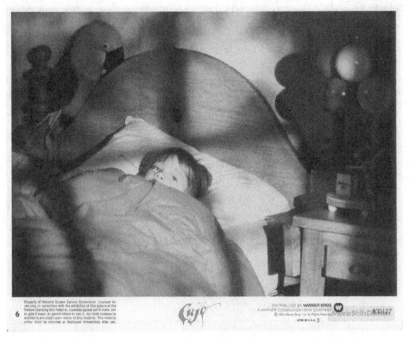

American lobby card of Tad Trenton (Danny Pintauro) in bed, fearing the monster in his closet.

CHRISTOPHER MEDAK: Working on something like *Cujo* compared to something like *Chained Heat* (1983) is complete night and day. The first film I ever worked on was *The Jazz Singer* (1980), I was a copy boy and tea boy and operator of the Xerox machine in a little office, that was my first job in the industry – and then coming in to do something like *Chained Heat* was once again completely different. It was such a bad B movie, it was shocking. It was absolutely insane, I remember the makeup artist knocking out the director. There was a wrestling scene and they were going at it and she climbed into the ring and knocked the director out. She was a feather of a girl too! But I guess the similarities between

57

Chained Heat and *Cujo* was the fact that neither films had a crew that had a love for their producer.

DEE WALLACE: I remember Lewis explaining the camera angle for the scene where Danny runs to his bed. Lewis was incredible. Also, the monster in the closet is real for every child, and Lewis wanted to do it in a very realistic point of view. That great shot of Danny running a very, very, long way to his bed gives you the feeling of the panic mounting up in this little boy and that begins taking the audience on its own ride because we all remember those times when we were little and so frightened about the boogeyman in the closet or the monsters at Disneyland. I mean look at all the Disney films, they have such strong monsters and villains.

CHARLES BERNSTEIN: It's a great, great gift when a filmmaker gives a composer the opportunity to just work with image and music; it is a gift that we don't always have. We're often under dialogue, we're often buried under sound effects, and so the scenes in this film are like gold to a composer, because our opportunity to be a major part to the storytelling is essential. I think most composers have a favourite scene or scenes they have done over time. I love the whole opening of *Cujo*. There is just a glorious moment when the little boy comes back from the bathroom and he turns the light off and he runs to his bed because he doesn't want to be vulnerable to any monsters from his closet. So he first tries to turn the light out and he fails and it always gets a little chuckle from the audience. Then he goes back and he really concentrates, and the music that carries him from the light going off until he gets in his bed, under the covers, is expressed by a brilliant shot by Jan de Bont, crafted by Lewis Teague, where the camera flips upside down and captures his run – and then when he jumps into bed the camera kind of catches him from another angle. It's a beautiful camera move and it gives the music the opportunity to really do something special. So I was able to play the theme with a descending shallow line, kind of a chromatic descending shallow line, and to me, it was just a cinematic magic moment, from the time the boy turns the light off until he kind of snuggles down into his bed. That was one of those moments where the music can do what it needs to do and not be interfered with. I treasure that!

PETER MEDAK: When I came onto the project, the original script by Stephen King was not very good. The producer Dan Blatt came to me and had this lady he was good friends with who was an excellent screenwriter, and this was the very talented Barbara Turner, who eventually refused to use her name on the project after I was fired, because she and I were incredibly close. I mean we were very, very close – we were best friends. So she was pissed off that I was fired and used an alias for the movie, which was Lauren Currier. She was so angry about that because she was so proud of her work on the film, and her writing was just perfect. The script she wrote for *Cujo* was excellent. Barbara was just beautiful. After we worked together on *Cujo*, she wanted me to work with her on a Jackson Pollock movie, and it was a major tragedy when she passed away. She remained a great friend until the end.

LEWIS TEAGUE: I wasn't trying to eliminate any of the supernatural elements when I first started thinking about it. That came later. For example, I really wanted to suggest something supernatural in Tad's closet that scared him at night; even though he couldn't convince his parents that there was something lurking in there. The thing that attracted me to the story was the fact that all the characters were real and well developed, and I saw that they were all reacting to fear. That had sort of been an interesting topic of exploration in my own life to try and distinguish between real threat and the imagined threat – to not be afraid of things that aren't real. For example, if I step out into the street and glance up just in time to see a Greyhound bus tearing down on me, that's something that deserves my fear and the fear will galvanize me to jump out of its path quickly. But, if I'm worried about how a film is going to turn out or worried about how I am going to pay the rent at the end of the month, or worried about a particular relationship – well those are all imaginary fears because they are not happening in the present. They are things that I am worried about that might happen! The problem with that is the brain; if I start worrying about paying the rent and get scared from that, then the brain thinks that it is a real threat and starts putting me through the biochemical changes that one goes through when there is a real threat. This goes back to caveman times when a sabre-toothed tiger would jump out from the bushes and the caveman would have a few seconds to prepare to fight or run. So the body goes through all these biochemical changes that would enable the caveman to fight or flight… fight or flee. And the problem is that back in those days the threat was over in a couple of minutes – the caveman either got eaten or got away. In any case, the threat was over and his body chemistry could then return to normal: the heart rate would slow down and the gastrointestinal track would start doing its job. He would stop flooding his body with adrenalin and cortisol and all that kind of stuff. But in today's society or in the society of *Cujo* and in the environment where the characters are living the threat was continuous. The father is afraid that he is not going to be able to feed his family when he loses the contract. The mother is afraid that she is going to grow old and waste away her life in this small town in Maine. And what the problem is when people believe that their fears are real – like she believes that she might waste away her life and then they start acting on the fear they start making stupid choices –for example she decides to have an affair with a local tennis bum. Choices made on the basis of fear are inevitably going to get into deeper trouble and that is what happens in that story. That is what I read and saw happening in that story. That was an important theme in my own life – it is a very important phenomenon that I have learned to deal with. So that I do not waste my time and energy worrying about things that aren't real and that is what I read in the book and that is what attracted me to the story.

MARCIA ROSS: I was working with a woman named Judith Holstra, who I worked with for eight years, and we had a company called Holstra-Ross Casting. Judith had a long relationship with Robert Singer and Dan Blatt, and Dan in particular she had worked with a number of times, and that's how we were offered to work on this film. I think Dee was attached from the very beginning, she had come into the project quite early. She had become quite the star, just coming off *E.T. the Extra-Terrestrial* and was a kind of motherly role and plus she had a name that we needed to go with the film. And then after we had Dee instantly involved, we started the casting process. The thing that I really remember the most was the fact that I went to New York. I went to New York City and Martin Gage who was a top agent, who is still alive and he's a wonderful man, let me use an office, like a room in his office, which was great. So I did auditions in a room at his office and one of the people I found from New York was Danny Pintauro. Daniel Hugh Kelly, Judith and I knew. We cast him in 1981 from a soap called *Ryan's Hope* (1975-1989), and Judith and I were big fans of his, so we had cast him in a pilot called *Murder Inc.* in the winter of 1981. So we knew him, Judith and I were big fans of his, and so we cast him in this pilot with Tovah Feldshuh for CBS. John Avildsen directed, so we knew Daniel.

LEWIS TEAGUE: All of the house's rooms were all actual locations. The only set we had was the elongated bedroom and that was shot in a warehouse somewhere in Mendocino.

ROBIN LUCE: I had not read the book, but I knew of Stephen King of course and was very excited to be invited to work on a Stephen King project. Once I read the script I thought it was going to be an excellent challenge for me, especially being the start of my career, this whole concept of being able to portray what these two characters will be going through

61

stuck in this car. I think I got the Stephen King draft of the script because I was brought in very early in the game.

DANIEL HUGH KELLY: I don't remember the connection *Cujo* was meant to have to "The Dead Zone" but maybe that was in the original draft that Stephen King had written which I never read. I still have a copy of my novel of "Cujo" and I have all the important sentences underlined in yellow. The script that Barbara Turner wrote was great, but the draft that Don Carlos Dunaway did – well, I didn't care for that. But I agreed to do the movie, so suddenly I was locked down.

MINA BADIE: My mother and Dan Blatt had a rough time during that project, but remained friends until Dan's death. I believe Dan Blatt told my mother that she "would never work in this town again" after my mother took her name off the film and used her pseudonym – created, I believe for that movie.

PETER MEDAK: Barbara and I decided to re-add the supernatural element into the story. Barbara's original screenplay opened with the little boy going to sleep in his bedroom and the closet door was opening and something was coming out – a ghost, or a spirit or something. The child screams and wakes up and we realize he is having a nightmare and the parents run in and so forth. Because of my kind of mania, when I did *The Changeling* with George C. Scott which was a great experience for me, I always wanted to do more movies concerning the supernatural and whatever picture I got I used to twist some kind of supernatural element into it; obviously not everything, but the films I could. Barbara and I had figured out that in the little boy's closet was the ghost of somebody who hung himself. This was an old house, and the ghost of a man who killed himself would haunt this little boy. He was a murderer. A killer with no remorse. Also, his ghost would later on infect the bat that would later on bite Cujo so there was a plot that was following it through. But had I made the movie, I would have made *Cujo* into a supernatural horror story. It would have been influenced heavily by Hitchcock. But of course I was fired.

LEWIS TEAGUE: I had seen the other films based on Stephen King novels and was familiar with them, but they really didn't enter into what I was doing at the time. I guess I really came out of a neo-realist school of filmmaking and Stanley Kubrick who did *The Shining* and Brian De Palma who did *Carrie* were far more expressionist in their approach. I'm more of the school of classicist realism which is why I didn't mind losing the supernatural element. I did try to keep the idea that there was something demonic in the closet that was scaring Tad; and I actually even shot something with that in mind adding special effects later. But it wasn't really working and it seemed a little hokey. It just seemed better to drop that and let it be in Tad's mind. What it was originally was a form of some monster in the foreground I concocted and lit with sheets of rubber, so when you are looking at it from the monster's perspective from inside the closet it looked frightening but looking at it from Tad's perspective it looked hokey. We started shooting and I thought this is not going to work, so let's take it out!

PETER MEDAK: I never met Stephen King. I doubt if Lewis ever met him either. By then, Stephen had become a massive writer. I remember "The Dead Zone" being a backstory for "Cujo", but that was never part of Barbara's script. Because of that, she and I developed an original idea which would involve a serial killer who kills himself in the boy's closet – he hangs himself, and his ghost returns there to haunt this little boy.

MARGARET PINTAURO: The producer Dan Blatt came to New York and asked for Danny to come and audition and he hired him immediately. So we flew out to California and that's how simple it was, that's how it all came about. I didn't know anything about the project. I don't remember any other boys auditioning for the role. Dan strictly came for Danny and Danny had the part straight away. For his audition he had to read from the script, but I don't remember what scene it was. Dan knew he wanted Danny from the start, because Danny was on *As the World Turns* (1956-2010), and Dan had seen him on that. Of course after doing *Cujo*, Danny had gotten the role on *Who's the Boss?* (1984-1992). That was all because of his work on *Cujo*. A woman executive from *Who's the Boss?* saw *Cujo* and she flew Danny and I out for an audition and he got that show straight away. Danny never went back to *As the World Turns* after *Cujo*. There was no screen test for *Cujo*, Dan Blatt came for Danny with Danny in mind.

PETER MEDAK: When I was a young assistant director I worked on some Hammer horror movies, which I loved. I was very fortunate. When I came to America I was just as lucky to work on *Alfred Hitchcock Presents* (1955-1962). I always had this keen interest in quasi-horror subject matter, so I really wanted to make a lot more of these films. The film I did before getting *Cujo* was *The Changeling*, and that was a supernatural ghost story. I was attracted to *Cujo*, but the film I would have made would have not been Lewis's, I'd have made a very different movie. I definitely wanted to give *Cujo* that supernatural edge with the serial killer and his connection with the dog. Stephen King had that in his novel with the killer from *The Dead Zone*, but here I wanted the killer to be a suicide that happened in the attic above the little boy's closet and he would go over and visit his own grave then return to the closet. Barbara fleshed it all out and she wrote that the boy's closet door would keep opening and there was a beautiful connection she made between the ghost and the bat that eventually infects the dog. I like what Lewis did with the opening with the dog going over the brook and chasing the rabbit and getting his head stuck in the cave, I mean all of that was mine. Not that I claim any credit there after all these years, but aside the years, there is all the work you put into it – but I think Lewis did a fabulous job.

CHARLES BERNSTEIN: In a lot of ways film music, when you trace everything back, sort of starts around the year 1600 with the beginnings of what came to be called "the classical opera." Opera did develop this concept over the years which was most fully realized with Wagner, of having themes he called "leitmotif" in German. This was the idea that themes were all stated throughout the process. But often in opera there is an overture and the themes are introduced. In musical theatre, in which Rodgers and Hammerstein were the highest manifestation of in America, is kind of modelled after opera and film kind of grew out of that era as well. So a lot of the earlier films, big movies, would have intermissions and walk in and walk out tracks. This is all part of the filmic musical experience derived by musical theatre and its ancestor the opera. For *Cujo*, I did not assign character themes, but I did assign circumstantial character themes, and by that I mean there were overriding themes like Cujo has his own personal theme, and the little boy has his piece of the main theme which is more delicate and more pianistic, like when the camera comes in on him in the bathroom in that opening scene; you start to feel the treatment of the theme for the little boy. Also, when the little boy has his "Monster Words" and the dad reads it and so forth; it's kind of a treatment of the theme for that tender boy moment, comforting the boy against the monster moment and so forth. So, in essence there are these overriding themes, but they are treated in certain ways for the mother and son and certain ways for the boy on his own, and for the father with the boy and certain ways for the unhappy martial issues and so forth.

DON CARLOS DUNAWAY: Barbara Turner did a super job on the Cujo siege, which tracks pretty much as she wrote it. She cut some of the advertising stuff, but not enough. There was quite a bit more Donna/ Vic stuff, maybe more Donna/Kemp. There was also quite a bit of explicit ooga-booga – supernatural things going bump in the night, special effects, etc. I took out everything I could on the theory that if you have a perfectly set up rational explanation for the bad stuff (rabid bat bites otherwise nice dog) the supernatural stuff is redundant and distracting. Writers like you yourself Lee Gambin, have stated that the film of *Cujo* is unusual for Stephen King simply because it lacks the supernatural; frankly, I can't remember if that was my impression of the novel or of the King script, but I'm pretty sure the Turner script had a lot of supernatural elements in there. I tried to squeeze all of it out of the script, but see in my copy of the shooting script there were traces of it in a couple of stage directions that Barbara wrote, so I must have missed them. I consider that my most important contribution to the film was eliminating the supernatural aspects. Lewis actually shot some kind of cheesy special effects in post for Tad's closet, but I'm pleased to say I was able to talk him out of using them.

PETER MEDAK: You know I have quit more movies than I have made. I think I have quit twenty movies in my career. When a director walks away from a film without making it, every frame remains in your brain. And this was the same with *Cujo*, but I completely closed my eyes to it. It was the most dreadful experience of my life. Dan Blatt used to be a lawyer working for Edgar J. Scherick, who was a New York producer, and Edgar came to me because he loved my movies *The Ruling Class* and *The Changeling* and various other projects, and he was always there in these meetings, and he would have this nervous habit of picking his nails. And I was going to make a movie for Edgar called *I Never Promised You a Rose Garden* (1977) with Charlotte Rampling and Mick Jagger and God knows who else, and the movie never happened, but that's how Dan and I knew each other, through Edgar.

The troubled Donna Trenton (Dee Wallace) comforts her sensitive son
Tad (Danny Pintauro), keeping him safe from imagined "monsters".

"NOPE, NOTHING WRONG HERE": The Trentons at breakfast and Steve Kemp pays a visit

Opening with Hanna-Barbera's longstanding cartoon dog Scooby-Doo on a small television set, this morning scene in the Trenton kitchen is a narrative centrepiece in that it establishes the hushed unease and quiet unrest that is embedded within the constraints of the *mise en scene*. *Scooby-Doo, Where Are You?* (1969-1970) featured "monster/ghost hunting" as its primary narrative infrastructure, however, in the final moments of each episode, our intrepid heroes Shaggy, Daphne, Velma and Fred, along with their dutiful titular Great Dane, would soon discover that these ghouls and supposedly supernatural menaces were, in fact, simply opportunistic or criminal deviants who wore masks and costumes. In *Cujo*, monsters are most certainly a constructed truth deeply rooted in primal and primitive fears and anxieties that exist in stoic realism.

These monsters are not werewolves, vampires or witches – instead, they are personal, societal and character-conceived demons that have materialized thanks to the horrors that surface from infidelity, unhappy marriages, careerism, alienation, lonely women, terrified little boys, sexually aggressive men and of course, rabid dogs. In Stephen King's novel, which opens with "Once Upon A Time…", discussion of Frank

Dodd (the perverted and demented serial killer and rapist from King's novel "The Dead Zone") is painted as a fragmented variant of American folklore meshed with the reasoning of complicated fairy tales. Dodd is referred to as a "monster" (a boogeyman that propels stories told by grandmothers who want to frighten unruly children) with the promise of a "new monster" emerging – in this case, the bloodthirsty St. Bernard with a nasty case of hydrophobia. "The monster never dies" is something that becomes a poignant and profound adage in King's book, and in the case of *Scooby-Doo, Where Are You?*, the "monster" will never cease to be a corrupt individual posing as an imagined fear – be it a yeti, a swamp creature or an alien from a distant planet.

Both *Cujo* and the popular Hanna-Barbera TV show share the concept of the changing face of the monster and the perpetually transitioning "perceived monster" – the violence perpetrated by a psychotic deputy eventually shifts to a foaming two hundred pound dog, and an old janitor with a bitter grudge can don a werewolf mask one day, then a woman with material gain on her mind can doll herself up as a local harridan the next.

Hanna-Barbera's Scooby Doo and his human counterparts.

In Lewis Teague's adaptation of Stephen King's source material, the concept of imagined terror and realized monstrousness is delicately intertwined and passionately examined. The sprinkling of pop-cultural reference as narrative commentary with the use of Scooby-Doo scooting across the floor and ceiling of a Hanna-Barbera fixed background, adds to the slice-of-life pragmatism while also defining the role/impression of the "monster" in innocuous surroundings.

While Tad watches Scooby-Doo skate around in a comic fashion, we get a fly on the wall glimpse at a household made up with personal divisions of concern, thought process and routine. Vic Trenton's mood is light and nonchalant, Donna Trenton is busying herself with innocuous duties such as preparing breakfast while harbouring firmly pent up secrets and worry, while their son Tad has just fended off monsters that "only come out at night". Vic asks his boy who would have moved the furniture around in his bedroom; Donna says it wasn't her, Vic also acknowledges that it wasn't him, and of course the actual culprit, Tad denies it also. The construct of this barricade that has blocked the monster from his closet is just as much a secret as Donna's extra-marital affair which will eventually come out and show itself in an ugly presentation later in the film; and this intricate and intimate portrait of three people locked together as a family unit are forced to face demons and confront personal monsters throughout the duration of the motion picture. This early kitchen sequence is a finely tuned handle on the balance between men, women and children and the domestic disturbance that can rear its ugly head at anytime and anywhere – the concept of fear both imagined and realized can manifest itself into varied embodiments of monstrosity.

Enter Steve Kemp (Christopher Stone), a rugged, sunkissed Lothario who strips the Trenton's furniture for them, as well as stripping Donna's humanity. Steve enters carrying a large wooden toy horse that belongs to Tad, and we get a sense of great familiarity here when he refers to Tad as "Tadpole" (another nickname bestowed on the boy, which is something that his parents also do – as earlier in the scene Vic addresses him as

"Tadder"). In a sense, Tad is rendered a communal child to be shared by the likes of busy fathers, complicated mothers and bearded heavies in the case of Steve Kemp.

Steve refers to the wooden horse saying that it "Looks pretty good stripped huh?" (a loaded line that stirs some unspoken cagey dealings going on with Donna), while Vic comments: "Maybe Mr. Kemp moved your furniture around?" Here there are more loaded lines intelligently powering the script – the idea of a man infiltrating the sanctity of the family unit happening to mysteriously appear and move around personal belongings to restrict a hidden monster is something poignant and profound. Another thematic connection is also peppered here where the role of furniture (a trapping of responsibility and "grown up" living) is connected to Steve who works with his hands and is "good with them". His presence clearly disturbs Donna (her shoulders drop on his arrival) while Vic remains oblivious to the situation at hand (a man completely in the dark). It is an interesting acting choice of Dee Wallace's to have Donna's back turned on her husband and child as she tends to breakfast – her shoulders shifting and her body language completely changing on Steve's entrance, and her nervous jittery dialogue when answering Steve's facetious teasing about wanting/not wanting a cup of coffee.

When Vic suggests that Steve was the person responsible for the "poltergeist" activity in Tad's room, he replies "OK, what did I do now…?", the question is an encumbered one, suggesting a sense of an irresponsible childlike mistake. The realized monster here ("No, the monster did it…") can be painted up to look like Steve Kemp, who is ultimately a very real threat to marriage and to family.

Donna's loneliness and suppressed inner-turmoil, as well as her boredom, forces her to remain quiet. During this scene, she has tiny snippets of dialogue, concealing the truths – both the truth behind her affair as well as the truth behind why she has taken this affair up. When Steve appears at the door, Vic calls out "Come on in Steve" and the idea of welcoming in the human monster is palpable and reflective: bringing in the "other", inviting the "disturbance". Donna's physical reaction to Steve being welcomed inside is masterfully delivered by Dee Wallace, who breathes every instance of insecurity, nervousness, guilt and personal restraint.

Merrit Olsen as the Sharp Cereal Professor (an invention used to peddle sugar-based breakfast) ensures that there is "nothing wrong here".

The reinforcement of there not being any "real" monsters propels the scene forward, however one is now in the house – Steve Kemp, someone who has polluted the sanctity of marriage. Adultery is a core focal point of the film, and what brings this very earthy "sin" against domestic bliss to the foreground is the intelligent way in which it is not discussed right away, but brought to light when necessary. A home invasion noir thriller, *Storm Fear* (1955), features a similar scenario of the other man inside the kitchen (a place of familial connection), and from this powerful orchestration of character and situation, an entirely methodically plotted character study would emerge and do its thing. This is very much the same case for *Cujo* – a film entirely dedicated to character, situation, story and personal struggle. This breakfast sequence quickly establishes characters living in the shadowy recesses of denial and shame, and as much as the sequence is shot with bright sunlight and an orange hue of cheery disposition, it is secretly concealing darkness – a very adult darkness, devoid of fanged monsters, but riddled with very human ones. The Trenton kitchen is a locale of varying degrees of domestic unrest throughout the film – first it is presented as a place of secrecy, then a place of disconnection (a very sombre dinner scene to come) and then finally the place where the ugly truth is revealed (the infamous "spilled milk" scene). The design for the kitchen is earnest and very real – a middle class family getting their bits and pieces together; a cluttered kitchen, a busy table, the noise from a bench set TV spewing out Hanna-Barbera cartoons and so forth.

Finally, in this sequence we are introduced to Vic's world – the world of television advertising. The Sharp Cereal Professor (Merritt Olsen) is a marketing invention, who peddles sugar coated breakfasts to young children everywhere. The Professor promises that his cereal is the best ("And, they're good for you") presenting a healthy façade as well as the concept of halcyon family living. Of course, this is a universe where reality is the key factor, and the fifties sensibility of happy nuclear families is a fabricated truth churned out by advertisers on television. In many regards then, Vic (who up until a certain point in the film) lives in a world of the made-up; here is a man whose entire life is based on selling product and creating a mythology of what "family" should be about. His breakfast cereals are reflective of a time gone by (a *Leave it to Beaver* (1957-1963) era, where children never feared monsters in their closets, and wives would never think of sleeping with another man).

In a film that examines unspoken truths, *Cujo* interweaves the delicate lives of Tad who is a sensitive child who picks up on things, Donna, a woman consumed by guilt and at a life altering crossroad and Vic, a man blinded by lies (both fabricated and really happening). Here, in this scene, the most together and not so distressed by the world seems to be Vic, and his counter/rival Steve, seems not too fussed about being paid straight up for stripping the horse. Steve's dark intentions seem to not be so much about making money, but more so about having the opportunity to see

Donna. When Tad states that monsters might not appear in the daytime ("Not in the day time anyway"), he sets his father and Steve into a chuckle but also taps into a preconceived notion that monsters don't exist in the glaring light of day – of course, they do (in the guise of adultery and human mistakes), and most certainly will manifest in realized confrontation (in the shape of a rabid St. Bernard). The Sharp Cereal Professor (a clear representative stand-in for Vic's career in advertising) also validates this fear of the hidden monstrosity, in that he is the "father of lies" to children all across America, when later it is learned that a little girl vomited up food dye which was thought to be blood. This "father of lies" in the Sharp Cereal Professor also acts as a divisive brick wall that separates two men locked in unrecognized competition – Steve comments on Vic's creation of the Professor ("Well your daddy's real smart isn't he?") while harbouring a silent resentment. The concept of the working class labourer Steve compared to middle class white collar worker Vic is palpable and something that *Cujo* seems to be invested in: classism and class is a huge overriding theme in both the source novel and the film.

The image of Donna eating her breakfast and looking quietly guilty – the adulteress woman distracting herself with the mundane – while the Sharp Cereal Professor sits over her shoulder throwing out catch phrases, is a masterfully designed shot, completely embodying the lies we tell ourselves and the lies we let the media spit at us. The scene closes with the adage: "Nope, nothing wrong here" and this is a perfect, finely tuned summary of the situation at hand. At the heart of the scene sits four characters with conflicting dramas to tend to: Donna's guilt and fear, Vic's obliviousness, Tad's confidence in daylight (which will soon change, when monsters can in fact attack you in broad daylight) and Steve's damaging influence that strips the family bare.

Along with the Sharp Cereal Professor reeling off a list of cereals – the idea of the sales rep being a professor and offering advice on health and healthy eating – the scene dedicates itself to keeping Donna in a perpetual state of solemn self-reflection (something that will keep at a constant for the early moments of the film), while the staging of each sequence will comment and foreshadow the events that will be blood soaked and brutal when she is trapped in the broken down Pinto with Tad. The image of Donna and Vic at either end of the dinner table, with Steve crouched in between them comes to represent a beast emerging from the middle of the family unit. Positioning Steve Kemp on the floor, also structures a ground level vision of the place a dog knows all too well (to be seated by the master while the master eats). An inexplicable link somehow develops between Steve and Cujo himself, two characters that will eventually trap Donna and corner her into a frenzied confrontation.

Domestic unrest: Donna Trenton (Dee Wallace) nervously hides a deep dark secret at the family breakfast table, while her lover Steve Kemp (Christopher Stone) draws a visible divide between her and her husband Vic (Daniel Hugh Kelly) and son Tad (Danny Pintauro).

LEWIS TEAGUE: Dee Wallace's character makes a bad choice and it is made because she is acting on fear. Personally, I don't think adultery is a good thing because I value integrity and honesty and commitment. I'm sure those characters innately also placed a value on those qualities, but she probably violated her personal inner beliefs because of her fear. Stephen King didn't really go into a deep Freudian exploration of that. But, to me, it is pretty clear that that was the cause and effect. She was out of her element in a small town. She wasn't being satisfied in a small degree, it was just a reaction to her husband's lack of attention, because he was totally obsessed with his work and hanging onto clients and supporting his family. So she turned her desire for affection in a different direction.

DEE WALLACE: When I perform it is always in the moment but it's the character of Donna in the moment. I find if that I'm the character in the moment than I would rely on the character doing whatever it is in the moment because that is always more interesting than what Dee would do if I worked on it the night before. So, I really do like to become her and see where she's gonna go and if the director needs a move here or a move there then I work with the character of Donna to find out how to make that real. Donna was always hiding secrets of her own which is very stressful and she was stressed out about Tad. In this scene she has her secret in the house with her, so on many different levels this is just another boogeyman in the closet and she has to hide it, and her life and death depends on not letting this boogeyman out of the closet which means having her husband being tipped off. Fear plays off in many different ways and *Cujo* is a perfect example of that.

DANIEL HUGH KELLY: I wasn't happy with the commercial they came up with. Lewis came up with the *Scooby Doo* reference in there. I didn't care for it when I first saw it when we were doing the scene, I thought that this was making me look bad, but then I thought, "Danny who cares what you think? Who are you?" It is really good stuff that is created. I mean what do you want to be watching on the television in the morning during commercial time, *Gone with the Wind* (1939)? I mean come on! The guy is an ad guy! This is what he came up with and what is really sick is that this is what is taking this guy away from his family.

I mean that ad with the professor is terrible, and that is what is really demented about it.

DANNY PINTAURO: I remember the commercial. I remember the "Nope, nothing's wrong here." I definitely have memories of filming that! I remember there was some tickling that happens in the breakfast scene with Daniel Hugh Kelly that wasn't planned. We were just having fun with each other. I really loved him. The funny part about it is, as an actor, or when I was acting, I had no concept of him being my movie dad, he was just this nice guy. This was the same with Christopher Stone. I knew that he was meant to be a villain in the piece, but he was so nice and charming. In the back of my head however, I was thinking "OK, he's a bad guy. He's the bad guy. I have to be a little cautious of him!"

Christopher Stone on set with Danny Pintauro's mother Margaret. (courtesy of Danny and Margaret Pintauro).

MARCIA ROSS: I don't remember casting Christopher Stone, I just remember that it was very important that there was a role for him because he had come with Dee Wallace as a kind of package deal. And that character, the lover she has an affair with, was the perfect role for him.

LEWIS TEAGUE: Dee Wallace was very sensitive and emotional and high strung and we got along great! She was a delight to work with because the results were so good! Yeah, she was great. And the boy who played Tad, of course, was amazing! He was cast under Peter Medak, so I was lucky that I inherited a cast that I was delighted with, and thankful for doing that! Yeah, I can't take any credit for that. It was already cast and I was more than happy to go along with it.

TONY RICHMOND: It was terrible for Peter when he was fired from this movie. Peter Medak is one of my oldest friends, I met him in 1959. We are very close and see each other all the time. I wasn't fired at the same time as Peter. Dan Blatt was a friend of mine; I was the only one that really knew Dan Blatt. He and I had worked together before, we had worked on a very good picture called *The American Success Company* (1980) starring Jeff Bridges and Bianca Jagger, and so I was the one that really had a close connection and history with Dan. So what really had happened was the weather cover was sixty miles away which was completely insane, and we got stuck in some pretty heavy rain, and when I got back to the hotel, I was in the bar drinking and Dan came in and said "I need to talk to you". I said "OK" and then he told me that he had fired Peter Medak. I was shocked. I said "You what?! You are crazy! Why on earth would you do that?" and Dan went on about how Peter was taking too long with decisions but it had nothing to do with that it was all to do with the weather conditions – so it was totally out of our hands. It was raining heavily, so we couldn't shoot! So once Peter was fired, he had asked me if I would leave with him, and I was definitely keen on doing that but I had to get Dan to fire me, because if I walked out I wouldn't be paid, but if I was fired I would get paid off. So that night I got very drunk. I was so rude to Dan that he fired me and I got paid off for the whole movie.

LEWIS TEAGUE: Well, the whole family had to suffer the karmic effect of the fear they were indulging themselves in. It is an indulgence to begin to live as if your fears are actually a real threat is an indulgence. There is a cause and effect relationship – it's very karmic in a sense. So in that sense, I always looked at the convergence of the dog and the family's life as an example of homeostasis in the universe. One of the most fundamental principles in the universe is homeostasis or the desire to achieve equilibrium and eventually everything corrects itself if it is out of balance. So the convergent path of the rabid dog and the woman and her son is real. Here the woman has committed adultery and her having to protect her son draws her husband back into that situation also, so it is an inevitable correction in the universe which could also cause karma. I don't look at karma as punishment, so I never felt as though she was being punished for her sins – I just thought that it was the universe trying to re-establish equilibrium. In this particular case, when she experiences the real lethal threat of this rabid dog and being trapped in this car, that puts everything into perspective and the universe's perspective – it is the idea that the only things that deserve our real fear are real threats.

PETER MEDAK: My eldest son, Christopher was the first assistant on the film. I think he was one of the PAs and it was one of his first jobs. He had stayed on the film all the way and he remained a good friend of Lewis's.

PATRUSHKHA MIERZWA (boom mic operator): I had no idea how the project came about. I didn't know about the book directly.

MARK ULANO (sound mixer): I haven't a clue as to how the job came about, really. I knew there was a novel, but hadn't read it.

DANNY PINTAURO: I don't know much and I don't remember much. I definitely have this vague sense of awareness of the idea that, you know, my job was to be there and know that something was happening in the background. But you know how kids are when they pretend that they're not a part of that, and like, they're scared in the background of their mind that something awful is going on. That they're not "I'm just gonna go. Dad's gonna take me, we're gonna go to the park. Everything will be fine!" I think I really played that a lot. What I internalized all of that was, I was the cause of it. For me, the way I look at it was I was externalising the stuff that was going on with my parents by creating this monster in a closet. I spent sometimes, sort of really, like I needed them to be there together to talk about the monster. That was a way to sort of bring them together. So that is how I sort of internalized the whole thing. All of this again, is really vague, and I don't know how to explain it. I was this weird, intelligent kid who had this whole concept of what was happening in my life, and yet it was all like I was being guided through all of this stuff. Because no six year old should really have any concept of any of the stuff that I was going through and certainly not an intelligent, sort of awareness of what would happen, and yet I was. I feel like it was a very fateful thing for that to be happening. Not just with *Cujo*, this goes for any of that stuff! A lot of my memories are me driving home from New York to New Jersey every day and lying down in the back of the Camino and sleeping and my mom promising me a pretzel if I did a good job at work that day. Then the dual side of it was I would show up, and I would just do these lines and cry and whatever it is they asked, and then we went home!

SEEN AROUND TOWN - Seven year old Abe Feran-Hickman and his St. Bernard, "EZ" have been seen around town advertising the appearance of noted author, Stephen King, to be here Saturday. November 19. The placard worn by the dog tells where the best-selling author will be appearing and the time. Truth or Consequences will be the only city visited by King during his trip through New Mexico. The event is sponsored by the Friends of the TorC Library. *11/17/83   Page 1*

A promotion for the novel of "Cujo". Here a young boy and his pet St. Bernard promote the book and promote literacy and the joys of reading for children in the suburbs of New Mexico.

"WHATEVER TURNS YOU ON": A tennis match of deceit

Following directly from the Sharp Cereal Professor's "Nope, nothing wrong here", we open on a sweaty and determined Vic Trenton lowering his head in preparation of smashing a tennis ball across a sunkissed court. Originally intended to be a longer sequence, the tennis match between Vic Trenton and Steve Kemp was plotted early in the piece to establish a competitive nature shared by these two very different men. Fundamentally the nature of their friendship seems to be considerably unlikely in that the two men differ in personality and even class. However, Stephen King is no stranger to writing relationships shared between men and teen boys that seem to exist within a realm of unlikelihood – the same year of *Cujo*'s release would see John Carpenter's adaptation of *Christine*, which would feature a remarkably unconventional friendship between a popular, handsome and athletic jock and a jittery, neurotic and pathetic nerd. However, the beauty found in King's writing validates these unions and fuels the dramatic intention and stitches together the emotional beats. Here in *Cujo*, Vic and Steve represent the polar opposites of masculine energy, which is essentially something that Donna bounces back and forth from. The allegorical energy of the tennis match makes poignant commentary on Donna jumping from one end of life's court to the other

– one of safety and conventional harmony, and the other of danger and sexual dynamism.

As much as Vic represents the middle class intellectual who is careerist and ambitious, in Stephen King's novel the character of Steve Kemp was an amateur poet, as well as local Lothario who was "good with his hands". This implies a sensitivity deeply hidden within the rough exterior regarding Kemp, and although his poetic leanings could also be attributed to his "slacker" sensibility, his interest in weaving words together is a somewhat quirky character ingredient painting up an originally complicated creation. However, in the film, Kemp's poetry is not even mentioned or even hinted at – even in the follow up scene where we get a glimpse at his shabby townhouse, production designer Guy J. Comtois doesn't pepper the environs with references to poets or great classic works, in fact the abode is barely dressed.

After Vic smacks the ball across the court, Steve swiftly strikes it back towards him, but it hits the net and kills the game. There is a sense of Steve letting Vic win – a condescending attribute heralded by the cagey and secretive Steve. It is as if Steve will let Vic win the unimportant tennis game, because it is a superficiality and something that pales in significance to what Steve has already "won" – or what he believes he has "won" – which is fundamentally the attention and affections of Donna. The visual brilliance commenting on Steve's hidden agenda comes with the poignant image of Steve having his tennis racket covering his face – a wonderful play on light, shade and composition. This completely reads as a man with secrets, and a man bathing in dishonesty. It is also interesting to note that the two men seldom look at one another in the eye during the entire short scene – there is an oppressive element of deceit here, matched with the sweltering heat in the dead of summer in Castle Rock.

"You're not getting tired of this, are ya?" asks Vic, to which Steve replies "What, are you kidding me? Getting my ass handed over to me every week, nah I love it, I'm a masochist!" The lines are loaded and beautifully concocted – this is not about a tennis game, this is about two men in

84

sexual competition (one unaware and the other concealing ugly truths). Vic follows this up with "Whatever turns you on…" which is a masterful throw to the following scene which establishes Steve's affair with Vic's wife. "Whatever turns you on" becomes something painfully close, and a direct attack on not only Vic, but the sanctity of the family unit.

Steve Kemp (Christopher Stone) conceals his face, remaining cagey about the extra marital affair.

DANIEL HUGH KELLY: The biggest difference between working on television and feature films was the wait time. With *Ryan's Hope* we shot almost as if we were doing this thing live, but with *Cujo* there was a lot of time on set waiting around. Film is much slower. With *Cujo* we would shoot two and half pages over the course of an entire day, and that was a lot and that to me was something incredibly jarring. I had to get used to that. However, it didn't bother me in a way because I had to learn how to play tennis. And Chris also didn't know how to play tennis, he had never played before either, so any time we weren't on set we would go to the hotel's tennis court and practice playing tennis. More so, we were practicing not looking bad at playing tennis. Lewis didn't think I was good enough in terms of playing tennis. He was bought on after Peter

Medak was fired, and of course it was Peter who hired me, and to be brutally honest, I wasn't sure if Lewis wanted me to continue on with the role. I came to really like Lewis, but when a new director comes on all you can think is "Hey, I'm not his guy!" so you're not sure if you're going to continue or not. I remember how hard Chris and I worked on getting our tennis game perfected, but I remember thinking about how I played and thought Lewis is not going to buy this and I look terrible pretending to play tennis. After *Cujo* I never tried playing tennis ever again. I do think that on the shoot they had lessons provided, quite possibly that was the case, but I just distinctly remember being out on the hotel tennis court with Chris any chance we got. I don't remember the intensity of the scene either.

Christopher Stone on the tennis court in between takes. (courtesy of Danny and Margaret Pintauro).

SMALL TOWN SCARLET WOMAN:
Donna wakes up in Steve's bed

Cutting from the close up of Steve Kemp's face hiding behind the net of his tennis racket, the following sequence carries on the thematic element of deception that runs through the contextual bloodstream of *Cujo*. As a core narrative component, the act of adultery sits as a structural centrepiece in the film, and the way this central character-driven and plot driving catalyst is presented, is through an honest (almost documentarian) lens. Steve's affair with Donna Trenton is introduced as a warts-and-all gritty reality, and director Lewis Teague, along with his artistic team, deliver a layered and yet silently sombre moment of self-reflection and hushed disorder.

Steve Kemp wakes up in his dishevelled bed and collects a rusty trombone, blowing it. Waking up by his side is a weary eyed Donna who is startled by the loud instrument; she lifts her head and is forced to face another hazy afternoon of lies and duplicity. Steve Kemp's abode is a messy shambles. It is a bachelor's den, free from the trappings of responsibility. Production designer Guy J. Comtois loads the place with non-descript articles of disperse necessity and questionability: in a cluttered mess – reflective of his recklessness – there are bits and pieces of scattered about belongings that seem to serve a purpose in the grand scheme of things, but are ultimately non-descript (piping, oil cans et al).

The sunkissed room suggests an already stifling oppressive heat (Castle Rock's worst summer) and it knocks out Steve's ability to hold on to more than a few notes from his trombone. His use of this instrument somewhat summarizes a mockery on the trumpeting of angels heralding in the morning, while Donna leaves his bed draped in a red dress marking her the "scarlet woman". This is an affair that is introduced to the film as something completely innocuous and blunt, with nothing glamorous in its foundation. Much like the rest of the film, the extramarital affair is very real and very earthy. However, it is packed up with deep symbolic resonance and pieced together by an air of mythic paragon that shall lead the film's heroine into a place of constraint, torture and trial by fire.

The image of Donna putting on her underwear underneath her dress with the perspiration on her lip – a combination of what might be sexual afterglow or the onset of sweltering heat – is made all the more provocative in that it is depicted in a reflection. She is staring at herself in a mirror looking incredibly sombre and completely consumed by an internalized guilt. This perplexed woman at some kind of crossroads in her life studies herself in the bronze hue while composer Charles Bernstein quietly drives in a maudlin and self-reflective musical motif that comes to embody an introspective and sorrowful thematic shift. Moments before Donna scrutinizes her reflection, she is in bed with Steve, who somehow comes to represent a sexually charged rugged bohemian – he works with wood and is initially introduced carrying in a toy horse, he has a trombone suggesting an interest in music and he is "good with his hands". The film denies Steve any kind of coverage into his personal life; instead it circles him and ensures that he is most certainly the "other man". Even suggesting his connection to music is treated as flippant throwaway, because his artistic intentions might be misconstrued as something that is attractive to Donna. Initially they share a laugh, but the tone swiftly turns sombre, escalating to Charles Bernstein's music which is both quietly sad and contemplative. This musical piece carries the audience off to the next scene and hammers the emphasis on Donna's loneliness and her isolation, as well as her desperate need to be happy or to find some kind of fulfilment. If her affair is treated as a warts-and-all slice of life, then so is her connection to her own husband Vic.

The original concept for introducing Donna and Steve's affair was much more graphic and explicit in tone, mood and visceral depiction. Director Lewis Teague initially shot a sequence where Donna would be on top of Steve and in the throes of passionate sex. Set to some established chamber music, it was intended to originally open with the idea that Donna was sitting at a piano playing a piece and losing herself to the music, however with the camera pulling back, it would reveal that she would be in fact on top of Steve, making love. This original concept plays up the provocative idea that Steve is a kind of "music maker" for the lonely and lowly Donna. That she can "play him" for a moment here and there and lose herself in the primal carnality of it all.

The adulteress Donna (Dee Wallace) catches a glimpse of herself in a dusty mirror at her lover's abode.

DEE WALLACE: It was so horrible to play out the sex scene. I mean doing a sex scene with anyone is stressful, but to do it with your real life husband is worse! We were stressing over it the night before and asking each other how we would do it, and there was talk of us not doing it how we would actually do it! Chris was so worried but he was adamant on protecting me and making sure there was nothing inappropriate, because there had been a lot of talk at the time because I was E.T.'s mom! And people did not want to see E.T.'s mom naked and screwing! The studio would have really loved to see this however! We didn't get any backlash at the time, but that was because we didn't do any nudity. I mean it was handled tastefully. I told Dan Blatt off the bat that I don't do nudity, but he said "We'll work it out", so we had me in a hot pink skirt with a dress over it so you don't really see anything explicit. We were getting ready to do this scene and I look down at Chris and I say "Dude! Where did you go? There's nothing going on down here!" and we both started laughing. He was hilarious, and so sweet because he was so concerned with how I would look and how I would be presented in this, but we just cracked up laughing. The best way I can describe doing sex scenes in a movie is like having your mother sitting at the bottom end of your bed watching while you're getting it on, there is nothing natural about it at all! The role of Donna was so powerful that it transcended a scene like this.

PETER MEDAK: I remember hating Dan Blatt and I then re-met him at one of Barbara's parties. She had these incredible Christmas parties with about one hundred or so guests and you had to bring one decoration with you and hang it on this huge Christmas tree. I couldn't talk to Dan at that party. I couldn't even look at him. For me, the only positive thing to come out of *Cujo* was my friendship with Barbara. When I was doing *Romeo is Bleeding* (1993) she was totally impressed with Gary Oldman, so I introduced her to him. She knew all my wives, all my ex-wives, I mean she knew my kids and I knew her kids and I remember Mina, her beautiful little daughter, would come into the living room while we were working on *Cujo*. She would look at us with those beautiful big eyes, and I would say to her "I will never forget you". It was a beautiful time. Barbara is one of my lifelong friends and I miss her terribly. We used to talk all the time and talk about her scripts and my films, and it was a beautiful friendship. She was a wonderful writer and woman and mother, and if you ever see pictures of her when she was young, she was incredibly beautiful. She was such an important part of *Cujo*. I just know for sure she was incredibly upset about me being fired and that is why she used a pseudonym. She said that Dan Blatt was out of his mind, and she was confused as to why Tony was fired. She was angry that his private life got him in trouble. I mean look at someone like John Huston who was drunk out of his fucking mind on every movie.

CHRISTOPHER MEDAK: Dad's attention to detail was crucially important, and he spent time with working on things and this opening is a testament to that. But bloody producers don't have that capacity to understand why he took that time. Dan Blatt was a fucking idiot. Dan didn't know talent from the backend of his asshole. All he cared about was the bottom line.

PETER MEDAK: The company was independent, they were called Sunn Pictures and their office was off Wilshire Blvd. I remember there was a tremendous lawsuit going on afterwards because the company refused to pay me. When you fire someone you have to pay them. If I was to quit, then that's fine. My lawyer and the Directors Guild fought Sunn and threatened to shut down the production. I was paid in the end.

ROBIN LUCE: I remember being in the room when Dee's haircut was taking place, and that was a big deal. This was a concern, because of continuity issues. Which was the same deal on the set of *E.T. the Extra-Terrestrial* I believe. Julie Purcell was the hair dresser on the film and I remember being more focused on the makeup, and I tried not to get tied up in the politics which were going on between the actors and producers and also even Julie on the film.

CHARLES BERNSTEIN: I had not read the novel, and so in a way, that is good for me, because the movie is quite different from the book in many ways, and it allowed me to simply deal with the movie on its own terms without being concerned with the things that are really happening outside of the story that happened in the book. So I really was only dealing with the movie as it was given to me.

PETER MEDAK: I absolutely adored Barbara. I worked on the script with her for two or three months, then I went off and looked for the locations while she wrote it. I remember finding the farm in Santa Rosa and the town in Mendocino, but I don't remember finding the apartment of the leading lady's lover, that was something else entirely.

"RUNNING OUT OF CONVERSATION": Dinner with the Trentons

The absence of dialogue in the previous scene ensures a less quiet, but even more solemn follow up. With cinematographer Jan de Bont's camera closing in on the Trentons as they are filmed through a wood panel arch, Donna seated to the left, Tad in the centre and Vic to the right, the sequence evokes a sense of hushed hysteria and silenced misery. These three characters are surrounded by enveloping darkness, and it must be noted that the scene is under-lit spinning out a nuanced sense of lacking light, denial of hope, disarray and despondency.

The minimal dialogue (as opposed to the previous scene which was entirely talk-free) is plotted and placed with strategic planning, and primarily comes from Vic as he senses a disconnect from Donna. Daniel Hugh Kelly handles this gloom with tenderness and care, as he observes: "This marriage is definitely running out of conversation". Vic Trenton, a man whose career is all about message-making and slogans, has finally realized that inside his very own household there is an oppressive and incredibly palpable failure of communication. Following this with "Maybe we should start talking about having another baby", Vic instantly introduces a direct reference to the family unit and also toys with the notion of extending such an institution. The suggestion of another child is doubly profound, it is both an extension to something that is already established (ie the family as a constructed entity) and also as an attempt to salvage what might be rescued. A crumbling marriage could quite possibly renew its loving dedication and association with the help of a second child.

The scene ends with Tad (who senses his parents' disassociation) breaking the tension – pulling his father to the ground to play wrestle with him allowing Donna to open up and let out a laugh. This would mark the first time we ever see her open and smiling; a fleeting glimpse of her happiness caused by the buffoonery of Tad. Tad's initial attempt to break the silence is when he turns the kitchen set TV on, however, of course he is told to turn it off and get back to his dinner. Tad internalising the domestic unrest and sensing that his mother and father are slowly becoming strangers living under the same roof is something that would lead the poor boy having delusions about monsters in his closet. *Cujo* responds to this in an intricate fashion where fragmented ideas of formative fears and illusions will suddenly become materialized and purposefully manifest. When Tad decides to bring his parents together with the gift of laughter, he jumps underneath the dinner table and brings his hand up, shaping it like a shark fin and running it across emulating the theme from *Jaws* (1975). By the release of *Cujo* in 1983, Steven Spielberg's innovative and iconic megahit would be part of the global consciousness, and having it referred to in not only the film of *Cujo*, but by its very real and very earnest characters, makes astounding sense. In fact, the concept of a fellow eco-horror movie loaning itself to character development and used in a pop-cultural sensibility, is a proactive extension to the attribute of fear – Tad's homage to *Jaws* (a film that dealt with the fundamental subconscious fear of the unknown and the depths of the unexamined).

Jaws would feature an all-consuming leviathan as its featured animal-monster, whereas in *Cujo*, there is an absolute unfortunate tragedy that leads to a once loveable pooch to turn into a relentlessly violent demon; after all, it is not Cujo's fault that he does the things he does.

Tad as saviour (bringing his parents together in unison laughter) is something that the film will employ for quietly restraint moments, however, by the end of the movie, it would be his mother Donna who would be outstanding in her delivery of strength. Her determination to keep Tad alive is the makings of masterful horror film execution.

By the end of the scene, Tad has successfully dropped Vic down to the floor while the finally cheery Donna calls out "Watch my chair!" Donna seems to be connected to material possessions which is something that the book emphasizes – her monologue late in the book goes into her collection of ceramic figurines and so forth while the music highlights the sadness, the disconnection and the alienation and becomes a theme that re-emerges throughout the film.

DEE WALLACE: We had the freedom to improvise anywhere. We had to improvise in the car. You had to. There were certain lines that we had to get out for the story, but whatever happened we had to have the freedom to go with that. In the dinner scene however, it was kind of written with very little dialogue and meant to be incredibly uncomfortable. This scene was meant to say: here's a family that is supposed to be OK, but they are not OK. Which is reflective of possibly three quarters of the audience watching. It is so real, and so poignant. We have all been in those situations of "this is pretend" and "I'm not really here and I'm not really committed to this, but I'll go with it right now".

DANIEL HUGH KELLY: You try and forget all the details in the character's intentions, you have to remember that you're making a movie and it obviously becomes hard when the crew is all there. What I usually try and do is escape from the reality of the situation and get out of being Daniel Hugh Kelly and become this guy – this guy who suspects his wife is cheating on him. It's not his fault that she is having this affair – I mean, look what I have built for her, there is this house, this great kid and I'm out working every day bringing in the money, and she's unhappy? That's what

I was thinking through these scenes. I never try and say "What would this guy do?" because then you have to question your own sensibilities as a person, and not so much as an actor, and you have to trust yourself to let the character take over. And if you do it right, then it will come through. That is why Dee and Kaiulani Lee are so damn good, because when they perform it is not them, it's their character, but it is also all them, and that is what makes them so special as performers. I remember talking with Lewis in the kitchen, and I was very nervous, and I remember quoting to him Laurence Olivier and saying "It's all the size of the portrait, isn't it?" and I said to Lewis "I'm not being too big am I?" and he said "No, it's a big screen, you're not on TV and you're not on stage". I remember that Olivier quote sticking out for me, and thinking about the cinema screen as a different portrait. For Dee, who had worked so much in film, made it look so easy. It was effortless for her, she was so damn good.

LEWIS TEAGUE: Well, Dee and Daniel are very different actors. Dee is very emotional and intuitive and Daniel was more cerebral, but it worked for the characters. It worked for the scenes. I don't ever remember any conflicts as a result of that.

MARGARET PINTAURO: Danny wasn't aware of the adultery in the film, he didn't know that his mother was having an affair in the movie. And nobody on set made him aware of that. He was far too young to understand that kind of thing – that issue is only experienced by adults. His acting was just so perfectly fine tuned that those feelings as a child came across on screen without him knowing what they were actually about.

DANNY PINTAURO: Lewis had told me to do something to break the mood so I did this *Jaws* reference. I guess Lewis liked it because it had that same sort of idea where another animal is evil in another movie. I would love to be able to say that I sort of created this moment that references another incredibly huge movie about an animal that kills people, but I don't actually know the truth to that. I do remember that I was told to come up with something to do, to get them and to get my dad to pay attention, and to sort of have them get out of that moment. But whether I was fed any of that, I don't remember. I do have very specific memories of feeling uncomfortable and having that feeling of that moment where you know not all is right with your parents, and that was a really powerful moment because as an actor who is learning lines scene by scene, I am sitting there with two actors who are very in the moment and the energy between them is very intense, so that was sort of painful for a child to feel. There was no question about it that that is inescapable for me to feel what is happening in the room in that moment.

The perceptive innocent: Young Tad Trenton (Danny Pintauro) senses and internalises the growing distance shared between his mother and father.

CHARLES BERNSTEIN: I had already worked for Dan Blatt, and I think that Dan had probably brought me in, but I knew Lewis, and had worked with him before also. He and I had worked for a documentarian named Fred Engleberg, so we knew each other from those days. This was Bert Schneider's production company, that produced many famous movies in the seventies with Jack Nicholson, such as *Five Easy Pieces* (1970). So, Lewis was part of that world and he and I had been in touch, but I don't think that he was the initial director set up for *Cujo*. I had worked for Dan Blatt, as I mentioned, and Dan had brought me in initially to meet with Lewis. We recorded at Warner Bros., at the recording stage which is now called the Clint Eastwood stage, but it was just the Burbank studios back then. I believe Bobby Fernandez was my engineer and we had an orchestra that was not huge. But my recollection was that it was maybe fifty players. We didn't record more than a couple sessions one day and then another session the next day. It was all recorded simultaneously. We brought in the electronic effects, we recorded them right there on the stage. I worked at home on the ARP; so some of those things were recorded on the Echoplex, put on the ARP and some other instruments on the stage.

"JOE CAMBER WILL DO IT FOR YOU": Vic visits the garage

Cutting from a dark interior sequence which presents one tiny moment of cheer shared by the troubled Trentons at the dinner table to an exterior tracking shot held in broad daylight, the next scene is solely in the service of plot development and adding to the building horror of circumstance which is what *Cujo* is essentially mounted upon. In Stephen King's novel, it is a combination of the mundane and the coincidental that merge in order to deliver a frenzied third act that will be gore soaked and highly intense. In Lewis Teague's adaptation of the novel, this ethos is presented in straight forward and right to the point detail where each scene, situation, development and structural plot point culminate in what will be a frightening siege that will genuinely upset, terrify and rattle. Much like in Brian De Palma's treatment of King's novel of "Carrie" in his 1976 stylistic and poetic film, each building block is essential to bring the horror home – in *Carrie*, each progressive element brings us to the prom, and here in *Cujo*, each narrative advancement is set to bring us to that busted up Pinto with mother and son trapped by a ferocious maniacal dog.

Opening with Vic Trenton driving through the sleepy town of Castle Rock in his stalling red Jaguar, the scene is completely grounded in the ordinary, innocuous and humdrum of everyday living. Here is a man, a professional urban type, trekking it through this Maine village, in order to get his car looked at by a trustworthy mechanic. Thankfully, Lewis Teague and his actor Daniel Hugh Kelly underplay Vic Trenton as a "fish out of water"; instead Kelly's methods under Teague's direction have him finding his own feet, sifting through the motions and taking an ease in establishing his place in such a rural setting. He is confident in starting to settle into small town living, and this is something that comes across in Kelly's acting choices and his ability to go with the flow.

He reaches a garage called Marshall's Body Repairs, and it is atypical of what you would find in a small town – a rundown shop, falling to pieces, cluttered with car parts and vehicles waiting to be tended, and with an equally rundown exhausted mechanic running what looks like a one man operation. Vic parks the Jaguar and steps out telling Harry (Terry Donovan-Smith), a greased up busy mechanic who lies underneath a car tending to its needs, that his car has a dodgy front wheel. Harry (who seems to be a replacement for the novel's character of Vin Callahan, who was a garage mechanic in the Castle Rock suburb of Conway) tells him to leave it parked next to the Dodson in what seems to be a semi-Irish accent. Castle Rock would eventually be established in Stephen King's universe as a combination of left over immigrant experience and very early settlers still holding on to founding dialects such as Irish, French and so forth. When Vic explains that he needs the car seen to right away, Harry cannot help. Luckily for Vic, Castle Rock's post man George Meara (Robert Elross), an elderly gent who seems to have been working in the postal service for his entire life, tells him to take his car to a shade tree mechanic named Joe Camber.

"Joe Camber will do it for you", says Meara, "He'll do a real good job and won't rob yer blind for it". Vic is intrigued, asks who Joe Camber is, and is not given any more information but just directions to his farm where he works on cars and the like. This is a classic story telling device in play here – the concept of a thus far unintroduced character who is referred to and "recommended" is an oft used trope in horror fiction and cinema (think of Dracula being mentioned to Jonathan Harker before he sets out to his Transylvanian castle), and here in *Cujo*, the set up and introduction of Joe Camber is earthy, but still harbouring on the mythic. Camber emerges from his foggy barn which acts as a make-shift shop, like a supernatural entity welcoming brand new prey – and here in this scene, Vic Trenton, an urbane polo shirt wearing, fitted Levi's adorning, tennis shoe sporting, gum chewing yuppie is sent out even further into uncharted terrain. In *Cujo*, Transylvania is the dusty plains of lower class rural living: the farming community. And here, while he converses with George Meara (a sunkissed local) and Harry (who is "too busy" to get a job done in one day), Vic is sent out to venture into the "wilderness" – giving the film a moment to capitalize on the thematic blueprint of class, cultural difference and restlessness, American suffrage and familial discontent.

The middle class Vic Trenton (Daniel Hugh Kelly) is forced to rely on the help of blue collar New Englanders represented here by Meara (Robert Elross) the mailman who advises the young advertising agent to seek help from mechanic Joe Camber (Ed Lauter).

TONY RICHMOND: Honestly the only good that came from it for me was being able to be in Mendocino which is a beautiful, gorgeous place. We started working out a shooting schedule and there was a huge, and I mean huge, night shot which was going to be absolutely fantastic, and then the rain came in.

PETER MEDAK: Barbara was a great friend of Dan Blatt and was a wonderful writer. Obviously Dan went to her and asked her for massive help, but she went off on her own to work on it. Once I was hired I worked with her. Now the film was very low budget at that time, there was no money for pre-production. But I do recall finding the locations, and I fell in love with Mendocino. It was an incredible locale for it. I don't know how long it took them to restart everything after I was fired, but it wouldn't have been longer than two weeks.

DANIEL HUGH KELLY: The scene where I get my car to the garage was shot in Mendocino as well.

TERRY DONOVAN-SMITH ("Harry"): I have a very small part. But I can tell you stuff about what happened. I was only at the location for two days. One day auditioning and another day shooting, so, you know. By the time I got there, Lewis Teague was the director. I auditioned for Lewis Teague. And so, I do not know how long they had been up there shooting. I was living in San Francisco making my living as an actor, you know, doing mostly TV commercials and the occasional TV show and this came up, and you know, it was not that high a budget thing, but I didn't even know what was going on, you know, when my agent called me and said "We're sending two people up there." In fact, the guy I was auditioning with didn't have a car, so I drove him up there and we auditioned, and he is actually a friend of mine. But I didn't know anything about the other director. I hadn't read the novel, but I had read *The Shining* and something else but in the breakdown I was told that it was a dog horror movie. I auditioned with sides. I knew that they had a lot of San Francisco actors in the show. By the time I got the breakdown, my agent had told me that there were some small parts peppered in and about this film and they were doing it as a piece deal for SAG, where they have to pay you to show up. So we even got paid for auditioning. It was a long drive from San Francisco but we got some gas money. I was going out there with a guy who was a little bit taller than me but we were both late twenties, and we had the "rough, garage mechanic" look. We were both white guys and just really average looking guys. So I think that's what they were looking for. But the Irish accent is the story that caused me to disavow *Cujo* for many years! I went out there with my buddy John X. Heart and we were in the house which was the house that they were using for the shoot – there were trailers everywhere and I didn't really realise what a low-budget feature was until I shared a dressing roo with Ed Lauter, who was one of the co-stars of the film! This was my first feature, so after I had done several more TV shows and features where I was getting my own trailer and everything, I'm going "Wow!. That really was kind of low-budget!" But it was nice because Ed Lauter was a really, really great guy! He was a terrific, well-known actor! So anyway, in the audition we just read the lines, as normally happens in these. The director was sitting there and there is the assistant director doing the throw-outs for us; there was no camera of course, there was just us. And it was just fine. We went out into another room, and they came out and said "Fine. Go have something to eat. We'll call your agent." John and I had the same agent. So I said "Okay. We'll drive home." I think we took a sandwich and took off. Then my agent called me that night and said "Okay. They want you the day after tomorrow on set. Seven O'clock blah blah". So I booked it! Great! I got a movie! This is cool! I call my girlfriend to tell her and then when I get out there, and of course, I am playing a mechanic so they really have to grease me up, I was out of makeup by 7:30, but I didn't get in front of the camera until the afternoon, so there was a lot of sitting around and all that. When I got there he said "So can you do that accent that you did in the audition?" Well, I didn't do an accent in the audition. So, right then I'm thinking "Oh, God. He wanted John and not me! He got the names mixed up!" Because what he wanted was like a north eastern accent. Now I am a dialect actor. I've shot television shows doing three, four different Irish accents and a lot of British accents, but I didn't have that. But I didn't want to make fun of the accent. I said "I didn't do an accent." He said "Yeah you did. At the audition." And I said "Nah. I didn't." So it happened he had the wrong guy! So when I saw the film the next year that it came out it wasn't my voice. I was stunned, because I knew they had to offer me the looping session, but I guess because I didn't do that north eastern accent – and it wasn't even a north eastern accent – but as you say, it was just a weird sort of non-Californian accent! I guess I don't have a non-Californian accent. But it wasn't me. It wasn't my voice. I called my mother and said "Don't go see it!" She said "I'm going to see your movie!" It was just one of the things that I was professionally insulted, that they didn't actually ask me to come in and do the looping session or the added dialogue session later. My agent said "We can get money out of them!" I said "I don't want to get money out of them! I just want to forget it!" So that was the story of the accent! Not me at all. If I had done an Irish accent, it would have sounded Irish. It could have been maybe now when they got into post they said "Hey, let's add this component since they guy doesn't sound like we want him to sound, so we will just add this in." I mean, I don't know what the thought processes are. We never get involved in post unless we are called in for the looping session. As far as my look for the film, there was a woman named Nancy who made me look all nice and dirty – the grease she put on me took a while to come off. I couldn't do an audition for like two days because I was still trying to get smudges off my face and hands! Daniel Hugh Kelly was lovely, but we didn't have much time to talk. I recall seeing the dogs being driven onto set, and I noticed the size of them by seeing the large tails wagging behind them!

"HIS NAME IS 'CUJO'": The Trentons arrive at the Camber farm and Cujo makes an appearance

In a brightly lit sequence reminiscent of a Norman Rockwell painting and purely capturing rural Americana, the meeting of the Trentons and the Cambers summarises the foundational core of Stephen King's original keen and acute interest in class resentment, the class system and the role of mother, father, child and family dog. The location of Santa Rosa, California with its large oak trees and dusty plains is a perfect environ for such a class divide. The very image of a bright red Jaguar (albeit run down) cruising down a dirt track towards a shade tree garage is symbolic of city folk entering the untapped domain of farm life. A decade or so before *Cujo* would be released, a pop-cultural rural purge occurred in film and television where anything remotely associated with hillbilly culture, white mountain folk culture and the non-urban living would be scrutinized and ultimately turned into something malevolent and disturbing. A film such as *The Texas Chain Saw Massacre* (1974) would ultimately validate this point in history, and nine years later with *Cujo*'s release, the idea of "cultured" and "sophisticated" middle class people paying a visit to the world of the underclasses and the farm dwelling and being tormented by that experience will resurface and formally resurrect in a full blown cultural expression of horror. In many ways, the drive to the Camber farm could be idyllic – the roof of the car is down allowing wind to blow through Donna, Vic and Tad's hair, the sunkissed grounds welcome them to untouched virginal landscape and so forth, however the bronzed earth and country aesthete is a totally different world for these characters, and as the Jaguar kicks up dust in its tracks, Vic, Donna and Tad are introduced to uncomfortable class division.

Shooting the Trenton arrival on the Camber farm.

The derelict farm comes to represent a place reflective of an already distorted family unit: Joe Camber (Ed Lauter) is a grim, mean looking redneck, his wife Charity (Kaiulani Lee) is a downtrodden, abused and neglected woman and their son Brett (Billy Jacoby) is trapped by his social conditioning – his only glimmer of any kind of happiness is his beloved dog, Cujo (who will eventually go through a horrific transformation). Castle Rock is presented as a working class terrain with middle class people such as the Trentons living there; peppering the town with an element of both "fish out of water" syndrome as well as "trying to build a new life" optimism. The parallels shared between the Trentons and the Cambers are palpable; not only do both families consist of mother, father and young son, but they are solidly connected in personal struggle and deep rooted turmoil. This is mostly apparent in the countering of Donna Trenton and Charity Camber, two very different women, but women both locked in the position of wife and mother. The poignant and incredibly beautiful shot that brings Donna face to face with Charity is masterfully crafted by both director Lewis Teague and his cinematographer Jan de Bont and the performances from these very gifted actresses in this very brief but incredibly telling moment is as naturally realized as any kind of effortless acting could be. Donna is confronted by the image of Charity, who is first introduced sitting under a tree plucking chickens. Here is a woman trapped by her rural surroundings and the epitome of the dutiful wife, serving her husband, serving her son and weatherworn by her sheer existence.

Character actress Kaiulani Lee would make an astounding impression with her performance as Charity – and although she had more screen time before the final cut came to the fore – she delivers a dedicated performance, brimming with soulfulness, sadness and a quietly determined desperate desire to live. The repressed Charity is a perfect character contrast to the lonely adulterous Donna who will end up trapped in the same surroundings and the film's acute exploration into the placement and displacement of women is outstanding, and profoundly feminist in its presentation and criticism of "woman in the storm" in response to women being trapped by responsibility and service to men and boys. Donna and Charity's brief dialogue is stunted and muted, and Donna's expression (more magnificence from Dee Wallace as an instinctive and intuitive actress) sums up the idea of "I could be this woman...but I'm not..." Screenwriter Barbara Turner would have this greeting occur right before the very first moment Donna comes face to face with Cujo – an excellent choice, a great condensation of Donna's inner-turmoil and the reality of monsters. Donna feels for the put upon farmer's wife Charity, shares some simple words, then is faced with what will ultimately become a force of punishment for spoiling the sanctity of the family unit.

Donna Trenton (Dee Wallace) comes face to face with Charity Camber (Kaiulani Lee). Here is a vivid polarisation of two very different women but both trapped by loneliness and desperation.

Charity Camber (Kaiulani Lee), the weatherworn farmer's wife repressed by her situation.

Adultery, domestic violence, familial unrest, childhood anxiety and the lack of communication are the rudimentary evils in the film, but the rabid St. Bernard is the tangible monster – the realised creature that will grab you by your throat and tear you apart. It is also interesting to note that Brett's first word of dialogue is "Pop!" (he calls out to his father when Vic drives up the farm) which instantly links him indirectly with Tad whose first word is "Mommy!" Here in *Cujo*, young boys are the product of their mothers and fathers and call upon them to save them from hidden monsters lurking in the closet or middle class red Jaguar driving designer shirt wearing men infiltrating the rural terrain. When Vic and Joe greet one another and shake hands, Vic instantly wipes his fingers clean from the grease and oil (denying the workload of the blue collar) and two very different husbands/fathers are bought together in a statement of servitude – this being, the urbane advertising agent requiring assistance from the toiling redneck mechanic. In *Cujo*, adult masculinity is divided in three components: sensitive provider (Vic), fiery desirable (Steve) and aggressive workhorse (Joe). Boyhood (and its sturdy connection to dog ownership and companionship) is also examined in the film, and Brett Camber's connection to Cujo is a thoroughly pure one, based on partnership, tenderness and playful mateship. In many editions of the novel, Brett Camber would be a character mentioned on many paperback blurbs as "Cujo's best friend" or in other instances, Cujo would be referred to as "the best friend Brett ever had" – in Lewis Teague's final product, this would underplay in development and representation, however in this sequence, the entirety of that union is displayed in earthy and unremarkable, stoic and earnest terms.

With Cujo plodding along the dusty road, this image of a large dog making his way towards the farm reads like a Disney venture again, much like *The Incredible Journey* (1963), however composer Charles Bernstein brings a sombre piece of music to accompany his arrival, suggesting that "not is all well in the world". This is the first time we see Cujo since he has been bitten, and when we get a close-up we notice that his bite mark on the end of his snout is red and raw with flesh ripped open and becoming infected. Strangely neither Brett, Donna nor Tad seem to notice, however the demure and friendly nature of this giant St. Bernard seems to eclipse this fact. Donna's initial response to Cujo is that she is instantly scared of him and wary of Tad getting close; however, Tad is desperate to befriend the dog.

The way in which the Cambers are all introduced is magnetically charged and nicely staged: Joe emerging from his barn like a foreboding presence complete with ominous fog (which will play up in theme later on with Cujo getting lost in the foggy vortex of rabies) is classic horror movie fare. Ed Lauter, who would make a career out of playing heavies and hardnosed toughs, looks as though he is a menacing hick with deep dark secrets, hiding out in his barn, working on his cars and quietly keeping violent outbursts hidden from the outside world. Charity is introduced "in service", with Jan de Bont's camera peering around a large oak tree to find her. She is viewed through the P.O.V. of Donna and from this perspective, we catch a glimpse of Donna's own sense of solemn judgement and personal regret. Brett is introduced playing baseball – he represents the "all American boy" (sporty and outdoorsy unlike Tad who is pale and scared of imaginary monsters). The fact that Brett toys with the great American pastime is an indication of preteen masculinity in contrast to a little boy who is hypersensitive and fretful. Baseball and the role of Brett's bat will also come into narrative play later in the film when Donna uses it to protect herself from the crazed Cujo.

Brett and his connection to Cujo is quickly established as the dog approaches him and the two embrace. Brett's love for his dog is apparent throughout the film and throughout Brett's scenes, and Billy Jacoby (who comes from a family of actors) plays this affection with purity, compassion and measured sentimentality. Brett Camber is also a character pushed into being stoic and not too emotional – a boy being rushed into perceived manhood, and this is something that Stephen King excels in writing about in the novel. However, for the film, Brett's character, as well as his mother Charity, would be modified and altered, so every moment they are on screen it matters and is revelatory without overstatement.

On Tad's meeting of Cujo he is told by his cautious mother "Gently", and then by Brett "Cujo. His name's Cujo". Tad embraces Cujo and the two of them share a tender moment. While her young son pets the loveable pooch and is told by the confident Brett that Cujo is not only a good dog but a "pretty smart one too", Donna remains nervous, looking over the animal and doubting the safety. Composer Charles Bernstein throws in a light musical motif while Cujo enjoys one of the last moments of clarity before his disease sets in, but closes the scene with "Cujo's Theme" which summons foreboding terror. In Stephen King's novel, the scene where Cujo and Donna lock looks for the first time ends with the writer mentioning "as if he was laughing" in response to Cujo's glare. The foreshadowing of this dog becoming a monstrous entity hellbent on killing Donna and her child (who at the moment is a "friend") is carefully noted here in this scene – Cujo as the angel of judgement, a morality measure looking over the ethics of familial harmony, ready to punish the adulterous woman.

Tad Trenton (Danny Pintauro) meets Cujo with the dog's best friend Brett Camber (Billy Jacoby) watching over.

From deleted scenes depicting the Trentons spending some time on the Camber farm and being charmed by the pre-ferocious Cujo.

Tad Trenton (Danny Pintauro) gets to know Cujo in this deleted sequence.

LEWIS TEAGUE: Ed Lauter was great! I had no problems with him at all. That was the same with Kaiulani Lee. I inherited the cast that was cast under Peter Medak's direction. It was probably Dan Blatt and him together making those choices. Clearly Dee Wallace was cast because Dan had worked with her on *The Howling* and she was somebody he was familiar with and pushed for the role. But Peter Medak must have had a veto power over that and recognised that she would be great for the part. And she was!

Actor Ed Lauter discusses his scene with director Lewis Teague on location in Santa Rosa.

DEE WALLACE: Kaiulani Lee was beautiful. Such a beautiful old soul, kind of hippy like. Just a gentle woman. We didn't have much time together, but I really enjoyed her peacefulness and gentleness, and she was perfectly cast in that role by the way. Ed Lauter was terrific. He was always cast as assholes, much like my husband Christopher Stone, and always stereotyped, but could not be further from that, just like Christopher. They got stuck in playing those kinds of characters, like I got the "mom" thing. I have made an effort to play all kinds of different roles in my career, and characters where I could be nasty, in such films like *The Lords of Salem* (2012) by Rob Zombie. Billy Jacoby was a sweet kid too. I remember a discussion with either Lewis or Dan because I played it very tense when I first saw the dog. Somebody said "Yeah but Dee, you don't know if he's not safe yet" and I replied "Exactly, I don't know". I can tell you as a mother, you would never let your child go up to a dog that you didn't know, so that is why I tell Daniel to get Danny and take him away. I keep my eyes fixed on Cujo until I know that he's OK, and in retrospect it kind of reads as a foreshadowing, but we didn't do it as a foreshadowing, it was just a real moment and something that Donna would do. I remember that in the book "Cujo", the dog is inhabited by this horrible guy that has died, and that is something we did not want to explore in the movie.

I never got the Barbara Turner draft of the script. I knew that it was a lot wordier than the final draft. But I am a big believer in what Jodie Foster says, and go through the script and get rid of what you don't need. If you can't play it and if you can't buy your vibration to let the audience know what you're feeling that you better go back and study some more!

IAN KINCAID (lamp operator): I really like Tony Richmond, he is a wonderful guy, but Jan de Bont was a real pain in the ass, I mean that guy's reputation is one hundred percent deserved. I was young, it was fun, we were in an amazing part of the country, it was a great time in my life. Now the character of Cujo was a composite of things. The animal trainers used four St. Bernards, there was also a stunt man in a St. Bernard suit, there was a Labrador in a St. Bernard suit, there was also a mechanical dog used that rammed the Pinto and so forth. Now, they also had a stuffed human dummy that was used to train the animals to attack, and this dummy had hair and clothes on it and one of my favorite stories about *Cujo* involves this dummy. We were working out in Santa Rosa at this house which acted as the farm house and it was kind of a spooky house. This was a big house and there was a giant walnut tree out in the front yard. Now I don't know why me and my buddies did this, but it was late and we were young, but I thought it would be funny to hang this dummy on a noose and hang it from the walnut tree. We put a little light on it, a six foot two light aimed up at this stuffed human effigy hanging from a hangman noose. We did this and then drove away. We got there the next morning and shit had hit the fan! The producers, the production manager and everybody else was freaking out about this dummy being in the tree! We were like "We don't know who did it! Why?" and they were like "Well if you didn't do it, who put the light on it?" and we were like "What's the big deal?" and then we found out. Apparently, somebody – say a previous owner – had hung themselves from that tree! We denied it and nobody to this day has admitted to it until now!

PATRUSHKHA MIERZWA: I remember the Camber farm had walnuts and they would fall from a huge tree in the front yard – people would get hurt. Also, we had a bee problem. We were always re-wiring to adjust to camera angles. We placed microphone plants in the car and I had a boom outside for slates and ambience or transitioning with the camera movement. The rest of the production crew was my husband Mark, so it was nice to have someone to be supportive, and commiserate with. The post people didn't reach out to us, and by the time they were on, we were staying low key.

VERN NOBLES (second assistant camera): Tony Richmond and Peter Medak were on board from the beginning. Me, Alex and Rich Osborne all came off of *Slapstick (Of Another Kind)*, and then we did *Cujo* almost straight after. I was second assistant cameraman and I kind of got moved up to first not knowing what to do. Then I got yelled at by Jan de Bont a few times. After Peter and Tony kind of got fired, we were all in Petaluma, California; we all thought we were going home. But we stayed for a week and then Jan came, but Jan didn't have an American crew, so we all stayed on with Jan until he gave us a place. And he said stay, 'cause I have to leave, 'cause Peter's leaving. But he said, "I have nothing. So you boys should stay." So we all stayed. We had a week off in Petaluma, and then we started with Jan. Then all three: me, Alex and Rich, we were with Jan, all the way up to when we done *Speed* (1994). The big deal was at that point HMI's were brand new, and he was using them. I think the biggest one was 40 back then. And that is when the bolt used to turn green… you didn't used to know till you saw it on film. There was a little learning curve there; we had a few green dailies. But Jan went for real hard stylized light. It was pretty good. Jan is so talented. I did all his movies; he used a lot of classical light and didn't make artificial light.

DANIEL HUGH KELLY: I complimented Lewis on that shot where the dog comes towards us on the farm. I really love that shot of the dog coming up moping over the hill, I thought "Geez Louise!" It was the first time I saw the dog and I thought "Holy cow look at the size of that thing!" As I recall that dog was Cubby, and Cubby was the biggest of the St. Bernards used in the film.

MARCIA ROSS: I knew Barbara Turner, she had written for television an awful lot and my recollection of the audition process was going by the draft of the screenplay that she had written. I don't remember Stephen King's first draft of the screenplay, I only recall Barbara's writing and her name being attached to the project. I never read the book, however I do think Stephen King is an excellent writer.

DON CARLOS DUNAWAY: I never met Barbara Turner. In the credit arbitration (written) I remember pointing out that her argument that I had so defaced her work that she wanted her name removed, kind of contradicted her argument. That since I had changed almost nothing, she was entitled to all the money. I didn't work. Barbara left the project and used a pseudonym on the project after her dear friend Peter Medak was fired.

ROBIN LUCE: Dee was a woman of not so much upper class or upper distinction, but she was cosmopolitan. I wanted to make sure that I enhanced her beauty. Even when she was stuck in the car, I wanted to make sure that her beauty, which is very natural and very striking, shone through. She was a delight to work with. I could subtract from her beauty as we went along. Dee had to look pretty enough in the beginning, that when she got into the dog sequence she could be a mess – a pretty mess. Kaiulani was more like a farmer and lower class looking character, so I played her look down. She was more like a Midwestern character, a plain Jane.

Makeup artist Robin Luce dresses Dee Wallace, turning the Midwest beauty into a woman damaged by overexposure to the elements and dehydration.

NANCY G. FOX (costumes): I was the costume supervisor on *Cujo* and Jack Buehler was the costume designer. I did some of the shopping for the film; sourcing clothes for mostly Dee Wallace. I did my first movie in 1979 with Jack Buehler and it was a movie that Ron Howard directed. I was nineteen years old Jack trained me from that starting point. *Cujo* was primarily a vehicle for Dee Wallace. She was so amazing in it. Dressing her was a treat. Jack and I designed her character to look like a woman stuck in a small town but wanting to wear clothes that a city woman would. I guess that added to the element of her being "trapped" throughout the film and having to break free from such trappings. Kaiulani Lee however, was designed to look like a farmer's wife. I think we aged her clothes and made them look weatherworn.

DANNY PINTAURO: Billy Jacoby was great but he was already a teenager though really, so there was an age bracket. It wasn't really quite the same and we really had very little interaction overall. Like we had a couple of scenes together and there are a couple of pictures of he and I.

DANIEL HUGH KELLY: Ed Lauter was wonderful. Just wonderful. He and I would work together a few times again, and we became very good friends. We would talk on the phone and catch up. I miss him. He was just a gem to be around, just a joy, a real Long Island guy. I think he thought he was Italian or something, I swear to God, but he was just wonderful. And so talented. He had the look that got him roped with roughies, but he was so gregarious and so quite the opposite of the characters he played. You know, I like to keep to myself and I like to go out by myself, but you can't do that with Ed. Not with Ed! I mean we were out in Vegas one time and he was like "OK come on! We're gonna go see Dean Martin and Sammy Davis Jr.!" and I was like "Oh come on Ed, we don't have tickets!" and he was like "Nah nah, I'll get us in! We'll go!" and sure enough we're sitting there watching Dean Martin and Sammy Davis Jr. and I thought how on earth did he do this but he was that kind of guy. He was the kind of guy that even introverts like me wanted to hang out with and drink with and have a good time with. He was a lot of fun. On another movie we worked together on I had to have a big fight with him and I was like "Damn that big nose of yours! It sticks out too far!" and so when I threw a punch at him it caught his nose quite badly, and he never let me forget that! I was so sad that he passed away. He was always saddled with these gruff roles but he wasn't that at all in real life. He could play that so well,

I mean that was a walk in the park for him, he could do those thuggish roles blindfolded, and he had that great look that went with it. I mean I love how he looks in *Cujo*, this greasy guy in a barn – he was such a good actor and I miss him.

Cultural crossover: Joe Camber (Ed Lauter) the shade tree mechanic starts work on Vic Trenton's (Daniel Hugh Kelly) red Jaguar.

CHRISTOPHER MEDAK: Dee Wallace was lovely. She was great and we're friends to this day. Daniel Hugh Kelly was another great guy and he and I used to drink at an English pub in LA, but I haven't seen him for years. Ed Lauter I also stayed in touch with. Kaiulani Lee was also awesome. They were such a great bunch and so willing to give their hearts and souls. They were definitely a beautiful gang.

PETER MEDAK: I remember casting Dee for the part and her husband and her lover and the kid. The kid was absolutely fantastic. I remember I was flying back to and from England to American and I was so exhausted and I was interviewing many actresses for the part of Donna. I remember feeling terrible at one point because when I got to listen to Dee read for the part, I fell asleep. It was because I was just so exhausted. It was one of those things where you fall asleep but you do hear everything. I remember Dee looking at me and being shocked, she said "I can't believe you fell asleep!" I felt terrible. I love actresses so much, and after seeing her in *Cujo*, she is just amazing. There was so little time and little money and I know I always rehearsed actors, and so we definitely having a reading when everyone was cast.

DANNY PINTAURO: I have always had dogs. I had dogs at the time of shooting. We had a poodle named Higgins. I missed Higgins; he was still in New Jersey with my dad, because my dad wasn't on set for the whole time. After the film, I never had a problem with dogs. I was acting! I had no scars from that movie whatsoever! One thing I was not allowed to do was have any interaction with the dog and that made me so mad because I really just wanted to play with them, because they were so cute and sweet looking and I just wanted to play with them. I was so happy for that one scene where I actually got to pet Cujo. You could sort of see the glee on my face. I was like, "Oh my god. I finally get to talk to the dog!"

PATRUSHKHA MIERZWA: I wasn't particularly "excited" that this film was to involve a lot of animal action, more so, this was a case of this film being an early one in my career; so it was a big project for me.

MARK ULANO: Having to work with animals wasn't a factor – I was excited, as this was Pat and mine's first studio project.

PATRUSHKHA MIERZWA: I was attached to the film while Peter Medak was signed on as director. He was quiet and lovely, and Mark and I were looking forward to the experience. He worked closely with his director of photography, and information flowed easily.

MARK ULANO: Peter Medak was gentlemanly with a good sense of humor. He liked to live well. He appreciated people for who they were and he had an artist's sensibility.

Mark Ulano on location. Patrushkha Mierzwa to the far right.

CHARLES BERNSTEIN: I was at a dinner party and Peter Medak was at the table and somehow the subject of *Cujo* came up, as one of my credits and there was some squirming on his part, and then I was later told that he had been the previous director! I haven't worked with Peter, but he is a very nice man, but I had no connection to him. When I came in, everything was pretty much done. The main players were Jan de Bont as the cinematographer, the editor was Neil Travis and the major players were producer Dan Blatt and obviously Lewis. I did not meet Barbara Turner either, nor did I have any connection to any previous screenplays that came about. Dan Blatt was a dream producer. He was hands on, very involved, and a very creative presence in the process. He had a vision. When I worked with him on *Sadat* (1983) – the biopic about M.A. Sadat of Egypt, and I worked with him on a movie called *Independence Day* (1983) that was directed by Bob Mandel, he was always a co-creator with the director; and someone who was present and had a lot of input. In regards to *Cujo*, I believe it was Dan who was describing to me what that opening credit to that card would look like.

PATRUSHKHA MIERZWA: I remember the turn over very well! The core company started the weekend before principal photography, setting up a moving night shot that travelled through the town to the bay. As I recall, it was a two-day set-up and shoot. Soon thereafter, the director of photography, camera, grip and electric crew were fired and we were shut down for several days in Fort Bragg. We were surprised that principal photography hadn't even started and people hired weren't trusted.

MARK ULANO: I remember Jerry Grandey always having a bemused look of disbelief at the events unfolding around him. He had a continual pained expression.

PATRUSHKHA MIERZWA: I don't remember having much, if any, interaction with Lewis Teague. He was not a director who partnered with his crew. There are directors who engage the crew, explaining what they're trying to achieve, and the crew works to give him/her what's asked for, and then some…the crew embraces the director's vision and, if invited, will feel comfortable offering suggestions from their respective departments. Lewis wasn't that kind of director. I remember being in the house while a shot was being set up; Lewis got a call from a French film magazine. To one of the questions, Lewis replied, "*Cujo* is a film about fear – economic fear…" he went on to name other fears, but that one stuck with me.

MARK ULANO: Lewis was the opposite of Peter. He was cold, reserved, calculating, and he behaved as if the movie was his big break. The film really was a break for many people.

DANNY PINTAURO: I really don't remember Kaiulani Lee very well. But I remember her being super sweet. I remember I have very vivid images of her plucking the chicken, because I thought that was so gross as a kid! But that is as far as I get with her, unfortunately. She seemed like a nice lady. But, as far as the farm went, there is a bizarre story there. My mom used to be psychic and connected to that sort of stuff. I mean, of course you have to be a believer in it for this to be interesting to you. But she was incredibly convinced for multiple reasons that the house we were filming in was haunted. There were many times she saw someone in an upstairs window just looking out the window. Then someone told her that the previous owner of the house had committed suicide in that room. She was constantly seeing a ghost in that room, in the upstairs window, while we were filming. There was also a swing set in the back and one day my mom was just standing there staring at it and somebody – one of the producers – came out and said "What are you looking at?" They look at the swing set and it's swinging. There was definitely a strange vibe at that farm house!

Danny Pintauro held up by Dee Wallace with Kaiulani Lee on location at Santa Rosa. (courtesy of Danny and Margaret Pintauro).

Danny Pintauro and Kaiulani Lee on location. Clearly the topsy-turvy weather was a cold point here during the taking of this candid. (courtesy of Danny and Margaret Pintauro).

TERESA ANN MILLER: A lot of the training that we do includes working the animals to the actors. I think most of the time when you see an animal that's looking off the eye line or in the wrong direction or away from camera – a lot of the time the trainers aren't able to speak to the animal while we are working and we have to use hand signals. Now, if it is silent on the set and the animal can't hear us they are going to look for us and that is when you are going to lose the relationship and it isn't as tight. Now if I can talk to my dog in a scene, I can tell my dog to go to the actor, stay there, look at it, look at him. Good. Look at him. Now bark at him. I can talk my dog through that whole scene without him having to look at me for direction. And in a case as something as big as *White God* (2014) or *Cujo* or *White Dog* (1982), the directors afford us the ability to

124

do that because it brings out the best performance from the animal, but that usually only happens in a pretty big animal show, you know what I mean, because a lot of times they are more focused and concentrated on the human actors as the main character. And of course, they don't want to distract from the actors, so most of the time we will have to do our work without speaking. And that is when you see that difference in how the animal is relating with the actor.

Animal trainer Karl Lewis Miller with "Daddy", one of the dogs used to play the titular role. Here he is on his ranch after bathing and giving the loveable St. Bernard a brush.

"MONSTERS STAY OUT OF TAD'S CLOSET, YOU HAVE NO BUSINESS HERE": Vic reads Tad "The Monster Words" and Donna says "goodnight"

Harkening back to the first time we were introduced to the Trenton household, this scene links it thematically with a distinguished return to Tad's nightmares and his intense fear of the imagined monster lurking in his closet. This exterior shot of the Trenton household at night is quick, but it serves its purpose in marrying the initial introduction to the troubled home to the secret world of childhood fears and anxieties. Charles Bernstein's music carries us into this sequence from the prior moment where Tad and Cujo have met, marking a poignant sensibility in that this now benign and friendly giant dog will soon transform into a monstrous realization for a sensitive and hyper-vulnerable boy.

Cutting to inside Tad's bedroom, we are deep in the dark recesses of his closet. Spectral blacked out images covet stuffed toys and children's games as Vic carries his boy through various points of his bedroom, ridding it of the monsters that haunt the shadowy corners. Here, Vic recites a piece of prose that he has created entitled "The Monster Words" which act as a mantra to protect little Tad. They read:

Monsters, stay out of this room!

127

You have no business here.
No monsters under the bed!
You can't fit under there.
No monsters hiding in the closet!
It's too small in there.
No monsters outside of the windows!
You can't hold on out there.
No vampires, no werewolves, no things that bite.
You have no business here.
Nothing will touch you, or hurt you, all this night.
You have no business here.

At the time of *Cujo*'s release, child psychology and the psychiatric treatment of children with anxiety disorders, paranoia, schizophrenia and various mental illnesses was widely discussed (globally and in the mainstream), especially after paediatric specialist Michael Rutter made a massive impact with his academic texts on the subject. Interestingly enough, in 1972, Rutter wrote a report entitled "Maternal Deprivation Reassessed" which was based on the findings of Dr. John Bowlby, a leading psychiatrist with a keen interest in childhood development. Bowlby's research (and Rutter's consequential report) argued that a child most definitely needs an intimate, warm and loving relationship with his or her mother in the earliest years of development, and without this, stress, guilt, emotional turmoil and self-worth issues will arise. This is a fundamental sociological construct used in *Cujo* – Tad will be seen for the first half of the movie in much more intimate situations with his father Vic, rather than with his mother Donna. However, once the film hits its intense third act, Tad will cling to his mother for dear life – forcing her to react, protect and die for her child if she had to. The bond between mother and son is born out of necessity, but for the scenes prior to this, there is a disconnect – subtle, but ultimately there. Donna uses "Over, done with, gone" as a method of ridding Tad of his problems, while Vic spends time developing

"The Monster Words", which acts as a prayer against adversity, struggle, inner demons and lurking beasts in the closet. Essentially, Donna will throw herself into the epitome of what child psychologists Rutter and Bowlby examine in their research; she will regress into a primal woman, desperate to protect and defend her child, and keep her offspring safe from menacing doom.

During the scene here, Lewis Teague and his cinematographer Jan de Bont choose artificial lighting, with a torch acting as a beacon of hope: shedding some truths and sparking the protection of children. In *Cujo*, children are presented as frightened sensitive creatures scared of darkness and afraid of the unknown (later, the more confident but quietly suffering Brett Camber will venture into oppressive fog to come face to face with the sick Cujo) while in earlier child-centric horror movies such as *The Bad Seed* (1956) which featured child as monster in the guise of Rhoda Penmark (Patty McCormack) darkness would be suggestive of magic and creative output. Rhoda's mother Christine (Nancy Kelly) reads her daughter "Inside the Castle Wall" – a book that seems to be made up for the film, however with strong ties to various classical children's literature that deal with protection and the necessity of creating out of darkness.

Vic is once again presented shirtless and in glowing light; he is open and vulnerable. Returning to bed and to Donna who is completely covered up with her blankets pulled up high, he mutters something about how late it is (another reference to his preoccupation with work and making deadlines) and notices her staring at him, smiling sadly. "What?" he asks. She replies "You're just really good with him, that's all", to which he responds with "How am I with you?" Director Lewis Teague would call this kind of back and forth as "economic dialogue" where everything said is necessary and important, but simple, straight to the point and loaded with subtext as well as narrative function and clear intention. Donna is complimenting Vic's methods with his son, but Vic is concerned that the same effect on her is missing. Donna responds with "Wonderful", but the line is stunted and consumed with marital unrest. Donna closes the "conversation" with "Goodnight" and turns out the light completely summarising the miscommunication, distancing and dark emptiness of their marriage. This lack of connection is just as shadowy and as scary as Tad's closet, and what lurks inside it is just as menacing and as dangerous as the monster that promises to eat Tad alive. Vic and Tad seem to share a unity (as simple as it may be), but Donna and Vic are at a loss – trying to rediscover something that may be gone. Infidelity hovers over their bed like a pendulous cloud (Tad trying to escape being swallowed by sadness as depicted by the camera angle that flips upside down earlier, throwing him into space) and later, it will be their bed that will be trashed by the vindictive Steve Kemp who reacts violently to Donna's calling the affair off. Adultery is a key monster in *Cujo*, and this is examined with full blown character driven mechanics here, however, the issue would prop up in other Stephen King novels set in small towns, such as "Salem's Lot" (1975) which uses it as an ingredient peppered throughout the plot (heavily influenced by the seminal New England 1956 classic "Peyton's Place" by Grace Metalious).

LEWIS TEAGUE: I wasn't there when Peter was on the project and directing the early scenes. I have however, talked to Dee Wallace about it and I've heard her comment on it. I wasn't there so I can't really say anything. All I know is that the producer called me after they had been shooting for about five days and said that they were going to make a change and asked if I still would be interested in doing the film. I had literally been pissed off and telling anybody I could – several months before that – "I'm supposed to be directing that film. Don't they understand?!" I just felt it in my blood. When I went in for that first interview, which just felt like all the forces in the universe were pointing in my direction! I read the book. I immediately fell in love with the story. I fell in love with the idea, with the theme and I had a great meeting with Dan Blatt. He told me the reason why he called me was that Stephen King had seen my film *Alligator*, and recommended me to Dan Blatt. So, it just did not seem right when I didn't get the job. I didn't get the job by the way, because there was some jerk over at 20th Century Fox in acquisition who didn't think I would be the right guy for it. What happened was, I had the meeting with Dan Blatt; we got along great, we talked about the material. He told me that Stephen King had recommended me for the job. And we shook hands on the way out and he said, "I'm calling your agent. I'm looking forward to working with you. This is going to be wonderful!" My agent started discussions with him. Then a few days later, my agent called me and said, "Somebody at 20th in acquisition was blocking my hire." So I went off and did another film. I did a film for Dino DeLaurentiis called *Fighting Back* (1982) (aka *Street Wars*). I had done *The Lady in Red* (1979) and *Alligator* and then I met with Dan Blatt for *Cujo*. And then I got blocked, and they hired Peter Medak. During *Fighting Back*, Dino and I got along great! We actually did three films together and I remember having a conversation, several conversations in fact, with Dino, and he asked what I wanted to do. I told him I really wanted to do *Cujo* but they hired another director. Then Dino called one day and said, "I hear that 20th have dropped the project", and so it was on hold! Dino said, "You call the producer Dan Blatt, and you tell him that if he wants to do the movie with you, that I will finance it!" So, I called Dan Blatt, and he said, 'I'm sorry. We've just made a deal with Warner Bros. So, we are going ahead with Peter Medak". So, I was having conversations with Dan Blatt during that time. So, I again expressed my disappointment; and went back to editing *Fighting Back*. I went back to L.A. and then Dan Blatt called me after they started shooting four to five days after they started shooting, and asked if I would still be interested. They were going to make a change and asked if I was still keen to direct. I said, "Absolutely!" I had never felt so positive about a film up until that point. I felt that in my blood and in my bone marrow that I was supposed to be doing that film! So, I can't talk about what it was about Peter Medak that they were not satisfied with, but I flew up there when they were shooting in Mendocino, to look at some of the footage. I said to

Dan, "I'd love to do it, but need to start from scratch, and bring in my own people, and reshoot everything." He agreed. I had several days to prepare. I think a weekend. And it was terrific because I was able to bring in the cinematographer of my choice, Jan de Bont. And the editor of my choice, Neil Travis. There were two Neils: Neil Travis and Neil Machlis. And Neil Machlis was the production manager, who was a great guy, by the way! A little anecdote by the way about Neil Machlis. We were shooting in the rain, and we were falling behind schedule; it rained for about four weeks when we were shooting. Everything at the farm where Dee Wallace is trapped in the car in that hot sun was actually shot almost in freezing weather in the rain! It rained for about four weeks! But every time that the rain would stop for a few minutes, or maybe there would be a break in the clouds, we would run out and shoot a few shots and then it would start raining again and everyone would huddle under umbrellas. I was huddled under an umbrella when Neil Machlis came walking up the hill whistling. I said "Neil!" and he said "What?" I said "What the hell are you whistling for? Don't you know that we are falling behind here?!" And he looked at me and stopped in the middle of the rain – rain pouring down his face – with a big smile on his face – and he said "Louie. Don't you understand it's just a movie?!" and he just wandered off whistling. I thought how cool is that? I had come out of the Roger Corman school where every second counted and Neil apparently had just had a son who had died of cancer, and he was able to put things into perspective, so it took a load off my back, when he did that. I didn't slow down at all. It didn't make me want to relax or get lazy but it took a lot of the pressure off! So I was able to do a better job. There were so many great people working on that film; there was the producer Dan Blatt that was one of the best producers that I have ever worked with, because he really knew the nuts and bolts of filmmaking, and he really knew how to show appreciation and knew how to get the best out of everybody.

MARCIA ROSS: One of the main things I remember was the casting of the kid, and trying to find that perfect kid for the role of Tad. We looked in Los Angeles first. I mean, the process is a lot different than it is now, I mean it is the same process in that you have to see everybody. But what's different now is the use of the internet and the expansion of the business. There are a lot of kid actors all around Canada and England that have representation and if you are searching, you can post the outline and cast kids from there. I mean I have cast kids from places you'd never imagine, and that's because the internet allows you to do that. We didn't have that then. That didn't exist. So back when we did *Cujo*, we read every kid that came through an agent or a manager, so that's why we came to New York because we scoured every kid in Los Angeles, and we went to various schools as well, and at that time there were a lot of kid actors in New York, and Danny was six years old when he came in with his mother, and there was something so poignant about him at the time. He read for me, and there was something so vulnerable and adorable about him. I am certain he did some screen tests with Dee Wallace, but the first step was me going to New York and making sure that we saw every kid in New York and I don't remember any other kid standing out at all, it was all Danny. Then when Danny was shortlisted, the producers came down and the director Peter Medak, who was the director at the time, and we had call backs. And at the call backs we narrowed it down.

CHRISTOPHER MEDAK: Dad had all these great actors like Dee and Daniel and Ed Lauter, I mean a brilliant fucking cast and he had this stupid producer who should have stayed in TV. When Lewis joined, there was no love for him. Here is a bloke who came in and whose greatest credit was *Alligator*, and we would look at this guy and go "What the fuck is this crap?" And this wasn't just because my dad was originally directing and now fired, but it was just a whole different execution and for the most part, Lewis just went straight from Dad's storyboards. I remember him walking around with the storyboards and directing them verbatim – my

133

dad's fucking storyboards. I mean Lewis came from low budget Roger Corman filmmaking, where everything was done quickly. I have to say, that once Lewis was on board the entire set just lost the warmth that we had – it was gone. Lewis is not the most engaging or warm guy, he is emotionally cut off. However Jerry Grandey the AD was very lovely, he was approachable and lovely. I feel like we lost our souls. I have to say, that there was a lot of hard work yes, but there was also a lot of fucking drugs on set. I saw everyone amp the fuck up. I mean the entire crew was getting into it heavily – the drugs and the booze. Everyone was getting off the deep end. And through the blow and the MDMA there was a bit of a feeling of "This is how we are going to get through this". I mean this is what happened in those days.

PETER MEDAK: I remember spending many days with production designer and artist Alan Roderick-Jones, who was an incredible talent from England. He worked on the first *Star Wars* (1977) movie. He and I came up with detailed storyboards for the dog sequences for *Cujo*, we wanted them to be as intricately detailed as possible because this kind of thing wasn't just something that you can bang out on the spot. Everything was drawn out with him. We had to figure out every frame. I was so upset about being fired, that I think I threw out all the storyboards Alan and I worked on.

DANIEL HUGH KELLY: I found working with Danny Pintauro very easy. All the father and son moments were very easy for me and there are two reasons why: first of all, I love little kids, particularly little boys that age. When I was doing *Ryan's Hope*, there was a child actor on that named Adrian who was a really sweet boy and before they would start wrapping a scene up to go to commercial I would go up to him and get him laughing. I feel really comfortable working with child actors. When I heard with Danny had arrive at the hotel – he had arrived on day two – I introduced myself to him. Before this, I had gone out to a hobby store downtown and

I bought a rocket, a really cool rocket! I mean this thing was like two and a half feet long, and that was the box alone! And it was very impressive, especially if you were a little kid like Danny. So me and Danny and his mom went out to a field and set it up and set the rocket off, and it was fun. I really liked Danny, I mean he was super intelligent, you could see that in his eyes and I take credit for him later getting into Stanford! I mean I gave him a rocket, how would he have gotten in if I hadn't have done that! I was so proud that he got into Stanford!

DANNY PINTAURO: That is the part that is profound to me, the point that this kid is completely convinced that there is a monster inside the closet and that the monster will end up being realized as a rabid dog! I remember feeling like that was very true. So that takes that whole thing to a separate level – that the monster has come to attack. I think that is really fascinating to me. But, as a kid, you know, the most tangible thing for me, in a lot of ways, because it was sort of my only prop, if you will, were "The Monster Words"; and that for me was everything! Like I was constantly reading them aloud, for preparation for any scene, and I don't actually think it was scripted. There were a couple of scenes where I'm just sitting there in the background reading them out loud. I don't actually know if that was scripted. I think it was just me reading "The Monster Words" because that was all I had. Everything I had was tied to those words. That brings my father into the room every time I'm reading them and the hope that my father will protect us from the dog, and that brings my mother and father together because they worked on them together; and she read them in the house when he wasn't there. So, for me, "The Monster Words" are like everything for me as an actor. If I could have anything, it was those words! That's why the paper was so crumpled, because I was always reading them!

CHARLES BERNSTEIN: Once the elements are there, part of the skill set of a film composer is to make transitions to treat things. I was recently talking to a group about *Casablanca* (1942) and Max Steiner's use of "As Time Goes By" and the other pieces he used which are based in Germanic music. The idea of taking the materials at hand that you have thematically weaved in and out of things and changing from darkness to romance. *Casablanca* goes from whimsical romance to menacing armies and what have you, so that skill set is just part of what we do. If the themes are invaluable and potent, it just makes it easier. The themes in *Cujo* were easy for me to work with, so I was able to move through the dark numbers and light moments as needed.

DANNY PINTAURO: I know there were local versions of "The Monster Words". The one that they used for the door of the room is not the same piece of paper as the one that I carried around, because if I'm correct, the stuff in the house was filmed after the stuff in the car, if I remember correctly. We had done all this filming, and then I remember all of a sudden they needed me again, and I thought we were done, and it was to show up on the set with a huge, extended bedroom. I feel like we may have filmed all of that bedroom stuff afterwards, after the car and the dog stuff. I could be totally wrong. But whatever the case, they were totally separate in the sense that the bedroom scenes are a set somewhere, and it was definitely before or after filming at the house. You know, all of that is totally separate from the car stuff. So there were different editions of "The Monster Words". The one on the set, in the car, like that was the one that held all the importance for me. I think if you look at the piece of paper that he tapes to the door or that is on the door, and if you look at the copy that I am holding in the car, they don't even look the same. Different handwriting as well!

Donna (Dee Wallace) "turns out the lights", while her husband Vic (Daniel Hugh Kelly) has doubts about their marital connection.

"IT'S NOT A MASS SUICIDE...": Children are vomiting red dye and Vic stresses about his job

Cutting from a nocturnal sombre moment where a married couple lie in bed coveted by secrecy and a repressive lack of communication, the next busy sequence ushers in a dramatic catalyst that will influence the course of action of not only the plot but fundamentally the motivations and journey of Vic Trenton.

With the Sharp Cereal Professor taking a spoon to his mouth and downing one of the many types of breakfast cereals the company peddles, the scene opens with the small television set in the Trenton kitchen delivering some bad news. Cleverly following up from the image of Vic looking at his wife lying in moonlight and hiding behind a mask of unhappiness and adultery, this brightly lit sequence opens with the Sharp Cereal Professor proclaiming "Nope, nothing wrong here" – a witty wink at the audience which marries the advertising motto for Vic's client with the fundamental domestic unrest that sits at the heart of the film. A news report tail-ends the image of the Sharp Professor with a slightly sarcastic Asian reporter (Clare Nono) responding: "Well....that's not entirely true". Here, this reporter makes commentary on the reality of truth and the perception of truth – that "Nope, nothing wrong here"

139

is in fact questionable and ultimately not at all the case. Actress Clare Nono (who would pop up as a newscaster in various films and television series contributing to a racial typecast in popular culture – that of the Asian reporter) delivers her story in front of a hospital, explaining that thousands of cases of internal haemorrhaging around the country have been reported, but in the end being a big false alarm in that the red dye used for the cereal was faulty and ran through children's systems terrifying concerned parents. What is learned from this quick news coverage is that the Sharp cereals were responsible for this health scare and this in turn sends Vic into a tailspin of stress, nervousness, paranoia and doubt about his career.

The financial fear that Vic embodies is his own tangible anxiety (the careerist under stress) as opposed to Donna's fear of growing old and alone and Tad's phobia of unseen monsters in his closet. What needs to also factor in a narrative and cultural structure is the great American health scare built as a social construct and this is an additive in *Cujo* that comments on the superficial terror whilst building a hidden agenda, where "kids all over the country are peeing and puking red dye" and "scaring the hell out of their parents".

An uncredited male reporter closes the story with "Nope, nothing wrong here, folks" to which Vic calls out "Cute" before slamming the television shut. While Donna tends to breakfast for Tad, she listens to Vic voice his concerns about his job and most definitely his company's Sharp account. This health scare has led to all the cereals being recalled and forces Vic's advertising campaign to be put under scrutiny. Donna remains calm and understands that Vic is a resourceful man, and that he will work it out because he has worked out how to handle these situations before. However, Vic protests "He (the Sharp Cereal Professor) comes into America's living rooms and he says to millions of kids 'Trust me!'" Here the film is invested in the distortion of trust – where wives can be found sleeping around with their husband's tennis buddies, where supposedly healthy cereal can cause panic and distress all across the country and big ole friendly dogs can turn rabid. Originally in Stephen King's draft as well as Barbara Turner's, the panic that arose from the Sharp cereal scare was presented in a much more direct manner – outside of getting information from diegetic television reporting, in the two former drafts before screenwriter Don Carlos Dunaway was hired by director Lewis Teague to streamline the story, a little girl screams out to her mother (more children calling out to their parents) to come quick and see what has happened to her in the bathroom. Her mother of course screams in terror when she finds what seems to be blood splattered all over the toilet and tiled floor, hence causing the course of action to hit right at the heart of Vic Trenton's career where children are reacting badly to dodgy food coloring.

This scene, which would come early in King's draft (ultimately following Cujo being bitten by the rabid bat) would be cut and along with it would be an extended television report featuring producer Dan Blatt in a cameo role as Dr. Merkatz who would discuss that this hysteria is all simply a major false alarm. This scene also rings topically aware when Vic makes commentary on Donna's nonchalance about the entire situation by mentioning the Sharp cereal scare situation not being as devastating as a "mass suicide". During the late seventies and early eighties, there was an acute awareness and understanding in the public consciousness all to do with cults and subcultural mind control with Guyana and the Jonestown tragedy. Screenwriter John Sayles would mention this horrendous event in his script for *The Howling*, and here in *Cujo*, it is subliminally referred to in relation to mass hysteria.

Also, in a very straight and actively serious horror film where humour is completely absent, this is one scene that lends itself to a quietly handled light moment of relief. Right at the very end of the sequence, the frantic Vic collects the telephone and tells his colleague Roger on the other end that "we'll work it out, we always have before" only to prompt Donna's exasperated expression moments after she has tried to calm her husband down and given exactly the same advice.

MARCIA ROSS: Judith and I had done a lot of television before we got *Cujo*, and to be honest, *Cujo* wasn't really the first film I worked on, because when I got out to New York, I was hired as Judith's associate and the first film I worked with her on was a film called *Southern Comfort* (1981), the Walter Hill film and then we also did *48 Hours* (1982), and it was by 1983 that I was sharing credit with her. But I think I had worked on several more films before 1983, but I do remember we did a lot of TV. I had worked in theatre in New York, I worked in a small talent agency, I worked at CBS television and that was my first job in casting. I became the assistant casting director to the head of casting on TV, I was the talent coordinator. I really knew a lot of New York actors. It was my passion. I only moved to Los Angeles in the summer of 1980 and I frequently went back to go to the theatre. My parents were still alive and lived in New York, but I really only went because of the theatre scene and to meet actors, and to work on things. For instance, speaking of Daniel Hugh Kelly being in that pilot, I remember working in the winter of 1981 in television, and Judith was a very, very big name in casting for television. We were constantly casting for TV, and films were something we were just starting to work on. Maybe we did one or two movies a year, but yes, mainly it was television. We were starting to build our business in film casting, and *Cujo* was one of those.

DANIEL HUGH KELLY: It doesn't matter to me if another actor wants to rehearse or not. I am happy to go either way. I have always been like that so it wouldn't have bothered me back then working with an in the moment actress like Dee. She is very talented and she is very real. She is the kind of actress who when Marlon Brando spoke about the fourth wall and what not is exactly that – she can be doing the same thing off camera that she does on camera and it's just real life. Dee is very pure and watching her you're like "Wow, she's really good". I did not know her, she was from California and I was from New York, but you could tell immediately that she was a very gifted actress. I had not seen *E.T.*

the Extra-Terrestrial and I don't think I ever have seen it, and that had just come out and so she had exploded, I mean she was very big. And I could see why, because she is so natural and so real. I don't get intimidated working with an actress as good as Dee is, in fact it is quite the opposite, it gets my motor running because I don't want to be the one that looks like the "Geez, who is this guy? What's he doing standing next to her?" It's a challenge but I remember her being very gracious on set, and very generous. I mean I didn't have any scenes with the dog, and when you consider what she had to go through with that dog, I mean wow, my goodness, and even Lewis for God's sake – here is Lewis's star and she's holding a young boy and they have this huge dog get excited coming close and holding him back four inches from her face, I mean it's like "Whoa!" That is some stress for a director and anybody involved!

CHARLES BERNSTEIN: The advertising jingle was a little thing that they got from an actual commercial library.

"WHAT WE'RE TALKING ABOUT HERE IS A LOT OF SCARED PEOPLE": Vic and Roger lose the Sharp Cereal account

"Well nobody got hurt, right? What we're talking about here is a lot of scared people" says Vic as the scene begins. Under the pump, Vic and his business partner Roger Breakstone (Arthur Rosenberg) frantically tend to separate phone calls in their office. While a fellow colleague busily works on her drafts for various advertising campaigns, the two men appear stressed, distracted, disorientated and defeated, whilst ultimately trying to keep their cool as their angry superiors tear through the other line. Roger stresses that it wasn't his fault that the red dye caused such concern and Vic attempts to defend his position while his boss aggressively asserts that the Sharp account is in dire straits.

While the issue and theme of economic anxiety trickles through the short and snappy scene, the opening line summarizes the surface purpose of horror as a genre – and that is to frighten its audience. Vic makes mention of "a lot of scared people" and this is what the genre thrives upon, and what artists such as Stephen King excel in. Preceding Vic's line is "nobody got hurt" which details the safety in the genre – that horror provides comforting scares, the kind that can be shaken off and dealt with. Where *Christine* (as aforementioned, released the same year as *Cujo* and also based on a novel by Stephen King) featured a line from actor Keith Gordon in the leading role of Arnie Cunningham, "You know part of being a parent is trying to kill your kids", in this film, parents have become terrified of what has become of their children after eating the once trustworthy Sharp cereals.

Roger closes the scene with "We lost the Sharp account" leading way to an urgent cut to the next scene which startles the audience with a loud buzzing from a welding machine. Here, director Lewis Teague jumps from cerebral business men anxious to keep their heads above water to a working class yokel welding and using his hands in service of a sturdy but struggling vocational choice. Before bouncing back to Cujo and the Camber farm, this glaringly different sequence set in the corporate world of advertising is a clinical and dry universe devoid of earthy reasoning – instead it is riddled with stress, the promise of "special" board meetings, taking the situation more seriously and angry unseen bosses.

The character of Roger Breakstone originally had a lot more to do in the King novel and also had an entire backstory painted up for him including a wife Althea and daughters. In the final draft of the screenplay by Don Carlos Dunaway, Roger is used as a springboard for Vic dealing with the Sharp account as well as being a confidant when Donna's affair is outed. Arthur Rosenberg plays the role with effortless realism – he gives Roger an everyman edge cemented in the world of advertising and he works out each line and each scene with the right amount of both defeatist grind slugging and stunted slight-ambition.

ARTHUR ROSENBERG ("Roger Breakstone"): My character was a victim of plot and focus I suspect. The audition was the usual – reading from sides and meeting the team plus I only ever remember Lewis being the director. Lewis was not, to my way of thinking, an actor's director. But the result was certainly good enough. I think actors, and certainly me, kind of prefer a more touchy feely director like Hal Ashby was and many others.

146

Roger Breakstone (Arthur Rosenberg) and Vic Trenton (Daniel Hugh Kelly) lose their account, while consumers are shaken by a nationwide health scare.

DANIEL HUGH KELLY: I never saw Arthur Rosenberg who played my business partner after *Cujo*. I know he was good friends with Lewis, but that is all. I think he may have become a rabbi!

MARCIA ROSS: Judith had a very long relationship with Robert Singer and Dan Blatt. She found people like Arthur Rosenberg for them. Judith and Robert and Dan had worked together for a long time, and I was on a lot of their projects also. Finally, Robert went his separate ways, I think he got a deal with a studio and I also drifted from Dan Blatt as well. Judith retired over ten years ago, I think she moved to Oregon, but not sure where she is now. It's been many years since I've seen her. She offered me a job and she was a great mentor and I learnt a lot of what I know from her.

ARTHUR ROSENBERG: The producer Dan Blatt was a very nice and humble man considering all the projects he did. I remember him as kind.

Also Robert Singer, his partner on some projects. I did the TV show *Reasonable Doubts* (1991-1993) with Marlee Matlin for them. So I am not sure if that is how I got this part, they knew me or if I got the part in *Reasonable Doubts* because I did *Cujo*. I recall we filmed the office scene in Santa Rosa outside of San Francisco. Lewis Teague directed them and Jan de Bont filmed them. So I don't understand what was second unit. We were first unit.

DON CARLOS DUNAWAY: Stephen King's script was a disaster and was way too long, with many, many pages about the advertising business, which he evidently found very interesting. In general, I remember thinking that he kept all the wrong things and cut a number of the good ones.

MINA BADIE: My mother was avid about staying true to the original book. It was one of the things that she and the producers fought about. She read and re-read Stephen King's novel and loved it. She wanted to stay true to the book.

PATRUSHKHA MIERZWA: Mark and I loved working on the scene at the Sharp account office. We were so glad to be in the city! One of the biggest tasks for me on set was making the crew a newsletter while we were out of the city.

Sound recorder/boom operator Patrushkha Mierzwa created a production newsletter for the shoot. This is the cover where she styled it after the first edition of Stephen King's novel from Viking Press. (courtesy of Patrushkha Mierzwa).

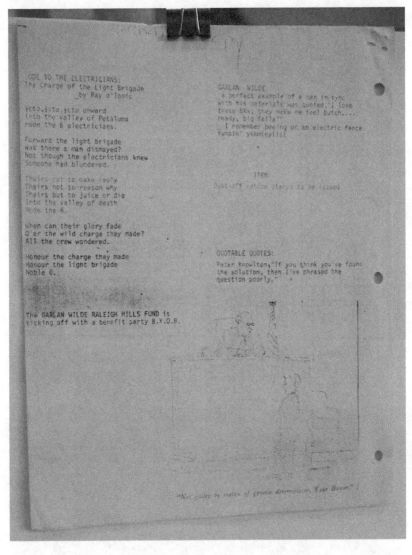

ODE TO THE ELECTRICIANS:
The Charge of the Light Brigade
        _by Ray d'Ionic

 icto,icto,icto onward
into the valley of Petaluma
rode the 6 electricians.

Forward the light brigade
Was there a man dismayed?
Not though the electricians knew
Someone had blundered.

Theirs not to make reply
Theirs not to reason why
Theirs but to juice or die
Into the valley of death
Rode the 6.

When can their glory fade
O'er the wild charge they made?
All the crew wondered.

Honour the charge they made
Honour the light brigade
Noble 6.

The GARLAN WILDE RALEIGH HILLS FUND is
kicking off with a benefit party B.Y.O.B.

GARLAN WILDE
  a perfect example of a man in sync
  with his materials was quoted,"I love
  these EKs; they make me feel butch....
  ready, big fella?"
  I remember peeing on an electric fence.
Jumpin' jiminy!!!!

            ITEM:
Burn-off ration stamps to be issued

QUOTABLE QUOTES:
Peter Knowlton,"If you think you've found
the solution, then I've phrased the
question poorly."

"Not guilty by reason of gross distraction, Your Honor!"

The interior of the newsletter. (courtesy of Patrushkha Mierzwa).

149

1. a bit of a spray
2. the upper part of a house-spoken through a cleft palate
3. bovine bellow
4. french fixtures for flagrant flooders
5. it falls mainly on the plain in Spain
6. what we're making
7. the only item really read on the call sheet (2 words)
8. the nightly retreat
9. Terry Southern' tasty title; craft services item
10. brings tears to their eyes
11. they used to be free every morning, but not anymore (sgl;2 words)
12. molotov or bean
13. when we finally get it right
14. lack of a sync point (2 words)
15. sync point announcement
16. paparazzi; Dee's pet peeve

1. the thing that brings Jan closer to people
2. falling death from above (pl.)
3. what we've got when it's not mud
4. the icing on a Cujo cocktail
5. Well, hello
6. it gets you hot (not sex)
7. the late, great Cujo
8. Karl's favorite "3 little words"
9. Monday money
10. one night stand (2 words)
11. usually goes along with guts
12. made by Tiffen (pl)
13. a former medieval torture device currently used on lenses
14. it's red and expensive to repair
15. we really only see them 5 days a week
16. attack command
17. he's not a crooner nor does he have blue eyes
18. we can expect this on a cold night
19. the sky turns grey and the sun goes away.......
20. what the crew does naturally and the actors need make-up for

A crossword puzzle was created for the newsletter. (courtesy of Patrushkha Mierzwa).

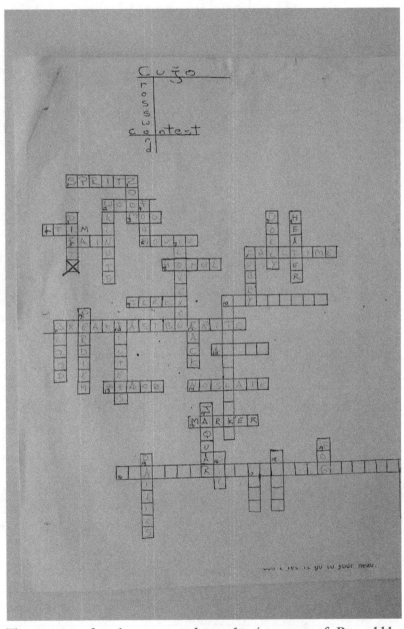

The answers for the crossword puzzle. (courtesy of Patrushkha Mierzwa).

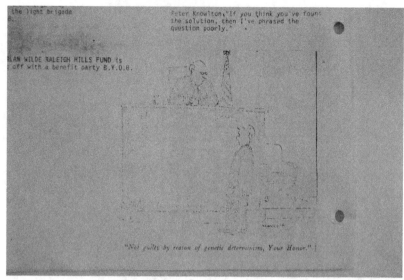

A cartoon added for the newsletter. (courtesy of Patrushkha Mierzwa).

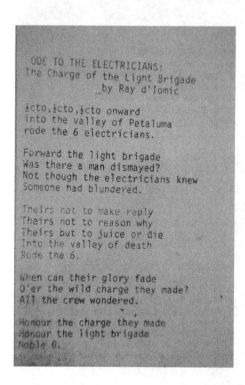

Patrushkja Mierzwa's ode to electricians. (courtesy of Patrushkha Mierzwa).

CUJO'S SENSITIVITY: Cujo and the welder

Immediately following Roger Breakstone's declaration of "We lost the Sharp account", we hear the incredibly shrill sounds of a welder in use. From the world of corporate advertising where men in suits, shirts and ties fret over financial ruin we cut to the dusty plains of a working class farm and shade tree garage. This scene surfaces and closes quickly, swiftly establishing a point in Cujo's declining health.

Opening with an image of the large St. Bernard trying to sleep away the excruciating pain that comes with the onset of rabies, and with his master Joe Camber in the distance welding down some car parts in his make-shift work shed, this tiny sequence sees the distressed Cujo slowly lift up his head, become agitated by the horrendous noise of the welder and trot away to find refuge underneath the Camber house. Joe calls out to his son Brett (here a reverse of youngsters beckoning for their parents) to help him with something and a clear distinction is thusly made where young Brett is an assistant to his mechanic father, and not just a boy left to his own devices. In *Cujo*, the differentiating of the two central boys is also an interesting component in the gender politics of the film. Brett is a rural dwelling kid forced to "man up" before his time and destined to be stuck in a rut (however honest his rut would be) whereas Tad is allowed to

153

have room to play and be a child, coddled and nurtured by detached but sympathetic parents. In essence, Brett is what would be socially considered "the real boy" and Tad would be a variant of boyhood – a sissified version, completely protected by a mother destined to face her demons in the form of a rabid St. Bernard.

Cujo tries to sleep, but the rabies virus keeps him restless and unsettled. Joe Camber's (Ed Lauter) welding doesn't help either.

In Stephen King's novel, Charity Camber fears that Brett will end up "just like his father" – something that she no longer finds admirable – and in both the book and the film, she will take him away with her to Connecticut in an attempt to give him a brand new life and the opportunity to become a better man than her husband ever was. This is also represented in the novel by the fact that in the closing moments it is learned that Charity has been able to afford to buy Brett a new dog – a healthy and vaccinated terrier cross – who will usher Brett into a newfound world of life without his father and proposed prospects.

While Joe goes about his day, working and angrily bellowing out to his put upon son, Cujo whimpers and slowly falls into the deep, dark vortex of rabies: the infected bite mark on his snout now open and pink, attracting flies, and his hearing being hypersensitive and not coping with sounds that once would have been comforting and reassuring.

TONY RICHMOND: I knew the book, and I knew of Stephen King, but I never read the novel. I just didn't think it was a very interesting story. The thing is with films, when you read scripts you sometimes think that this is going to make a terrific movie, and it turns out to be a piece of shit, then you do another one and it's been hell all the way through working on it and all the while you're thinking it is going to be a load of rubbish and then it turns out to be great, you just never know. There are only three movies that I worked on that I thought were going to work from the beginning and they turned out to be absolutely wonderful, and they are *Don't Look Now, The Man Who Fell to Earth* (1976) and *Candyman* (1992). That stuff just fell off the page!

MICHAEL HILKENE (supervising sound editor): It's important to keep in mind that, as the Supervising Sound Editor on the filmmaking crew, I am striving to help create a sound track that captures Lewis Teague's directorial vision of telling the story of the *Cujo* screenplay. Motion picture sound tracks are mixed down from recordings that fall into three major categories, dialogue, sound effects and music. On *Cujo*, as the sound editors worked on the dialogue and the sound effects, Charles Bernstein, the composer, wrote and scored the music for the picture. In 1983, we were still working on 35mm film. Consequently, the shear bulk of film limited the number of sound tracks that Neil Travis, the picture editor, could have at his disposal as he edited the picture. Oftentimes, the work tracks for films were as simple as an A and B dialogue tracks that were made from the production recordings on the set with a few sound effects thrown in when there was open space on one of the tracks. To start putting a sound track together for a picture like *Cujo*, the first step of the sound editing process was to spot with Lewis, Neil, and the producers,

Dan Blatt and Robert Singer. From the beginning of the spotting session it was clear to me that Lewis recognized the important contribution that the sound track was going to play in telling his story. As we went through the picture scene by scene, Lewis gave detailed notes on how he wanted the picture to sound. Those notes were key, because they established a clear guide of how he envisioned using sound in *Cujo*.

"I'VE GOT THIS TERRIFIC HUSBAND AND THIS TERRIFIC KID...": Donna ends her affair

Charles Bernstein's incredible musical motif for "Cujo's Theme" transitions from the guttural menace of the low end French horns (as Cujo trots towards the Camber house) into the emotionally stirring response to human turmoil which compliments the distressing melodrama that follows in this sequence. Opening with Donna driving down a sun-bleached Castle Rock street, this chapter of the story has our heroine end her affair with Steve Kemp. Here, Donna wishes to reclaim and rescue her crumbling marriage and refers to both her husband and son as "terrific" (the first time we physically hear her acknowledge her family). During this quiet and yet tumultuous sequence, the adulterous Donna anxiously puts aside her own personal needs and desires and severs a purely sexual connection in favour of a conventional familial union.

Driving in the beat up Pinto that will serve as both her protective fortress as well as her stunted trap in the latter part of the film, Donna nervously takes the wreck of a car to her lover's house, passing through the quaint New England street. Of course the scene was shot in Mendocino, California, however it is a perfectly disguised small town that can easily pass for coastal Maine – a showcase of some terrific work from location scout Jain Lemos. Working class in its set up (cruddy back alley ways adjoining to the shabby street etc), the area is a blue collar dystopia occupied by dishonest and opportunistic men like Steve Kemp. Donna walks into Steve's place without knocking – a familiarity established; clearly this is something she has done many times – and she abruptly wakes up the sleeping Steve which would be the second time he is seen awakening in his soiled and sunkissed bed. In this scene, Donna wears a blue summer dress which is the polar opposite of what she was wearing in the first scene we see her in bed with Steve which was the scarlet red dress (a symbol of fiery passion and sexual freedom). Here, in blue, she is matronly, maternal, almost on par with the Virgin Mary – something that actress Dee Wallace would be associated with in her role of Mary in *E.T. the Extra-Terrestrial*, which would heavily draw from the Bible as a source of narrative and thematic inspiration. A red belt would sit around her waist as a reminder of her "sin" – like a marking or branding that will forever "stain" her consciousness, and this is all the wonderful work of costume designer Jack Buehler and his wardrobe assistant Nancy G. Fox.

Originally intended to be a lengthier scene with Donna expressing her feelings for her husband Vic and making mention of her son's Tad's sensitivity and near-awareness of the situation at hand, the scene is to the point and direct. Screenwriter Barbara Turner intended to have the scene play out as a confessional and then confrontation, however follow up writer Don Carlos Dunaway designed the scene to be blunt and without too much discussion. Director Lewis Teague delivers the two-hander moment as a documentarian – a fly on the wall approach – that has Donna stand in the doorway calling off this extramarital affair that has left her feel used, empty and damaged. Dee Wallace's performance here is elegantly handled as she presses on with a woman convoluted and pinpricked by loneliness and a desperate desire to be loved or at least admired. She opens the dialogue with "I can't see you again, Steve" to which Steve asks "Why?" Donna doesn't beat around the bush; after admitting that she may in fact have a good life populated by good people

("I've got a terrific husband and a terrific kid") she brands her affair with Steve as a "stupid mistake".

Infidelity in film would become part of a structural narrative function throughout the history of cinema and when it was the core backbone it still served to assist the fundamental plot. In *Fear* (1954), Ingrid Bergman's affair sends her into a mentally deranged state, *Human Desire* (also 1954) had Gloria Grahame question her own moral fibre after she sparks up a condemned romance with Glenn Ford, while in the French production of *Lady Chatterley's Lover* (1955) infidelity is romanticized and even championed. All of these films prominently feature extramarital affairs as dynamic centrepieces, whereas in a far more perceptive film such as *Cujo*, adultery is a firmly cemented, ever important plot ingredient that reads as both allegorical and evolutionary. If the St. Bernard is bitten by a rabid bat and is infected by a disease that is carried through the bloodstream, then similarly Donna Trenton has been affected by the onslaught of a "stupid mistake".

In 1987's *Fatal Attraction*, Michael Douglas would be tormented by the after effects of an affair with Glenn Close who turns out to be a living and breathing disease hellbent on avenging her "honour". She plots and plans an attack, just like a crippling virus – much like rabies, or even more socially responsive at the time of the film's release, much like the AIDS crisis. Incredibly similar to Dee Wallace in *Cujo*, Michael Douglas's infidelity has polluted the sanctity of the family unit and Glenn Close's psychotic jilted lover infecting the domestic domain becomes a direct antagonist that will stop at nothing to cause distress to the stability and comfort of domesticity. Douglas is forced to defend his family, however it is his own wife that comes to the rescue; whereas in *Cujo*, ultimately, the "woman in the storm" will resurrect a force of primal power and build up the courage, wisdom, strength, determination and zeal to save her child, her world and most importantly herself.

Legendary screenwriter and librettist Arthur Laurents (*Rope* (1948), *West Side Story* (1961), *The Turning Point* (1977)) would discuss the concept of "woman in the storm" as a narrative function and story trope in academic essays and script doctoring lectures and argue that adulteresses throughout literature and film history have been made to "suffer" and be "put out in the metaphoric storm" that will act as a systematic test. In *Cujo*, this is most certainly the case.

This scene in question, with Donna ending her affair, is a testament to the leading up to the picture belonging to the "woman in the storm" trope, and with Steve reacting violently – angrily getting out of bed and chasing after Donna – the film will become emotionally invested in the concept of personal struggle inside and outside of horror movie trappings (ie the terror that unfolds when the rabid Cujo lunges at the busted up Pinto and torments mother and child). Steve follows Donna outside and protests the end of their affair, only to have Vic Trenton drive by and spot them – his dissatisfied wife with the "local stud".

TONY RICHMOND: Barbara Turner became a very close friend of mine. She was a wonderful writer. She was also a very dear friend of my wife's. She also knew Dan Blatt well. She was a fantastic writer and she didn't take any shit from anyone either. Peter and Barbara got along like a house on fire, they were very close and that played into it big time, Dan went off the deep end and lost his marbles. There was just not enough time between reading the script and then planning to shoot it.

Jan de Bont and Lewis Teague take a coffee break.

"OVER, DONE WITH, GONE": Donna picks up Tad and heads home

Racing out of school is Tad Trenton. He carries his Pac-Man lunchbox, runs through the crowd of screaming children, gets tangled in a little girl's skipping rope and jumps into the banged up Pinto greeting his mother. Donna Trenton looks weary and sombre, but she shifts energies and embraces her son acknowledging his new drawing ("Hey! That's real nice!"). She notices a mark on his forehead and asks about it, to which Tad replies "I got hit by a swing!" Tad's delicate body and vulnerability are highlighted here; a tiny scratch is going to be completely dwarfed in severity come the third act of the film, where the poor boy will be struggling to breathe and trapped by a menacing realized monster in the form of a rabid St. Bernard. Tad's forehead injury would be another point of conversation when his father Vic spots it and voices his concern. Back in the Pinto, Donna tells Tad she can make it "better" and kisses him, offering the reassuring "Over, done with, gone" that he repeats. This tiny scene with Donna and Tad in the decrepit Pinto will foreshadow the impending third act where they will be imprisoned by the vehicle and forced to face personal demons, rather than flip them off with superficial mantras.

163

When they take off, the car stammers and stalls, jolting back and forth and making Tad laugh. They drive past a cemetery which is the same cemetery used earlier in the film by originally assigned director Peter Medak (the discarded sequence involving the supernatural element that was originally intended for the film from the screenplay of Barbara Turner). Pulling up into their driveway, Donna and Tad are singing their favorite nursery rhyme:

I see your heinie, nice and shiny
If you don't hide it, I think I'll bite it!

The lyrics are subtly humorous in that it sparks the notion that Cujo himself will want to bite both the "heinie" of Donna and Tad while he has them trapped in the Pinto later in the film. The song will be reprised when Donna and Tad hit the road to get the car fixed at the Camber farm.

Peering through the blind shades is Vic, watching his dishonest wife park and step out of the car. Tad runs to his father and the two share a warm moment with Vic protecting Tad from taking out the groceries, and offering to play baseball. Donna and Vic exchange some dialogue that is deep rooted in fear, disconnection, caginess, stress and disloyalty. Much like the earlier scene with Vic and Steve Kemp who used his tennis racquet as a shield of secrecy, here, Donna lies to her husband through the glaring windshield of the Pinto – which she will later smash to smithereens. Her pent up internal struggle, her marital trap, the prison of responsibility, domestic banality ("groceries, errands") and her sense of self are both a veiling and masking of insecurity and overwhelming sadness and then finally shattered and washed away – Donna will be reborn by the end of the film; bloodied and bruised as if she has been in battle, she will emerge out of the movie a warrior and a mother determined to rescue her child and herself.

Vic watches Donna lie to him, while Donna remains frustrated by his detachment and false promises ("Yeah, I've heard that before..."). The final line of the scene is Vic's "He's (Roger Breakstone) still in mourning for the account" – an indication that his profession will be the perfect distraction for him while he deals with Donna's infidelity, which will soon be outed and exposed.

DEE WALLACE: I think the distinction is that I was never a mother physically but I had always been a mother to a lot of people. I had been a high school teacher, a dance teacher and I took care of a lot of kids and I was raised by a mother who took care of a lot of people. That's what she did, she took care of people. It was very natural for me. Probably one thing that affected it mostly was the fact that my father was an alcoholic all my life and my mother had to work, so I took on the world of taking care of my little brother. So I had really been a mother in the real sense of the word – sheltering him, loving him, taking care of him, making sure he was OK. I didn't give birth to my brother, but spiritually, physically and emotionally I definitely took care of him, so that was very good practice.

DANIEL HUGH KELLY: They had built the huge façade of the Trenton house on the coast of the ocean in Mendocino, and that was typical Dan Blatt. And it looked like a real house, but it was just a façade. The first shot I had to do was when Dee comes home and I am supposed to look through the blinds and that is when I met Lewis. I think my hand just comes in and you see the blinds move, watching her arrive home.

ROBIN LUCE: *Cujo* was a big deal because I had very little experience and it was the third film I had worked on, so it was daunting at times, but I always found that I worked well under pressure. I found that out at a very early age. I always liked the challenge of trying to figure out how to deliver what they were looking for!

Danny Pintauro and his stand in at a clothing store where costumers Jack Buehler and Nancy G. Fox sourced some of the costumes. The t-shirt worn here would never make the final cut. (courtesy of Danny and Margaret Pintauro).

"I WON THE LOTTERY": Charity buys Joe a gift and wants something in return

(Also, extensive coverage of a deleted scene as told by actor Robert Craighead)

Incredibly gifted actress Kaiulani Lee would make an impression in a tiny role in the 1981 horror film *The Fan* starring Hollywood legend Lauren Bacall and upstart Michael Biehn. Lee would play Biehn's concerned sister who begs her movie and theatre obsessive brother (who manifests his obsession into violence) to reconnect with his family. Later, she would play one of the feminist cultists who cut out their tongues in solidarity for a child rape victim in the provocative drama satire *The World According to Garp* (1982). But here, in *Cujo*, Lee gets more than one scene and is permitted to speak dialogue, and her performance is poignant, delicate and beautifully handled. She breathes effortless life into Charity Camber – a woman completely trapped by domestic imprisonment and suffocating isolation, who finally gets a glimmer of hope from coincidental magic when she wins the lottery and decides to flee a miserable life, in hopes of starting a new and enlightened one.

Countering Lee's elegant performance is the brilliant and magnetic

Ed Lauter as her husband Joe, who had already made an impression in varied versatile character roles as seen in films such as *The Longest Yard* (1974), *Breakheart Pass* (1975), *King Kong* (1976), *The White Buffalo* (1977) and *Death Hunt* (1981) to name a few. In 1978, Lauter would play Ann-Margret's jilted, gruff husband in the horror film *Magic*, which would possibly be the closest relative to Joe Camber as far as crotchety and cantankerous earth-stained working men would go. Both Lee and Lauter play out this sequence in *Cujo* with earnest realism, and complimenting their earthy delivery is the perceptive and bright Billy Jacoby as their "aware" son Brett.

Prior to the scene set inside the Camber kitchen, the sequence opens with Joe finding a brand new engine hoist – still wrapped up in its protective packaging – sitting in his garage, while the sickly Cujo descends under the house to escape the painful noises that come from his humans (the roaring motor from Joe's pickup truck, the clanging of cutlery that hits the kitchen bench and so forth). Cujo's twisted face now bears the effects of rabies, with thick gooey yellowish green ooze seeping from his drooping eyes and long hanging saliva stretching towards the dusty plains. Not able to stomach water anymore, Cujo's final moments of good health and sanity are rapidly drifting away. "Hydrophobia" would be the old world name for rabies and it refers to the latter stages of the disease where the inability to drink or swallow liquids is prevalent. Films such as *Old Yeller* would use the horrible condition as a point of tragedy, while in *Cujo*, the disease would act as the monstrous entity inhabiting a normally benevolent dog. Interestingly enough however, the term "hydrophobia" would be first mentioned in a comedy, that being George Cukor's innovative and thoroughly witty *The Women* (1939) which had Rosalind Russell bite Paulette Goddard in a fight sparking Goddard to remark "Yeah! Gotta be careful of hydrophobia!" (a coded way to refer to Russell being a "bitch"). Earlier in the film, Joan Crawford would make the snappy remark: "There's a name for you ladies, but it isn't used in high society...outside a kennel!" which adds more wonderful word play that link mouthy and opinionated women to dogs. But outside the comic antics of legendary and very talented actresses of the late thirties, in *Cujo* we are presented with a dog undergoing a tragic transformation, from happy and healthy St. Bernard in his prime, to a sketchy, unsure, addled unfortunate.

Feeling the devastating effects of the onset of rabies, Cujo's sensitivity to loud noise flares up.

However, this scene with Joe driving into his farm, finding the hoist and Cujo whimpering and hiding under the house, would originally have a sequence precede it which would feature young actor Robert Craighead as a delivery man dropping off the engine hoist with his postal partner where they would encounter a progressively aggressive rabid St. Bernard.

DEE WALLACE: Robert Craighead was one of my students at the time, and I asked Dan Blatt to audition him and get him on board. *Cujo* was his first film, so I was pretty chuffed.

The first time the term "hydrophobia" is mentioned in a Hollywood film – George Cukor's *The Women* (1939).

The musical *Ameritage* was produced by Dee Wallace and Christopher Stone and where the duo met actor Robert Craighead. (courtesy of Dee Wallace).

ROBERT CRAIGHEAD ("Joe MaGruder" from a deleted scene): I was doing the world premiere of a musical called *Ameritage*. Dee Wallace and Christopher Stone were producing this musical and Dee was very nice during it and then eventually helped me get this role in *Cujo*, which was my very first film! Dee did the choreography for the musical and everything and this was while she was working and finishing up on *E.T. the Extra-Terrestrial*. We worked on this project for quite a while. We ran for, I guess, six months, in Beverly Hills. It was a kind of "history musical" similar to something like *1776*, except this was a comedy and was in the vein of Monty Python. There were like eight actors and we had one basic costume that you had to run off and grab, then add a hat, change, come back and we'd be somebody else doing a whole bunch of songs and dances. It was a really funny show! So not long after that I got to read for *Cujo*. Dee got me the audition. I mean, she got me a few auditions while we were working on that show together. She was so wonderful. I read for the lead role in *Gremlins* (1984). I think that was my very first audition for a film. Dee always encouraged me. So, I went and read for the casting director Marcia Ross and the next thing I know, they said "You've got the job!" and this was exciting because not only was it my first film role, but I was a huge Stephen King fan! I mean, in the early eighties, he was king! Also, if I'm not mistaken, Stephen King was there on set. This was the first film he had actually written the screenplay based off of. I mean, he wasn't there the whole time, but I just have a rough memory of him being there, when he was there for a few days. I went up there and filmed my part. I think I was there for like maybe a week and then the show closed. At the end of it all, Christopher Stone came down and asked me if I would help him, because they wanted to bring one of their cars and their dogs. So, I drove back with them, and spent another week or so up there. And that is when I got to see the phenomenal work that Dee did in the car! She was just amazing! Watching what she did, developing that off camera – I mean, watching her preparation was really inspiring! The scene that I was in for *Cujo* has me making a reference to getting that cherry picker that is

171

going to be delivered to the farm. So we show up to deliver it, and we're looking around for Joe as in Ed Lauter and he's not around, so we put it down there in the barn and my partner says "Leave it in the barn if he isn't here". So we unload it and put it in the barn, and that is when the other scene opens up with Cujo jumping out and that was pretty scary because they wouldn't let you be around the dog. I think they had around three different dogs on set and we were not allowed to meet them because they wanted to maintain that element of fear. I have a fear of big dogs anyway so when that dog jumped up on the table; and they squirted orange juice in his mouth and he was drooling, it was truly scary. I remember the trainer. I remember him being off camera, and he's doing this thing with a fan hat would make Cujo start growling and bark at us. I don't really re-member having much interaction with him, but I do remember them say-ing "We want you to keep your distance from the dogs." The scene I was in was shot all in one day, I believe. We might have got part of it down at the end of one day and then we shot the other the next day. We did some interiors of the barn and exteriors at the house and stuff. The dogs were extremely well trained! And we didn't get into any trouble whatsoever, but believe me, I was scared! But of course, my scene is cut. Dee and Chris told me after they went and saw the dailies that I was in the master cut. But then they went and saw the final cut at a private screening. They called me up and we get together and they broke the news to me, that the scene was gone. It was good coming from them. But of course I was devastated because *Cujo* was my first film. Of course they explained to me why these things happen and Chris was great because he kept saying "They cut a lot of my stuff out! When I trash the house! That's all gone!" I have no idea if the scene still exists. From my understanding, it was in the master cut. If there is a copy of the master out there somewhere, then chances are that as well as several other scenes. I know that the scene that Chris was really upset that they cut where he destroys the house was filmed. Any actor is going to be upset, especially a scene that you really poured your heart into. My stuff was pretty much true to the script. At that time I was a theatre

The deleted sequence from *Cujo*. Here, Robert Craighead and his partner are startled by Cujo, who leaps up at them growling and snarling. In this scene, Craighead's character would deliver the engine hoist that Charity Camber (Kaiulani Lee) would buy for Joe (Ed Lauter). Upon delivery, he and his associate would come into contact with the rabid Cujo, but make a successful run for it. The scene was dropped because director Lewis Teague felt it read as slightly "comical", and definitely not apropos for a film so serious in tone. (courtesy of Robert Craighead).

trained actor and we're trained that the script is the bible, so you have to follow along. But overall the shoot was excellent. Dee even got me to read for the lead in *Gremlins*! She is just a beautiful soul inside and out and so is her daughter – I love them dearly. As far as the rest of the *Cujo* crew, well, I can't even think of the actor who played by delivery partner. I never saw him again after that. I never really had any communication with him after that. I'm not really sure. He was a great guy. I really can't remember his name. I don't know what happened to him. They had me a hotel room and everything. But Dee said "Well, I want you to stay at the house." She

173

meant the house that she and Chris were put up at. She said "I want you to stay with us." So I was like "Oh. Okay. Great!" So I stayed at the house with them. Like I said, when I came back up there, I hung around for a while and watched them shoot. It was a great experience! Besides the beautiful and brilliant Dee, was Lewis Teague. I loved Lewis! I come from a theatre background and that was my very first film and he was very helpful as far as helping me work in front of the camera, because he had to take everything down a little bit and to stage the film which I was aware of. He really worked with me as he was directing. I've come across him several times since. So he's a real sweetheart. Ed Lauter was one of my heroes growing up as a kid. I mean, I'm a big western fan. Ed was in a lot of westerns. Kailulani Lee was a very deep person and individual. I remember the wardrobe girl Nancy Fox very well. Actually, Nancy was also the costume designer on the musical I did with Dee and Chris and Dee introduced me to Nancy and I think she was trying to set us up, I believe. Also, one of Dee's stunt women had an accident with one of the dogs and another woman I felt horrible for because she had really long, beautiful blonde hair and they cut it all off to look like Dee.

Robert Craighead and Dee Wallace on set. (courtesy of Robert Craighead).

Lewis Teague on location with Robert Craighead. (courtesy of Robert Craighead).

Robert Craighead and Ed Lauter on set. (courtesy of Robert Craighead).

The production
bomber jacket for *Cujo*.
(courtesy of Robert
Craighead).

The original production's call sheet for the "I Won The Lottery" sequence which would also include the delivery of the engine hoist which would ultimately be cut from the film. (courtesy of Robert Craighead).

Lewis Teague talks out the scene with Robert Craighead.

"I WON THE LOTTERY" (cont'd)

Shot on a low angle (as if from a dog's perspective, which will eventually become a thematic aesthetic delivered by cinematographer Jan de Bont) Joe enters his house already agitated and unimpressed by the appearance of a brand new engine hoist. He confronts Charity about it, while young Brett pleads with his father explaining that "You kept telling me that you needed one". Joe's glare at Brett suggests a "back of the hand" or an "undoing of the belt buckle"; there is so much disdain and silent rage in Ed Lauter's expression who has such a dedicated handle on this kind of stoic, hardened and damaged man.

In eighties America, the idealistic enterprise of capital gain and unadulterated wealth and status is lost here in the impoverished "white trash" small towns of rural Maine. In essence, the Cambers are left-over hillbillies. These are North Eastern Yankees lost in socio-economic woe, thriving on scraps and living outside the construct of the established town. As poor white people living in rural Maine, the Cambers somehow understand their place: whether it be in service of the middle class (which is epitomized in the scene where Joe takes a look at Vic Trenton's car) or fixed in their own social carpentry as a family unit. The dark cloud that lingers over the Cambers is the fact that there is a hint of domestic violence that exists under the shabby roof. Joe reacts violently when he finds out that Charity has bought him an engine hoist. Instead of being thankful and grateful and honouring this extremely kind gesture, he lashes out and cusses (the first "fuck" uttered in this R rated feature) and grabs hold of her arm. Cujo also responds to this, with Lewis Teague having his editor Neil Travis cut from Charity being under attack to Cujo hearing this onslaught and lifting his head in worry, whimpering.

It is suggested that Cujo has seen such hostility in the household and possibly seen Joe be rough on Charity and never liked it for one second. Also, what this does for an audience eager to see some bloody carnage is that it sweetens the eventual killing of Joe – if he is a horrendous man to begin with, then his demise will be welcomed. In the grand tradition of ecological horror movies, the unsympathetic loutish man who is killed by the animal threat is a slaying happily welcomed. Ernest Borgnine's succumbing to the rats in *Willard* (1971) is applauded because he spends the entire film being an awful bully, Ralph Meeker being killed by giant rodents in *The Food of the Gods* (1976) is understood because he is opportunistic and self-serving, the shady rich political figures chomped down in *Alligator* are killed because they are the reason innocent (non-wealthy) people have been eaten, and so forth – Ed Lauter and his drunken friend Gary (Mills Watson) are both killed by Cujo and their deaths are somehow warranted.

Charity explains that she has won the lottery and therefore can afford to get Joe his gift (which will no doubt benefit his business as a shade tree mechanic) and in return she asks her husband if she can take Brett to Connecticut to "visit" her sister. The weatherworn Charity, in her simple summer dress, wishes to be granted this "gift" and it is hinted at later that this will be the new start that she wishes to undertake – an escape from the abuse and a brand new life for her and her boy.

Connecticut would forever be known as a state of white upper middle class security and esteem. In the horror film, Connecticut can also be another place of dark secrecy and hushed violence (as seen in *The Stepford*

Wives (1975)), but here in *Cujo* it is a place of refuge for Charity. In Stephen King's novel, emotional and intellectual abuse simmers in Connecticut when Charity's snobbish brother-in-law voices his opinion on his wife Holly's working class roots which are now in his face and living under his roof in the form of Holly's sister Charity and her son Brett. Throughout the passages of the novel that chronicle Charity's stay at Holly's, it is learned that she wants what is best for her son and also – eventually – in service of what she needs for herself. Physical abuse sits at the heart of the Camber household with Charity being a victim of domestic violence, whereas her sister Holly is subjected to intellectual berating by her supposedly "sophisticated" husband linking the Maine set *Cujo* with a former piece set at turn of the century New England, the Rodgers and Hammerstein musical *Carousel* (1956). In this dark fable, two young millworkers Julie Jordan (Shirley Jones) and Carrie Pipperidge (Barbara Ruick) are subjected to two kinds of abuse – Julie is beaten by her swaggering barker Billy Bigelow (Gordon MacRae) and Carrie is continually undermined by her professional fisherman betrothed Enoch Snow (Robert Rounseville).

When Joe grabs Charity's arm and roughs her up, we cut to Cujo underneath the house listening and grunting – a dog falling under the effects of a physiological disease catching glimpses of his family struggling to be happy and comfortable. In the novel, Stephen King writes profound messages of beautifully realized prose from the dog's point of view. There is a moving passage that discusses the notion that Cujo wanted to be a good dog, that he loves the Man, the Woman and the Boy, and wanted to be their protector and friend. The tragedy in *Cujo* is that – much like desperate wives and lecherous loutish husbands – the loyal and the devoted can turn. If Joe Camber can beat his wife and Donna Trenton can cheat on her husband, then this unfortunate St. Bernard can succumb to a terrifying fate as well and wreak havoc on the fragile psyche of a little boy stuck in an overheated dead car, gasping for air.

The Camber household is only made "liveable" because Charity has

181

made an attempt to keep it well-maintained and when she asks to go to Connecticut with Brett to visit her sister, there is a balanced reasoning behind it – she has done what she can to satisfy and work for her husband, and all she wants is a moment for herself and her son. However, as we learn later in the film, this moment will become a full blown attempt at escape. Author Stephen King had been quoted in saying that he based portions of Margaret White, the religious zealot mother of the telekinetic teen in "Carrie", on a woman he knew who used to be obsessed with buying lottery tickets. This theme would pop back up in his work for "Cujo", with the thrifty Charity (her namesake even evoking feelings of desperation and a desire to "make good").

This loaded and beautifully performed and directed scene encapsulates the story device and thematic hoist of chance and the notion of circumstance and coincidence. The lowly and desperate Charity has won the lottery – something that is completely granted by luck – and this gives her the opportunity to break free from the trappings of a loveless marriage, an abusive husband, a tonally bland existence on a dead-end farm and Kaiulani Lee delivers a heartbreaking performance, and it is a tragedy that more of her work in the film ended up on the cutting room floor.

LEWIS TEAGUE: I remember watching all the footage that involved Kaiulani and Ed and just thinking it was so good, but that it was also too long. I can't remember which were the scenes Barbara Turner wrote that we left in and the ones that we had to take out. But ultimately Barbara had kept a lot more in of the Cambers' life and sadly that's what I had to take out. It was all good material, it just wasn't necessary, and it was too long.

CHRISTOPHER MEDAK: The farm house in Santa Rosa always stuck out in my mind. It became as much of a story and as much of a

Originally the film would examine the domestic violence aspect that permeated the Camber household with Joe Camber (Ed Lauter) being an oppressive force, constantly belittling and berating his wife Charity (Kaiulani Lee). This element would ultimately be cut from the final film.

character as everyone else. That great tree in the middle and that barn, I mean the whole thing was just fantastic and it made us feel that we were in the world of *Cujo*. The land itself was the story and that was just great to be immersed in. The attention to detail was great. I mean the disrepair and the degradation that Guy J. Comtois created was just special. The farm house itself was desolate and the people who had owned it had lost their son. Their son had hung himself off the tree that features in *Cujo*. The house had not been lived in for quite a while before *Cujo*. The only way we found out that the previous owners lost their son to suicide was that one of the grips had hung a dummy that we used for the film off the same tree and then we were told the story. When the location manager came down to the farm, he freaked out and screamed "Take that fucking thing down!" The grips thought it was funny and were like "Oh no one will know!"

MARCIA ROSS: Kaiulani Lee was an actress I knew. She was a New York actress. Kaiulani was someone I bought in when we had the casting sessions in New York. I knew Kaiulani from New York because I went to the theatre all the time and I worked as a stage manager, and then went into casting. My passion was going to the theatre and a lot of these actors I saw on stage, and Kaiulani was one of those actors. I knew her well from watching her on stage. She had a wonderful face. She didn't look like other people. First of all, she had a small town look to her face, she looked like she was a woman who lived in a small town. She had that complete feel of someone who looked as though she lived her whole life, and probably will live her whole life, in a small town. There was such an earthiness and realness to her, and she was a wonderful grounded actress.

ROBIN LUCE: It was very easy to make up Ed Lauter. The thing I love about makeup the most is less is more. If someone is meant to be grubby and redneck looking, then it really is all about less is more and highlights and shadows. It all translates in the face with the lights and camera. Ed had a great gruff look to his face and I just added to it to highlight features of his face that made him look even more agitated and edgy.

Billy Jacoby as Brett Camber: the all-American boy and best friend to the ailing Cujo.

Charity Camber (Kaiulani Lee) tells her husband Joe (Ed Lauter) that she won the lottery: the magic of circumstance and chance is a major thematic element in *Cujo*.

"I'LL SIC MY DOG ONTO YOU": Joe Camber and Gary Pervier make plans

"Boston?!" yells out the drunken Gary Pervier (Mills Watson) over an establishing shot of his decrepit, shambolic, ruin of a home. Gary is a loutish redneck, guzzling beer and agitating poor Cujo who lies down by his master Joe Camber. Cujo is heard whimpering and feeling the painful sounds that envelop the scene. Sound designer Michael Hilkene decided to exaggerate the audio which in turn made the smashing of beer cans, the shattering of the icebox, the banging of pots and pans as well as Ed Lauter's high pitched whistle all the more annoying for the struggling Cujo. Heightening their intensity affects the doomed dog who groans in secret anguish, as the two booze addled men discuss plans to visit Boston.

In Stephen King's novel, the character of Gary Pervier (a French surname, harking back to Castle Rock's European background as a result of years of immigration and bastardisation of cultural diversity) is written as a far more complicated and even sympathetic buffoon than what he is presented as in Lewis Teague's film. It is noted in the book that Gary is misanthropic, however truly feels compassion and even love for Joe Camber, his son Brett and most especially Cujo. As distanced Gary is from the rest of the world, he feels a passionate connection to

187

the mechanic, his boy and the hulking St. Bernard – who he refers to as "someone who understands" him. In the filmic treatment of Gary Pervier, he is stripped of any kind of empathy and any kind of humanity, and is rendered an obnoxious, grotesque, loutish pig of a man who lives in his own filth. Character actor Mills Watson would make a big impression in pop-cultural iconography as Deputy Perkins on the hit TV series *B.J. and the Bear* (1978-1981) and here he loads up the unappealing character of Gary Pervier with a poignant sense of disdain, disregard and contempt for the world. Gary, in Teague's film, is essentially fodder for the bloodthirsty and enraged rabid Cujo who will eventually kill him, making him the dog's first victim.

This scene is primarily filmed from yet another low angle which emphasizes the omnipresence of Cujo, and although the dog is physically there lying beside the kitchen table, his energy permeates the mood, distortion, unease and murkiness of the sequence. During the conversation shared between Joe Camber and Gary, the two men indulge in heavy drinking and the dialogue is matched by the faint sounds of Country and Western twang heard from a nearby radio. The entirety of the scene is clouded by jarring sounds and grimy bleakness in color, tone and light. The men's alcoholism and the vortex that it spins them into is reflected in cinematographer Jan de Bont's choices of angles and camera movement, which also comments on the dog's declining health. While Joe and Gary make drunken unwholesome plans for a trip to Boston, Cujo moans and is agitated by oppressive noise – a perfectly composed juxtaposition marrying selfish and ugly intentions of mankind with tragic and unfortunate transformation in a normally joyful, pleasant beast.

Joe's objectives in Boston are made clear – he wants to sleep around, get drunk, gamble and spend some hedonistic days away from his work and family. He plans to use the lottery money won by his wife Charity; however he wishes to share the fun of the trip with his friend Gary. "Broads, booze and baseball!" declares Joe in an eager attempt to convince Gary to join him – and it works. Once again, the film manipulates its characters to drive them out of the situation that Donna Trenton and her son will soon be entrapped by; Joe Camber is set to go to Boston with the neighbouring Gary, and therefore (along with Charity and Brett off to Connecticut) there will be no one around to help the terrorized Donna. Horror movies – such as this one – heavily rely on isolating characters and plopping them into situations that are not only desolate and burdened by lack of contact or communication, but also devastating and dire in their very set up. Of course, for both Joe and Gary, their intentions of hitting Boston are severed as soon as they come into contact with the frenzied Cujo who will maul them both to death.

This particular scene also importantly highlights the fact that Cujo's violent nature is something completely unnatural and utterly out of character. When Gary says "You couldn't sic that dog on me if I was coming at you with a straight razor in each hand!" it is a clear indication that Gary has only ever known Cujo to be a gentle and loving dog – something that will change as soon as the rabies finally sets in and the Cujo he and Joe once knew is gone forever.

MICHAEL HILKENE: One of Lewis' directives was to make sure that all the sound elements that we used to emphasize Cujo's increased sensitivity to sounds, were as shrill and piercing as possible. He wanted the sounds to be as unsettling to the audience as they were to Cujo. Scenes like the grinder scene and the drinking scene in the kitchen where Joe Camber (Ed Lauter) and his buddy (Mills Watson) are smashing things in the icebox and crushing the beer cans, were a few examples of where that was done. Likewise, the attack scenes were laced with high-pitched sound effects like Cujo's nails on the windshield, as well as shrill screams from Donna Trenton (Dee Wallace) and Tad Trenton (Danny Pintauro).

ROBIN LUCE: I was pretty much responsible for every character that went through the film. It was Julie, the hairdresser and I, and we were solely responsible for all the looks for each character.

189

CHRISTOPHER MEDAK: Jan de Bont is an absolute dickhead. He was arrogant and horrible to the crew. Even though Tony Richmond wasn't a friend of my father's but instead a friend of Dan Blatt's, there was a charm to him and he and my dad had a camaraderie and solidarity that was obvious. Jan, much like Lewis, was not at all warm or engaging, but cold and detached. It became a dictation. I mean there is no question that Jan is a great DOP, and he has a great eye, but on set there was no love for Jan.

TERESA ANN MILLER: St. Bernards are a tricky breed to train. German Shepherds are brilliant. Labradors are great. A lot of your mutts are very good! What happens is you get a dog with various backgrounds and specialities bred into this one dog. So a lot of times your mutts are great, but the purebreds are challenging. I remember there was one particular dog for *Beethoven* and boy oh boy it took him like a week, I don't remember what I was trying to teach him. It wasn't something very difficult. Maybe just to wave his paw or something. It took him over a week, he just didn't get it. Like he was going through the motions, like he just doesn't understand it, then all of a sudden he would just do it. I was so excited, then the next minute he had no idea what he wanted. I mean it was really just a funny challenge in contrast to working with a German Shepherd, which I have worked with since 1988, I guess on *K-9* (1989) with John Belushi. My father and I got the Shepherds and I have been working Shepherds almost non-stop since then. I did *Inspector Rex* (1994-2008) for sixteen years. I did ten years in Vienna...eleven years in Vienna, then five years in Rome – the Italian version. We mostly had domestic animals growing up. You know, maybe my father was 5 foot 6, he wasn't a very big man and he always said he didn't work anything bigger or meaner than him. So we didn't have a lot of exotic or different animals in that sense, we had a lot of domesticated animals. The pigs are still to this day my favourites to work with. We had done a couple of test pigs for a movie that never really came to be, and that was before getting *Babe*

(1995). Working with the pigs is very rewarding and just fascinating, it is so funny to see them learn and they learn quite quick. They learn quicker than a dog. Much quicker. However, it is a different way of working. A dog will work for a reward such as anything from a toy to food to praise. Whereas the pig works strictly for food. He's got one job and that's it! But it causes them to learn very quickly. I think the most obvious challenge is the emotional expressions. I don't want to say control but the reaction that the animal feeds off you and your body language and your tone, because that's very unique... that's very unique. Most the training you see in stuff that you have dogs do in behaviour and tricks but they're just doing it as dogs. For my dad to specialise in dog Jekyll and Hyde dynamics and be able to manipulate the dog's emotions and reactions that they're acting as opposed to just doing tricks and behaviour was very unique to him.

Animal trainer Karl Lewis Miller and "Chris" who played Beethoven in the movie of the same name from 1992.

"YOU HAVING FUN AT SUMMER CAMP?": Vic collects Tad

In earlier drafts of the screenplay, scenes depicting Tad Trenton at summer camp would be elongated and inserted to make a methodical point. This would be an element of the story that would be meatier and intended to emphasise the fact that Donna needed time out of playing "mom" for long stretches of time. However, in rewrites, this aspect would be underplayed and ultimately this sole scene with Tad not enjoying his time at summer camp being picked up by his father and taken home would be the hangover of that attribute of the script.

With the red Jaguar pulling up to the grassy plains of the summer camp, the scene is picturesque and lit with crisp, vibrant colors, set to the noisy sounds of children having fun. Tad is seen on his own, alone in his own world, finger painting. Vic, hiding a degree of sorrow, regret and stress, collects his son into his arms and plays up the role of loving father. *Cujo* presents a world of men consumed by their work, however these same men will also come to the "rescue" of children caught in the middle of domestic disputes and uncertainty. Tad is presented as a child susceptible to torment bought on by the perils of isolation and disorder, and this scene, as well as the previous scene where he attempts to hide his bruised forehead from his mother, highlight the delicate nature of the boy, who will ultimately be in the throes of terror and torment in the third act of the film – left stripped, wet with perspiration, choking on the lack of air, dying in the heat and scared out of his wits by the rabid two hundred pound dog who longs to tear out his throat.

Danny Pintauro would play this sensitivity, vulnerability and elfin-like whimsy with flawless precision and this frailty is something that sells the character's insecurity and anxiety with driven intelligence, perception and almost ethereal resonance and poignancy.

Danny Pintauro getting some playtime in on location in Mendocino. (courtesy of Danny and Margaret Pintauro).

DANIEL HUGH KELLY: Danny's mom was from Jersey and I was from Jersey, so yeah I got her. It was her first movie set, she was very protective of Danny, and sometimes very nervous on set. I had heard that there were some problems later on with some people that were associated with the film, but that had gotten ironed out pretty quickly. I met his dad as well, and his dad came out on the shoot early on but I don't recall him being there a lot during the course of the shoot. I think Danny's mom was named Margaret, but she went by "Peggy" and she was very "Jersey". Dan Blatt was a wonderful guy and a wonderful producer, and I think he took care of whatever issues that came up regarding Peggy.

DANNY PINTAURO: I remember the rocket ship for sure! I totally do! I felt like Daniel Hugh Kelly and I had a really great connection. We didn't even have to really do anything to get to it. Again, it just sort of happened, and it was all fun. He was my dad! I loved him, and was worried about him, because something was happening at work, and all this stuff...just the way a child sense things and worries, I was like, "Oh God, I hope everything was going to be alright! I know he's gotta go into work now all because something is wrong with the commercial!" Even at that young age I got all of that. Then those scenes sitting on the car where he was telling me that he had to go out of town, well that was very real, and I do remember all of that. But if you were to ask him or I about rehearsing or going over themes or motivation, we didn't sit down and talk about it at all. We literally just ran through it and with great ease as soon as Lewis said "Okay. Go!" I mean, he was probably having lots of conversations with Lewis about what is happening in that moment and voicing his concerns, but I don't really think that Lewis or the three of us were really having those conversations. I think that we he was just turning the camera on and we would go. But I really loved Daniel, I thought he was an excellent actor and more of a friend than a TV dad. Much like Tony Danza in a way on *Who's the Boss?*

Lewis Teague finger paints with Danny Pintauro in between takes.

VERN NOBLES: Well, we were all kind of bummed when Peter Medak was fired, we all thought we were going home. He had great ideas from the get go – not only with the dog stuff but just the human stuff. I mean, there was a few days where we didn't know if Tony was going to stay or Tony was going to go, then Tony talked to Peter and he said he was going to go. We were all on nights that first week, so there was a week of transitions to just wake up and figure out what went on. And then when we got it and spoke with Tony, we were all bummed and then it was interesting to work with Jan, because, I think Alex worked with Jan one other time – he was the first assistant. I think that might have been his last movie as first assistant and then we started working with Jan and then we were using the Ultracam… we weren't using Panavision yet. So part of the reason that we stayed too was because Rich and I knew how to fix the Ultracam, cause we did a lot of movies with the Ultracam. And then Jan had a few problems, I mean, he got rid of the Ultracam and then we were Panavision.

Danny Pintauro has fun on location. (courtesy of Gale A. Adler).

SPILLED MILK: Donna's affair is outed

Donna Trenton drifts through her shadowy house tending to mundane domestic duties such as carrying a wash basket, plopping it down and trying to fill her days with purpose and meaning. She stops in her tracks and looks outside for a moment, rubbing upon her flat belly (a beautiful gesture and acting choice from actress Dee Wallace) lost in thought and smothered by boredom, isolation, frustration, personal despair and overwhelming loneliness. Wallace's choice in coveting her belly during this moment makes an unconscious reference to childbearing and childbirth – that this woman, empty in her own life, has in fact born a son that has become her entire world. As the film progresses, this element will be the core fundamental character driving force, that this woman will put aside everything (least of all personal happiness and contentment) in order to protect and save her vulnerable child. As Donna crosses over into her kitchen (the first time the room is completely her own domain, and not shared with husband, child or lover), she gets some water which in a sense hints at the oppressive heat that will sit as the backdrop for the rest of the movie. Director Lewis Teague has his cinematographer Jan de Bont film Dee Wallace from behind, closing in on her and stalking her.

The character of Donna will be visually "stalked" later in the film with her first encounter with the rabid Cujo in the third act of the movie. Here, however, she is not only stalked by the narrative lens, but by an intruder who is lurking in the shadows and who reaches out to touch and to terrify the troubled woman ("God you scared the shit out me!").

Steve Kemp has been hiding in the Trenton home – the "welcomed guest" now a trespasser. Steve's hand touches Donna's bare back and she jumps out of her skin, welcoming a wonderfully composed horror movie trope of the monster or threat creeping up on the hapless victim. Steve is inexplicably linked to the tangible traditional monster of the film which will ultimately be the two hundred pound rabid St. Bernard, and throughout this scene he is filmed in a way that foreshadows the terrifying canine that will relentlessly attack Donna by the film's final act. When he lunges at Donna and forces his mouth upon her own, it is incredibly on par with the frantic action that will surface later in the piece when Donna is fighting off the foaming, bloodthirsty dog.

Presenting the frightened Donna with a pink carnation, Steve whispers "I'm sorry". Symbolically, the pink carnation represents "a mother's undying love and devotion", which is precisely what *Cujo* in essence is about (or what it will eventually be about). The irony here is that it is the man who has polluted the familial bonds that tie mothers to their children (as well as to the fathers of their offspring) who has offered this mother – with her undying devotion and love for her son – the pink carnation, making this a wonderfully perverse reversal in morality and connection. It could be argued that this may be read as a mockery of maternal values, that Steve's delivery of such a throwaway offering could be an intended sarcastic commentary on an adulteress now wishing to reclaim her position as devoted mother (and wife).

Ignoring how he got inside, Steve explains that he has recently "stripped" and "refurnished" a new piece of carpentry and left it outside. Here is a character whose role it is to remodel work ("it's a beautiful piece of work") and in saying this, he is there to reconstruct situations at hand that are entirely selfish and self-serving, but also act as an offering of distraction from an alienated existence in Donna's sheltered and unsatisfying life.

Christopher Stone would play unsympathetic characters in many films, and this scene is very similar in tone to a moment in Joe Dante's *The Howling*, where Stone – who in that modern werewolf classic is once a sensitive and morally supportive husband – becomes an aggressive abuser. In *The Howling* he slaps Dee Wallace who plays his onscreen wife, forcing her to leave him. Eventually, she will shoot him in defence while he is in his full blown werewolf state, but before his infidelity with local lycanthrope Marsha Quist (Elisabeth Brooks), Christopher Stone's Bill Neill is a loving and considerate husband. In *Cujo*, there really is no time to spend with Steve Kemp – and therefore, no chance or opportunity to understand his personal motives and his own pathos. Instead, he is presented as "something to do", a "play thing" for the lonely Donna Trenton. In Stephen King's novel, Donna would describe her affair in great detail to her husband Vic, offering an insight into her infidelity. This intricately and brilliantly penned piece of prose from King would later find its way in the screenplay adaptation by Barbara Turner, however would eventually be completely omitted by follow up writer Don Carlos Dunaway, who under the direction of Lewis Teague, cut it to save on time and costs. Dee Wallace would welcome this change wholeheartedly and deliver the entire dialogue with a simple gesture, look, demeanour, physical presence and in the moment poignancy that the actress champions so critically. By the end of the scene, Donna is left on the kitchen floor surrounded by spilled milk, and the analogy is crystal clear – the old adage of "no use crying over spilled milk" springs to mind, and also, this conceptualized visual of a woman in the midst of a mess is an expressive, heartrending image of a flawed human being caught out at making a silly mistake. Wallace's co-star Daniel Hugh Kelly would find the omission of her monologue stressful and unwarranted, protesting the lack of verbal insight into Donna Trenton's choices, however, as aforementioned, the irony would be that the actress set to perform the lengthy soliloquy would opt for the "economic dialogue" response and do all of that lip service justice in choosing expression, physicality and manner. When director Brian De Palma came to the closing moments of *Carrie*, he wished that the final speech delivered by Piper Laurie as Margaret White was to be cut, however the seasoned actress fought for it and got to perform the electrifying dialogue ("All that dirty touching all over me, and I liked it..." and "I should have given you to God when you were born") – a completely different situation to this incident in *Cujo*. Both novels "Carrie" and "Cujo" would showcase Stephen King's excellent take on not only character driven horror, but also a superb display of creating very interesting, dynamic and complicated women. Donna Trenton is a marvel of texture and intricacy, and Dee Wallace's interpretation of her is outstanding. In a scene such as this one discussed here, this is most certainly on display. Here is the moment in the film where Donna's agony and torment start to propel a transitional arc for a woman who will eventually be forced to become a warrior.

Donna beats on Steve's chest, screaming at him "This is my goddamn home you bastard! My goddamn home!" Interestingly enough, Dee Wallace would holler out a similar sentiment in *E. T. the Extra-Terrestrial* when the "men in black" invade her home ("This is my home!"). Dee Wallace would make a career out of playing women protecting her children, something that the actress would be incredibly proud of in future years, expressing this sentiment in many interviews, at horror conventions and in genre associated press. Shooting from yet another low angle, Jan de Bont evokes a sense of the forever omnipresent Cujo, observing and taking everything in. As Steve closes in on Donna, he corners her into a section of the kitchen that is a trap and the film makes remarkable commentary on the role of women being cornered and trapped by men and boys. Steve tells Donna that he "misses her" and proceeds to attack her with violent kisses. Donna fights back, determined to get rid of this pollutant that has stained her ego, consciousness, morality, self-worth and spiritual centre. Donna's guilt has now transitioned from soul destroying ailment to a forceful resistance to a man who has literally come in and tried to dominate her and her situation. When she pushes back his advances and bashes onto his chest screaming at him "This is my home goddamn it!" she is forcefully reinstating her previous conversation with Steve about having a "terrific husband and a terrific kid". However, here Donna is also fighting back and protecting the sanctity of her home. She rejects the sexual freedom and liberties that can be represented by Steve Kemp and, in this, is defending the moral code and domestic equilibrium. This is also the first time Dee Wallace gets to lash out and get violently angry and physically proactive – something that will become the basis of the dynamic in her performance of the final sequences of the film during the siege sequence with Cujo himself.

Steve Kemp (Christopher Stone) threatens Donna Trenton (Dee Wallace) in her own home; desperate to keep their affair alive. His ruthlessness foreshadows the relentless violence eschewed by the rabid St. Bernard in the scenes to come.

When Steve pushes her back into the wall cabinet (possibly another piece that he has "stripped"), Donna knocks over some household items including a jug of milk that spills all over the kitchen floor. Steve barks out "Who do you think you're talking to?" which exposes his narcissism and egotism, two traits that are profoundly ugly and turn this Lothario into something grotesque and mean spirited. Steve's violent nature is exposed here, a rapist eager to "get some more" from the woman he has been sharing spare time with. Racing into the kitchen is young Tad who stops in his tracks, startled by the image of his shaky mother upon the floor surrounded by spilled milk. Concerned he asks if she is okay, and soon he is joined by his father Vic who gets the entire picture loud and clear. His fear is realized and then eventually confirmed when he asks "Yes or no?" to which Donna replies "Yes". Here, Don Carlos Dunaway's economic dialogue rings out in its sharpest manner; Barbara Turner's screenplay would have Donna shift into a lengthy soliloquy examining her situation and the reasons behind her extramarital affair, but with this "Yes or no?" from Vic, the entire passage would be discarded for action, no words. The rest of the film will eventually follow this trend and become increasingly less wordy and far more concentrated on mood, emotion, raw primal energies and an extreme emphasis on physicality and action.

Spilled milk: Donna Trenton's (Dee Wallace) affair is outed.

dinner. What drove women crazy, she thought suddenly, wasn't really sexism at all, maybe. It was this mad, masculine quest for efficiency.

'I don't know if I can explain. I'm afraid it will sound stupid and petty and trivial.'

'Try. Was it . . .' He cleared his throat, seemed to mentally spit on his hands (that cursed *efficiency* thing again) and then fairly wrenched the thing out. 'Haven't I been satisfying you? Was that it?'

'No,' she said.

'Then what?' he said helplessly. 'For Christ's sake, *what*? Okay . . . *you asked for it.*

'Fear,' she said, 'Mostly, I think it was fear.'

'Fear?'

'When Tad went to school, there was nothing to keep me from being afraid. Tad was like . . what do they call it? . . . white noise. The sound the TV makes when it is—'t tuned to a station that comes in.'

'He wasn't in real school,' Vic said quickly, and she knew he was getting ready to be angry, getting ready to accuse her of trying to lay it off on Tad, and once he was angry things would come out between them that shouldn't be spoken, at least not yet. There were things, being the woman she was, that she would have to rise to. The situation would escalate. Something that was now very fragile was being tossed from his hands to hers and back again. It could easily be dropped.

'That was part of it,' she said. 'He wasn't in real school. I still had him most of the time, and the time when he was gone . . . there was a contrast . . .' She looked at him. 'The quiet seemed very loud by comparison. That was when I started to get scared. Kindergarten next year, I'd think. Half a day every day instead of half a day three times a week. The year after that, all day five days a week. And there would still be all those hours to fill up. And I just got scared.'

'So you thought you'd fill up a little of that time by fucking someone?' he asked bitterly.

That stung her, but she continued on grimly, tracing it out

as best she could, not raising her voice. He had asked. She would tell him.

'I didn't want to be on the Library Committee and I didn't want to be on the Hospital Committee and run the bake sales or be in charge of getting the starter change or making sure that not everybody is making the same Hamburger Helper casserole for the Saturday-night supper. I didn't want to see those same depressing faces over and over again and listen to the same gossipy stories about who is doing what in this town. I didn't want to sharpen my claws on anyone else's reputation.'

The words were gushing out of her now. She couldn't have stopped them if she wanted to.

'I didn't want to sell Tupperware and I didn't want to sell Amway and I didn't want to give Stanley parties and I don't need to join Weight Watchers. You —'

She paused for the tiniest second, grasping it, feeling the weight of the idea.

'You don't know about emptiness, Vic. Don't think you do. You're a man, and men *grapple*. Men grapple, and women dust. You dust the empty rooms and you listen to the wind blowing outside sometimes. Only sometimes it seems like the wind's inside, you know? So you put on a record, Bob Seger or J. J. Cale or someone, and you can *still* hear the wind, and thoughts come to you, ideas, nothing good, but they come. You clean both toilets and you do the sink and one day you're down in one of the antique shops looking at little pottery knickknacks, and you think about how your mother had a shelf of knickknacks like that, and your *aunts* all had shelves of them, and your *grandmother* had them as well.'

He was looking at her closely, and his expression was so honestly perplexed that she felt a wave of her own despair.

'It's *feelings*, I'm talking about, not facts!'

'Yes, but why —'

'I'm *telling* you why! I'm telling you that I got so I was spending enough time in front of the mirror to see how my face was changing, how no one was ever going to mistake

me for a teenager again or ask to see my driver's license when I ordered a drink in a bar. I started to be afraid because I grew up after all. Tad's going to preschool and that means he's going to go to *school*, then *high school* —'

'Are you saying you took a lover because you felt *old*? He was looking at her, surprised, and she loved him for that, because she supposed that *was* a part of it; Steve Kemp had found her attractive and of course that was flattering, that was what had made the flirtation fun in the first place. But it was in no way the greatest part of it.

She took his hands and looked earnestly into his face, thinking – *knowing* – that she might never speak so earnestly (or honestly) to any man again. 'It's more. It's knowing you can't wait any longer to be a grownup, or wait any longer to make your peace with what you have. It's knowing that your choices are being narrowed almost daily. For a woman – no, for *me* – that's a brutal thing to have to face. Wife, that's fine. But you're good at work, even when you're home you're gone at work so much. Mother, that's fine, too. But there's a little less of it every year, because every year the world gets another little slice of him.

'Men . . . they know what they are. They have an image of what they are. They never live up to the ideal, and it breaks them, and maybe that's why so many men die unhappy and before their time, but they *know* what being a grownup is supposed to mean. They have some kind of handle on thirty, forty, fifty. They don't hear that wind, or if they do, they find a lance and tilt at it, thinking it must be a windmill or some fucking thing that needs knocking down.

'And what a woman does – what *I* did – was to run from becoming. I got scared of the way the house sounded when Tad was gone. Once, do you know – this is crazy – I was in his room, changing the sheets, and I got thinking about these girlfriends I had in high school. Wondering what happened to them, where they went. I was almost in a daze. And Tad's closet door swung open and . . . I screamed and ran out of the room. I don't know why . . . except I guess I do. I thought for just a second there that Joan Brady would come

out of Tad's closet, and her head would be gone and there would be blood all over her clothes and she would say, "I died in a car crash when I was nineteen coming back from Sammy's Pizza and I don't give a damn."'

'Christ, Donna,' Vic said.

'I got scared, that's all. I got scared when I'd start looking at knickknacks or thinking about taking a pottery course or yoga or something like that. And the only place to run from the future is into the past. So . . . so I started flirting with him.'

She looked down and then suddenly buried her face in her hands. Her words were muffled but still understandable.

'It was fun. It was like being in college again. It was like a dream. A stupid dream. It was like he was white noise. He blotted out that wind sound. The flirting part was fun. The sex . . . it was no good. I had orgasms, but it was no good. I can't explain why not, except that I still loved you through all of it, and understood that I was running away. . . .' She looked up at him again, crying now. 'He's running too. He's made a career of it. He's a poet . . . at least that's what he calls himself. I couldn't make head or tail of the things he showed me. He's a roadrunner, dreaming he's still in college and protesting the war in Vietnam. That's why it was him, I guess. And now I think you know everything I can tell you. An ugly little tale, but mine own.'

'I'd like to beat him up,' Vic said. 'If I could make his nose bleed, I guess that would make me feel better.'

She smiled wanly. 'He's gone. Tad and I went for a Dairy Queen after we finished supper and you still weren't home. There's a FOR RENT sign in the window of his shop. I told you he was a roadrunner.'

'There was no poetry in that note,' Vic said. He looked at her briefly, then down again. She touched his face and he winced back a little. That hurt more than anything else, hurt more than she would have believed. The guilt and fear came again, in a glassy, crushing wave. But she wasn't crying any more. She thought there would be no more tears for a very

From Stephen King's novel, Donna Trenton's detailed monologue about growing lonely and tapping into the reasons she had the affair with Steve Kemp.

DON CARLOS DUNAWAY: I do, generally, prefer less is more, and I like a lot of the dialogue as written and shot. Seeing it again thirty five years later, there were bits that felt underwritten to me, that I would have like to fill out. Then again, a few days later I found myself thinking that this was supposed to be a horror movie, and maybe it would not have been right to develop the characters too much more. I was sorry to have to confine Donna's entire "Morris the Explainer" speech about getting old and so forth, to a single scene. It would have been better to thread it through several pieces of their life. After cutting thirty pages, in the overall economy of the film, there was only room for it in one scene, and even then it was cut down.

LEWIS TEAGUE: Yeah. I'll give you an example: there is the scene where Dee Wallace's husband comes home, and she's cleaning up some spilt eggs from the floor... some broken eggs; and he comes running in with Tad, his son, and looks at her on the floor and looks at the tennis bum on the other side of the kitchen and right away nothings has to be said, he senses what is wrong; and he looks at Dee and says "Yes or no?" And she says "Yes". Now, when I read that, I thought, "Boy, that is way too lean. I'm going to cut it." But we decided to try it and we rehearsed it and the actors made it work! I just thought "I love that moment!"

DEE WALLACE: Jan brought so many brilliant ideas and expanded the film so much, and he and Lewis were such choreographers. I loved the metaphor of the spilled milk. Steve Kemp and Cujo are both monsters, and we all have monsters in our lives and sometimes we create them ourselves. And sometimes they come out of nowhere.

DANIEL HUGH KELLY: I definitely think that monologue that Donna has in the book about being lonely should have been in the film without question. Some of the endless changes from novel to script to screen were mind blowing to me. Every time I would hear that there was a change, I would get incredibly upset. I have so many examples of these changes that really pissed me off, but I just don't want to go into them. It was upsetting and things such as this scene where you have the chance to hear Donna's personal problems being explained, well that would have been excellent, but instead they are tossed out of the picture, and that really upset me. It would have been nice to have heard her give Vic the reason why she started up the affair. I remember marking that speech in the book and I analysed it and liked it. However, I have to say, overanalysing things in art does not make you friends. You don't want to upset anybody – and I may keep to myself, but I have these thoughts, but I don't want to upset anybody. I ain't that bright, but I ain't dumb, and I know what works. My background is repertory theatre for God's sake, I mean I also worked at Joseph Papp and everything, I know a good script. I have come to respect the work of a writer, and when you have great material being constantly changed and altered suddenly, well that is just a tragedy. And it wasn't just a matter of changing a line or two, it was changing entire scenes. And that angered me immensely, because changing these scenes would then ultimately change a character's intentions or motives – it was a very trying time for me.

LEWIS TEAGUE: Stephen King's screenplay adaptation wasn't that good. It departed a lot from the book and no one was that fond of it. What we decided to do in my very first meeting with Dan Blatt was to go back to the book and restructure everything from the book and use as much material from the book as possible, including dialogue. So that was a deal we made at the first meeting, and that's something that he pursued with Peter Medak also. They brought in Barbara Turner. She was a great writer and she went back and almost did a cut and paste job from the book and took out the best scenes. She did a really terrific job of structuring it according to the book and streamlining it a great deal. Now I'd say she did a really good job, however, when I came on board the first thing I did was look at the script. And I've done enough movies that I can accurately look at the script and time it. And I could see that it was way too long and we needed to make some cuts. She'd taken out most of the subplots but there was still material in there that had to come out. It didn't really help the story or was necessary and it was also too long. She'd worked on it quite a bit and did not want to make those cuts, so I brought in Don Carlos Dunaway and he did a good job of streamlining it and writing some new scenes. He also was great at writing some very economic dialogue which I liked a lot. A good example of that is the "spilled milk" scene.

DANNY PINTAURO : My memories of Dee Wallace spring to mind once we get into the car. I was the kind of kid where the only things that stood out to me as a six-year-old were really huge things or really exciting things. I have two memories from the five years I worked on *As the World Turns* . One of them is they set the set on fire. My mother on the show and I were locked in a closet by some awful man and they literally set a fire on the downstage! I was so fascinated by the idea that they could do that and not burn the whole building down that I actually have a specific memory of that. The other one was they sent us up to Spain for filming for a couple of weeks. So for me, the memories from *Cujo* don't really start until I have this really specific memory where I got into the Pinto that they had cut in half! Because I was so fascinated by the idea that there was no engine! I was like, "Oh my God! That's so crazy!" Then I have this very specific memory of the rocking horse that Christopher Stone had. I have a very specific memory of Dee with the eggs on the ground because that was a very emotional moment. I have a really specific memory of that! But for the most part, I have a lot of specific memories of the car. I also remember saying goodbye to my dad in the car, partly because I was so fascinated. But that wasn't a real house, the Trenton house, that was just a front. I thought that was really cool!

CHARLES BERNSTEIN: A lot of the music in this film comes out of just concentrating on Dee's face: her eyes, her brow, her expressions and everything in between. Because music comes from the depths of the film's characters and it always helps a composer if there are great performers or performances in the film. I think this film has some excellent performances. I mean that little boy, my God! But Dee really brought a depth and strength to that role and she had a vulnerability mixed with fierceness that is so hard to do well. I mean, what a great character she creates in this film and it just feeds the music. Don't forget a composer sits and looks over and over again at these scenes and gets the musical elements and this is all thanks to a performance like Dee's. What a role for a woman and what a brilliantly conceived performance she delivers.

PETER MEDAK: I love women so much, and I love actresses. Barbara is an excellent writer of women and *Cujo* was a perfect opportunity in this regard seeing that it is a movie about a woman. For me, as a director, I have always been attracted to projects featuring women as the protagonist. I mean something like *Negatives* (1968) with Glenda Jackson is one of my favorite films I've done. Barbara wanted to make *Cujo* a very realistic story about a very real woman with problems and flaws. She wrote a wonderful snapshot of a small town and the social structure of characters all intertwined within it. For example, the extramarital affair is so well written and Lewis did a great job showing off the different aspects of it. It is wonderful when the husband is driving and he sees Dee having an argument on the street with her lover and then he can't find them when we turn back. Then he goes home and she arrives and she can sense that something is wrong but doesn't say anything, and you can feel that wonderful tension. Those scenes are just wonderful. Lewis did such an excellent job with those scenes. He probably thinks I have hated him all of my life, or at least held onto some kind of resentment for losing the job to him, but I most definitely do not hate him, nor do I hold a grudge. It is an incredible thing – say thirty years later – to have another director tell him, or at least let him know, that what he did with Barbara's material was just fantastic. Barbara and I worked in one of her living rooms and every time I went there she had put out a huge spread of cherries and other fruits and there was this cupboard in that room and that is where the ghost was in our mind. We put a teddy bear in a child's chair in front of the cupboard and that was always there every time we worked on the script. That closet represented so much to me because I have such a connection to shut closet doors that make me think of my dead brother. I mean us artists always draw on things that have happened to us even if we don't realise it. Barbara and I created our own fantasy in her house while we worked.

DANNY PINTAURO: That look from Dee Wallace was amazing! Oh, my god! That look! It was just heart breaking! My parents may have been privy to her monologue being cut and to script changes. You have to remember what I was doing at the time, and that I couldn't really read. So my mom is reading the whole scene to me and then I memorise the lines before mine, so that I know when to speak and then I memorise my line. I'm not only memorising my line, but I'm also memorising theirs. And that's all I know. Like I don't really know what's come before. I certainly don't know what's going to come afterwards. I just know what is happening in the moment. I guess that is sort of what makes the performance, it's that I am not creating this arc of the character. I am just literally living in whatever pages of the script that my mother is having me memorise that day, and whatever emotional content is happening in that moment, and that's it. I don't think a kid needs to have more than that. I think kids do live moment to moment and that's it! That's the truth!

"THE THING ABOUT 'THE MONSTER WORDS'...":
Vic reassures Tad

Vic Trenton, dressed in a polo shirt (a symbol of the middle class), is bent over the bonnet of his busted up Pinto and angrily tries to tend to the engine. Clearly not a man who can "fix things", he is desperate to try and tie up loose ends (the dying Pinto being one of them) before heading out into the city to save the Sharp account. Distracting himself from the newfound knowledge of Donna's extramarital affair with Steve Kemp, the advertising agent notices his golden haired son, dressed in his pyjamas, watching him. Tad voices his protest against his dad leaving and also cries out that he doesn't want to go to day care, to which Vic suggests he "give it another chance". When Tad mentions "The Monster Words", Vic forgets everything and embraces his boy. Tad asks "Who's gonna say 'The Monster Words', mommy don't know 'em" and this brings Vic home – a centred, wholehearted home. Here, Vic is capable of being a vital and important figure in his son's life; in essence, he is the parent responsible for a mantra/prayer that keeps monsters out of his sensitive son's life. When he lifts him into his arms, Charles Bernstein brings in the delicate piano motif that responds to the frailty of human compassion and familial sacredness. Vic promises that he will write "The Monster Words" down, and that because they would be written down, Tad's mommy can also read them – in short, Vic is inviting Donna into his world of "protecting Tad".

Donna enters the scene, calling out for Tad to take his nap. She breaks the intimacy shared between father and son ("I love you sport") and is aware of it – her head low in solemn guilt, her body language tight and rigid, riddled with a deep rooted knowledge of doing something wrong. More brilliant astute loaded dialogue follows with Donna asking "Did you fix it?" to which Vic replies "No. I don't have the tools." Obviously they are referring to the rundown Pinto, however, in classic Film Noir style, the line that Vic throws out to her has an imprint of subtext. He mentions that he doesn't "have the tools" – a subtle reflection of his inability to satisfy his wife. Donna has reached out to the handyman Steve who seems to be capable of "fixing things" (stripping furniture, polishing, refining etc) which has rendered Vic "incapable" and "impotent".

The magic in this quiet and intimate scene is that it is shot outdoors and looks over the glorious view of the Californian coast and rich, green forestry of Mendocino which is all "acting" as Castle Rock, the Stephen King fictional town in Maine. The Trenton household, a brilliant façade constructed by incredibly talented designers and carpenters, overlooks the stunning view which is lit by the broad oranges and blues of a romantic sunset. Why this sequence is "magic" is because even in the sorrowful melodrama of the piece which is painted up by a man crushed by his wife's infidelity, a woman's sad regret and a child's frailty and delicate innocence, it is set amidst the idyllic beauty of the natural world (the ocean, the forest) and domestic bliss (the large house, the rich garden).

Following this comes a night time sequence that is bridged by Charles Bernstein's magnificent piano spot, where we are once again inside Tad's bedroom. Cinematographer Jan de Bont has his camera pan across the bedroom, starting from Tad in a deep sleep in his bed and closing in on "The Monster Words" which now hang on his closet door. Much like a string of garlic or wolfsbane protecting hapless maidens from bloodthirsty vampires. The final shot is of Tad, asleep, comfortable, unaware of

The crew set up a crane shot for the exterior of the Trenton house façade in Mendocino. (courtesy of Danny and Margaret Pintauro).

The crane hovering over the Trenton façade. (courtesy of Danny and Margaret Pintauro).

DOP Jan de Bont overlooking the crane shots.

The camera crew and riggers hang out on the Trenton house façade rooftop, overlooking the shot.

monsters. The next scene will finally introduce the film's "monster" in his last moment of benevolence; he will disappear into the foggy vortex of madness and frenzy.

DANIEL HUGH KELLY: I remember the scene where I'm working on the car out front of the house and I remember thinking "Gee, if they just had fired the director and they now have this new guy and he doesn't like me, then does that mean I'm gonna be fired?" Plus I was not happy that there were constant changes in the script, none of which that I thought were improving the story at all. The overall story was not what I read in the book.

I remember reading the script and thinking it was all different and I didn't think that it was better than the book. I may have been very young and not really understanding the fact that you can't always get everything from the novel into a script. That being said, I think that changes were made unnecessarily. You know, I'm in my sixties now and I've had a long career, and not only as an actor but as a writer, and I gotta say that writing is everything. If you don't have the writing then you have nothing. You can have big names, incredible actors and what not, but if you don't have a good story and an excellent writer to sell that story, then you got nothing. At that point in time, I just thought that the scripts were not at all reflective of the book, which I thought was great. I remember that Stephen King himself wrote a draft, and people said that it was completely unreadable. And I was like "Wow! He wrote the book!" But that is the difference I guess from a movie script to a novel.

DANNY PINTAURO: When I first went to audition for *Who's the Boss?*, it was very similar to what happened with my lines learning in *Cujo*. I memorized Judith Light's lines and Tony Danza's lines before mine. Then I would say my line. But I guess Tony and Judith had been there all day auditioning child after child, and they were kind of at the point where they were just paraphrasing and I literally stopped them in the middle of the audition and said, "I'm sorry, but could you read the lines as they are written on the page, because that is how I learned them and I can't do it otherwise." They were literally like "That's the kid!" The one who's got the balls to literally stop Tony Danza and Judith Light and be like "Can you read the script as it is written? Thank you."

PATRUSHKHA MIERZWA: I remember little Danny Pintauro designing a shot where he pushes a toy car across the floor; I was impressed that someone so young had an artistic grasp of shot design.

The camera crew relax in between takes.

CUJO IN THE FOG: Brett calls out for his beloved dog

Disney's *Old Yeller* would present the curse of rabies as heartbreaking tragedy. When the loyal, loving and trusty Labrador Retriever Mastiff mix contracts the fatal disease whilst defending and protecting his humans from a dangerous rabid wolf, young Travis Coates (Tommy Kirk) is forced to shoot him dead. In *Cujo*, a film that uses rabies as a form of "possession" in a sense, the unfortunate St. Bernard loses all comprehension of sanity, peace, understanding, compassion, order and companionship, as he disappears into the foggy recesses of the dreaded virus.

Cutting from an image of a sleeping Tad Trenton, comforted by the now penned-on-paper "Monster Words", this sequence opens with a ghostly shot of the Camber farm suffocated by thick, ominous fog. Out onto the porch comes Brett Camber, a young boy taking on the darkness of early morning to find his dog who has recently "not been himself". Stumbling outside and trekking through the distorted wilderness, Brett bravely ventures out to find Cujo. He hears him whimpering in the distance, painfully crying out for help. Into the foggy terrain, Brett moves through over hanging oak branches, spots a busted stump in the middle of the moist plains, feels the heat brewing, is startled by unnerving sounds that seem to be coming from his dog and finally comes face to face with his once healthy, loving Cujo.

217

The brilliant manner in which Brett comes face to face with the frothing and snarling dog is delivered with acute swiftness – Brett is frightened by his surroundings, backs off from the broken tree stump and steps towards the path of the diseased and ravaged dog. Shocked by Cujo's appearance, Brett trembles with fear asking "Cujo? What's the matter?"

Here the solid loving union shared between a young boy and his dog is made perverse, disorienting, distorted, troubled, sinister and malevolent. Cujo is covered in fresh blood, his muzzle completely coated in froth and bile, his eyes dripping with ooze and his breathing heavy and unsteady. He spurts out some growls, spits out some foam, lower his head in uncertainty and looks into Brett's eyes with confusion, fear and brimming malice. While Brett pleads with his dog ("Take it easy boy. I'm not going to hurt you…"), the tragedy of this sequence is made clear – here is a good dog who is sadly falling into a vortex of incurable horror. The transition from terror to tragedy is perfectly demonstrated in the dog's performance as he starts off viscous and threatening and then ends the scene showing his last traits of sensitivity, compassion and honor. He stares at Brett with a knowing confliction and here we witness a dog fading off into foggy turf lost in torment. Brett is the last person he shall see before rabies finally turns him into a deadly, unstoppable violent force.

This vivid image of a young boy exploring the eeriness of fog rings similar to an earlier Stephen King filmic adaptation in *Salem's Lot*, where the young Glick brothers walk home, encountering the darkness that will soon envelop the entire town. In the novel of "Cujo", Brett Camber suffers from sleepwalking and it is made a point of in Stephen King's book as an unconscious response to his insecurities being the son of Joe – who is a distant and stoic figure. This scene in the film is the sole moment that young Brett gets solo onscreen time and thoughts will trek back to the issue of sleepwalking for viewers who know the novel very well.

Performed with measured intelligence and nuance, Billy Jacoby gives his Brett a necessary sensitivity and a tremendous warmth – he ensures us that this is a young rural dwelling boy who ultimately loves his dog.

Billy Jacoby (also known as Billy Jayne) comes from a family of actors. His older brother Scott Jacoby would feature in some of the most popular cult movies of the seventies such as the made-for-TV classic *Bad Ronald* (1974) as well as the haunting Jodie Foster vehicle *The Little Girl Who Lives Down the Lane* (1976). Billy would also feature in a horror cult favorite *Bloody Birthday* (1981) which allowed him to be a nasty *le enfants terribles* and then would follow up his role in *Cujo* appearing in the progressive gender bending teen comedy *Just One of the Guys* (1985).

Composer Charles Bernstein would use sustained notes to exaggerate the tension and evoke unsettling implications, while Jan de Bont's camera would manipulate its audience effectively bouncing from Brett's P.O.V. to angling in on Cujo and then to narrative "stalking" which by now is a visual style oft used in this stylish and sophisticated motion picture. A fog machine would be used for this sequence – one that would previously be used during wartime to hide coming ships from the enemy – and the concept of fog in horror movies is an age old aesthetic that has been employed since the earliest incarnations of both supernatural and naturalistic horror. Evoking feelings of the unknown and setting mood, fog in *Cujo* is used as a representation of transition, loss, confusion and blurry disconnection.

MARCIA ROSS: Billy Jacoby I cast in Los Angeles, but I was reading boys for that role in New York too. I remember he came from a family of actors and he was a prominent child actor. I knew his brother Scott too.

IAN KINCAID: We encountered huge fog one day and then it rolled in off the ocean and we filmed. It was a continuous scene so we had to film the following day, but there was no fog. So the SFX team suggested to bring in a naval fogger, and the producers were like "What's a naval fogger?" In World War II when allied forces were moving around the Pacific, they would take a small boat and use a diesel making fog machine that would race around in front of the fleet or in front of the enemy to hide and conceal ships. The SFX team scrambled and got themselves a naval fogging machine and attached it to the back of a truck and drive it up and down the street to make an enormous fog bank. It stunk and was awful. It is diesel oil and exhaust and it took about half an hour for the fire department to race towards us, sirens going and thankfully they were just a local fire brigade so they laughed about it. That fog was awful, it was horrible to be in there. I distinctly remember that scene with Billy Jacoby and the dog in the fog, and that was just awful to be in.

MARCIA ROSS: I remember Sarah Jessica Parker coming into my office during the auditions for *Cujo*. She wasn't reading for me of course, but she had a sibling, a brother with her, who did. I remember going out to talk to her in the lobby, and that's when I first met her and she was barely sixteen. She was accompanying a sibling to the audition, I must have seen her in *Square Pegs* (1982-1983) or something, so she must have been working in film and TV already, so I went out and talked to her. I would always go out and talk to the kids waiting to see me in the lobby. Sarah Jessica Parker's younger brother was actually after the role that Billy Jacoby got, the role of Brett Camber.

GARY MORGAN: Oh, the fog was a disaster! The fog was a huge fuck around! They used this big fogger at the back of a pick-up truck. What they used for battle ships when they needed to help ships disappear. It was a diesel fogger that was used to fog up the forest and everybody was getting sick because it was just diesel smoke! All the crew had masks on and the actors were getting sick from the smoke! Their eyes were runny and it was like being in a garage with a diesel bus or something. Of course it was outside but they had to fog a lot of area in the forest. These were just not good working conditions.

CHARLES BERNSTEIN: In my mind the St. Bernard in this picture was not necessarily generating a theme that would come from any aspect of geography. In other words, I didn't ever have the idea of using Swedish instrumentation or Scandinavian tones for the piece. However, I do remember something I wrote many years before this film that did have a St. Bernard in it for a theatre piece. John Rubenstein, who won a Tony Award on Broadway for his role in *Children of a Lesser God* (1986) got his Tony and he was thanking people who had gotten him to where he was, and he mentioned me because I had written this song that he had used for the audition up until that point. Anyway, he mentioned the song that I had written for him in a musical back in college; and in the musical his name was "Bernard" and I wrote a song called "Poor Bernard." The lyric went:

> *I know that people call me 'Poor Bernard'*
> *Snickering they whisper 'Poor Bernard'*
> *They think I'm dull and clumsy and they think my*
> *head is hard*
> *But no one knows the true Bernard*

And it ends in him saying:

> *This brain is packed with learning, smart Bernard*
> *My stocks and bonds are earning, rich Bernard*
> *And when my fellow man is down, I'm there and*
> *on my guard*
> *Oh, someday men will call me St. Bernard!*

Then the chorus starts singing "St. Bernard" over and over again and getting intoxicated with the notion of being a saint, not realising that the audience is snickering because they are picturing this lumbering dog! The musical was a fantasy I had written about a carnival and a young boy named "Bernard" who is the son of the trinket salesmen at the carnival. It's just a little parable about a girl who comes to the carnival and is disillusioned.

TERESA ANN MILLER: It was different than from a lot of the work my dad had done, because physically the animals had to be able to retain memory of behaviours and tricks – the St. Bernards are not up there on top of the list, you know what I mean? They are a little more difficult to teach and master a specific behaviour, you know. So that in itself was a challenge for him to work with that type of a breed. But, it is just a matter of finding out what works for each animal; and that is not each breed alone, that is each individual animal that we work with. Each one is going to learn on a different level and sometimes it is going to take a little longer for him to learn something, and sometimes they are going to pick it up quite quickly. But what you find is, the more experience the animal has of course, he learns how to learn. And so it is easier to teach him new things. And once he has had the exposure of learning and early training. But that is the most definite thing with that breed is: physically they are limited because they are so cumbersome, and also mentally they are not necessarily bred to work so closely to man; they are working dogs that are bred to work out in the field and more of a companion dog.

"I'LL TAKE CARE OF IT…": Tension out front the Trenton house

With an establishing shot of the Trenton household in the hours of early morning, the seeping fog that was so present in the previous scene sits at the top right hand corner of the frame. It is as if the lingering ghostly horror of what we have already seen (with the rabid Cujo now lost in the throes of his sickness) is now infiltrating the world of the Trentons, or about to affect them. Lewis Teague's masterful interlocking and acute manner of juxtaposition is sharp and inventive: the director successfully manages to interweave two stories that will eventually catch up to one another.

The horror of circumstance sits as the film's backbone, and the dual-narrative (Donna and her family and Cujo's descent into the torturous world of rabies) starts to meet at the centre as the final act of the film takes shape.

Donna, in her dressing gown, nervously watches Vic move his luggage into his red Jaguar. He is off to "take care of business" and rescue what can be saved of the Sharp cereal account. Tad voices his protest ("I don't want you to go for ten days, I want you to go for one day") while Donna pleads with Vic to understand that her affair with Steve meant nothing and was well and truly over. Vic remains cold and detached, not even looking at his wife, who is teary eyed and desperate. She crouches over the door of the

A French lobby card featuring Vic Trenton (Daniel Hugh Kelly) bidding a farewell to his son Tad (Danny Pintauro), en route to "save his career".

Jaguar and begs forgiveness, but Vic isn't biting. Plot exposition has Vic let Donna know that he "forgot to take the Pinto to Joe Camber's" which indicates his muddled brain at the moment, dealing with his career and more importantly his wife's infidelity.

Donna responds with "I'll take care of it" – and come the third act of the film, she most certainly does. Donna transforms from sombre and lonely woman to complicated adulteress caught out to a force of nature, destined to either die or survive, but with saving her child as her number one priority. Dee Wallace would revel in these kinds of dynamic and interesting roles offered by the horror genre.

This scene would have additional imagery shot as one scene on a lobby card depicts Donna racing across the grassy hillside, chasing after Tad.

An American lobby card depicting a scene that never made the final cut.

Jan de Bont leads the crane shot over the façade of the Trenton household.

DEE WALLACE: I really love to play arcs – really strong emotional arcs. I love to start out in one place and go through this whole journey and end up somewhere else with a lot of hills and valleys in between. To have a career where I'd just be doing light comedies my whole life would bore the hell out of me! So I really love these films, these horror movies because I love to really push myself dramatically and also because I really love to do highly dramatic material. And *The Howling* really presented an opportunity to do all that. I really loved Joe and Dan Blatt. Dan was so available and accessible to everyone that worked with him and for him and this was all very important to me, having this family feel, coming from Kansas to feel safe and taken care of. And Dan did and so did Blake Edwards on *10* (1979). In the eighties when I was coming up all the work for women was great, it was all highly dramatic and emotionally stirring and excellent to do because you had so much to do as an actress. All the major horror films right through to the movies of the week were all these dramatic women-in-peril movies, so I was in heaven! It was all female driven and I mean every opportunity presented to me was that kind of role, whether it was a horror film or not, I mean the role could have been that of a battered wife rising above her abusive husband or the mother of a child with AIDS and so forth. There was always some major arc that needed to be solved with a lot of colors in between and that's the most exciting work for me.

LEWIS TEAGUE: That was on the coast outside Mendocino. The house was just a façade, it was not a real house. It was a façade that was built on a hillside, so it would have that spectacular background view.

DEE WALLACE: Since Daniel came off day time television, he wasn't used to rehearsing a whole lot, and that worked really well for me. My whole acting technique involves very little rehearsal. It is to learn the scene, be in character, be in the moment and shoot it. On camera we worked

226

really well together, off camera we didn't have too much to do with each other. He was not readily available to socialize. This is also my perspective of back then, and as we know our perspectives now may not always be so truthful when you're talking about the past, but I do remember him not being completely available if you know what I mean. I remember one time outside the front of the house, there was some kind of disagreement between us. Dan Blatt was once again just brilliant and he would talk to him and talk to me and was always a gentle man and always was able to bring people together. I think the argument was all about us seeing the scene in different ways. In this very difficult movie, we both came together and created a relationship that worked on screen. When you're playing these kinds of roles often times the character falls over into the personal relationship and that is very hard to keep that finite line down the middle.

CHRISTOPHER MEDAK: For the most part we just showed up and executed what was on paper. It wasn't really a case of us giving our souls to the project to making something even better. Everything changed when my dad was let go. It was such a blow to the system to see my dad get fired by Dan Blatt and then everyone else just putting themselves into his shoes and clocking on going to work without what my dad had in mind, even though Lewis used his storyboards as a guide. I mean on one hand it was my very own old man getting fired, on the other hand you stay behind and do the job.

GARY MORGAN: Lewis is really a chilled guy! I really love Lewis. He is actually the second director. Had a first director that had been fired after about a week! That was Peter Medak. I worked with him for a couple weeks. He actually hired me. He was a really nice guy! I don't know what exactly happened, I feel like the producers weren't getting what they needed, but I don't know why they fired him. He was a sweet guy. I liked him. It happens on movies for some reason, I don't know if it is a personality thing or if they don't get a shot that they want, and people get fired. It's not the first picture I have been on where a director has been fired.

PETER MEDAK: I was very concerned as to how we were going to do the dog and how we were going to get the dog to do what he was supposed to do. It was going to be tricky for us to get this dog to fight Dee and kill the cop and kill the drunken friend and of course the guy who owns the garage. So I remembered we had several ways we were going to do it. We put a young stunt guy who was very small into a dog suit and I was working with him for a tremendous amount of time. Gary Morgan was a very small guy. He was perfect for the dog suit. I am certain he did most of the action in the film. We also had various dog heads on wheel-burrows and dollies, what I did intend for it to be was a very realistic looking film. I wanted the dog to look incredibly real.

Stunt man Gary Morgan was fitted for a St. Bernard costume and did stunts in place of the dogs for the animals' safety.

Boom operator Patrushkha Mierzwa holds up her mic on location.

The crew take a coffee break shooting outside of the Trenton house façade.

Cinematographer Jan de Bont sets up a crane shot.

DANIEL HUGH KELLY: I remember being let down that they weren't going to shoot the film up in Maine, and I didn't know that Stephen King's stuff takes place up in Maine, but I thought, there is no way they're going to shoot up there.

MARK ULANO: We used Schoeps, Sennheisers and Trams.

PATRUSHKHA MIERZWA: At that time we used Sennheisers: a 415 and an 815, and some plants in the car. There were a few times we had Trams (and radio mics) on the actors. I do remember a scene with Daniel Hugh Kelly in an undershirt at the car. The shots were designed so that I couldn't get a boom in close enough. That's where I worked out my superior rigging for thin shirts – most people run a wire straight up the front under actors' shirts, but that cable shows with some movements. I ran Daniel's from the side seam up, around the neck in the small banding. It was impossible to see, no matter the actor's movement.

MARK ULANO: The film used practical locations except for the house façade in Mendocino.

PATRUSHKHA MIERZWA: We were there to see the change of seasons. It is always a lovely area, more so at that time of year. The setting helped balance the work environment.

MARK ULANO: The setting was beautiful.

"I'M WORRIED ABOUT CUJO": Charity packs up for Connecticut

From another wonderfully placed low angle back on the Camber porch (suggestive of Cujo's P.O.V.), we see Brett head out of his farmhouse carrying two weighty suitcases. He drops them to the dusty plains and drifts across the dirt track deep in thought. His hands wedged in his jeans pockets and his mannerisms concerned and worrisome; Brett is clearly distressed about the state of his dog from earlier that morning. Cujo is on his mind – Cujo's whereabouts, his health and strange behaviour. However, there is not much time to think about the unwell St. Bernard as soon enough his father Joe pulls up in his pick-up truck. Joe doesn't let his son rest for one second and whips his boy's back with his grubby hat and tells him to "get the rest of the bags". The dutiful Brett does as he is told.

During this sequence, Charity Camber is about to leave Joe for good. Gathering her strength to leave an abusive man, she is first seen collecting a treasured photo album that seems to feature a lot of photos of Brett as a baby, infant and small child. Inside the Camber living room, Charity (wearing a pale blue dress which is creased down the back but clean and presentable and all ready for a fresh start) quietly and steadily packs personal belongings. From her demeanour and actions it is clear that Charity is not simply going to "visit" her sister in Connecticut, but she is determined to leave her life in Castle Rock, Maine for good and leave the cold, unfeeling and hot tempered Joe.

Actress Kaiulani Lee owns this scene with a great sense of earthy ease – she moves through her motions with a careful thorough understanding of a brow-beaten woman longing for something more. Even in her presentation – the light blue dress, her prettiest cardigan draped around her arm, her sensible but feminine shoes clopping upon the floorboards – she is ready to take on a new existence free from the burden of the farm and the heavy hand of the mechanic she once loved. In Stephen King's novel, the subplot of Charity and Brett living in Connecticut would feature prominently and act as a go between. It would pop up after the reader would be subjected to the horrors facing Donna Trenton and Tad who are stuck in the Pinto while Cujo keeps them trapped. It would also bounce from the stress levels Vic Trenton experiences as he deals with worrying about the whereabouts of his wife and child as well as the ailing Sharp account. During these textual visits to Charity and her plight, we understand that she and her sister Holly have an estranged relationship, that Holly's husband is a snob, that Brett is struggling to be a "man" and that his concerns for Cujo linger and so forth. Stephen King's screenplay would offer a glimpse into life with Charity and Brett but not delve into it too much in fear of detracting from the core purpose of the third act which would be the showdown between Donna and the rabid dog. What King does present however, in his novel, is the notion that mothers and sons have complicated and fragile relationships. The newly single Charity needs to be strong for her boy to grow, while the dehydrated and desperate Donna needs to remain strong for her son Tad to survive.

In this quiet intimate scene shared between the gifted Kaiulani Lee and Billy Jacoby, mother and son make a deal (to call Joe later that evening and suss out the health of Cujo) while Charity plans her secret fleeing from the oppressive farmhouse.

Brett calls out to his mother and tells her that he's worried about Cujo. He explains that he saw him covered in blood and with foam coming out

Charity Camber (Kaiulani Lee) sets out for a new life with her son Brett (Billy Jacoby).

Ed Lauter, Billy Jacoby and producer Dan Blatt on location.

of his mouth. Charity looks worried but reacts semi-angrily when Brett makes the suggestion to tell his father. Protecting Brett from having to spend more time with his cantankerous father, Charity insists that "No, you do no such thing!" and that if Brett was to tell Joe about Cujo's condition it would delay her escape. Charity also tells Brett that Joe loves Cujo which is the first time we ever hear any character say anything positive about this dishevelled, easily agitated mechanic. There is of course discussion of Joe being a "good mechanic" who "won't rob you blind", however this is the first sentiment leaning towards a tiny glimpse of pathos. Joe's "love" for Cujo would be his one redeeming feature – however, there is not one scene that really showcases his affection for the dog. Charity leaves packing her suitcase to actively stop Brett making his way to Joe ("he'll come mooching around your dad and your dad will take care of him") and then closes the sentiment with a promise. Secretive decisions are being made here in *Cujo* – Charity is leaving for good and taking her son with her, Joe is set to enjoy a hedonistic trip away from responsibility with his friend Gary Pervier and Cujo suffers in silence as he succumbs to rabies.

The final image of this sequence depicts a sickly rabid Cujo strolling across the sunkissed plains of Castle Rock, plodding along as the summer's sun burns bright and hard.

DANIEL HUGH KELLY: Kaiulani Lee was so good. I thought she was going to be huge. She was so talented and she had that kind of talent that you are born with and the kind of talent that the camera really likes. There was something about her – she was very quiet, and very sweet, but when she does something on camera you just cannot take your eyes off her. I mean she could do something simple with her arm and you get lost looking at her. She was not this outrageous beauty, but that made her even more attractive. I haven't seen her for a long time. The last time I saw her was at looping for *Cujo*. Now, I don't usually do this, but for some reason I had gone out with some friends of mine from Jersey who had come down to visit me. We had gone out and gotten very drunk, and I had a looping session the next day, and I was very hungover. I was laying down on the couch while Kaiulani was doing her looping, and after one take I groan "Oh man…" Now I didn't mean this at all, it was not at all a comment on her looping! It was just that I was so hungover that I felt awful, and she looked over at me and I thought she thought that I was commenting on her take. Which I was not. I was just hungover like bat shit. Allison Janney reminds me very much of Kaiulani, these very natural actresses who have these God given talents.

GARY MORGAN: I was around for everything. I was around for every take and everything, except when the dog wasn't around. Young Billy Jacoby was great and it is interesting because his big brother Scott Jacoby was a Broadway actor. He was in a musical called *Golden Rainbow* around 1971 and my sister was in a musical across the street called *Curley McDimple*. Scott's mom would drop him off on matinee days and Scott would hang out with my little sister and my mum and they would go to the movies. She would babysit Scott Jacoby! So Scott came to the set of *Cujo* with Billy and act as his guardian; Scott was there all the time taking care of Billy. Billy right now lives in Laurel Canyon. I bump into Billy at the market from time to time.

The front porch of the Camber farm was a real location out in Santa Rosa, CA. (courtesy of Danny and Margaret Pintauro).

237

Producer Dan Blatt surveys the front of the Camber farmhouse.
(courtesy of Danny and Margaret Pintauro).

"I DON'T GIVE A SHIT!": Gary is killed by Cujo

Gary Pervier is a repugnant character, and this is an intentional choice by the writers and designers for the incarnation of this Stephen King creation. As aforementioned, in King's original source novel, Gary is presented with at least a tiny iota of pathos and sentimentality, however in the film adaptation Gary is devoid of any humanity, compassion, warmth or sincerity. He is ultimately loathsome and unsympathetic, so when he is killed by Cujo it is accepted without apathy. Gary doesn't even have a wife who can vouch for him or give him credit in any sense. Even Charity Camber tells her son Brett that her stoic and abusive husband still "loves Cujo" – giving Joe a tiny sense of considerate affection – however, in Gary's case, he is a character that lives in a vacuum of dense disdain for his fellow man and therefore is a much welcomed victim. Much like the callous and vindictive Chris Hargensen from King's first novel "Carrie" and subsequent film adaptation from Brian De Palma, Gary is a mean spirited bully who is killed by the book/film's featured monster (be it the telekinetic prom queen or the rabid St. Bernard).

Opening outside Gary's shambolic abode which is even more of a mess from the outside than what we have seen earlier in his kitchen, the scene plays out with shrewd classic horror movie stalk 'n slash sensibility.

239

Gary carries a bag of trash out to a massive pile of trash that sits out front of his shack. He empties the contents and hears something approach; a distant growling. It is Cujo. This is the first clear image we have of the rabid dog in all his grotesque glory. Cujo is covered in grime, wet with blood, frothing at the mouth and snarling angrily. His body language is in attack mode as he trots towards the startled Gary. Gary mutters: "Cujo, what are you growling at…?" indicating that he has never heard the dog ever even growl in his life, and yet here the St. Bernard has his eyes fixed on Gary himself. Letting out some frothy barks, Cujo leaps into action and chases after Gary, set on ripping him to shreds. Rabies has now taken over the dog's sensibilities and he is completely dedicated to destruction from here on in – Cujo is now in full blown movie monster form and there is not one moment from this point where Cujo shows any sign of his old good self. This dog is now a killer, and to kill is his sole purpose.

Gary Pervier (Mills Watson) is slaughtered by Cujo.

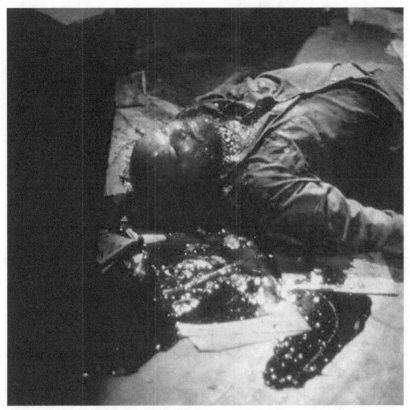

Gary Pervier's (Mills Watson) dead body.

Boasting some fantastic animal action headed by phenomenally talented animal trainer Karl Lewis Miller, this scene is the first of incredibly violent and blood-drenched sequences that will eventually make up the rest of the movie. Miller manages to get the dog in question performing this scene to do some stunning animal acting; for example, the moment where Gary manages to push Cujo off him, and stares directly into his eyes screaming "I don't give a shit!", the dog stares back with eyes filled with rage and bestial brooding intelligence. There is so much anger and hatred in that glare that it is hard to shake off as simply circumstantial, this is an animal who understands his trainer's intentions and is performing magnificently. All the dogs used in production who make up Cujo do a superb job at their allocated position – some would be masterful at running and lunging, some better at the attack sequences and so forth, and here in this frenzied scene, the dog doing all the damage is an excellent attack dog, lunging at actor Mills Watson and his stunt double with tremendous force and zeal.

Mills Watson's performance matches this intensity with dedicated fury, so that when we hear him scream out "I don't give a shit!" we completely understand that this man is now accepting his lot in life: a world consumed by shit, cluttered with shit, destined to remain shit and ravaged by shit. Through this statement comes the notion that this is also a man who really doesn't care if he lives or dies, and although he attempts to load his rifle to kill Cujo, he is completely defenceless and helpless when it comes to fending himself from the crazed dog.

Cujo tears through Gary's flyscreen door and pins him down, ripping into his chest with his mighty claws, shoving his muzzle into his flesh and chomping at bloodied flesh and thrashing the pathetic man across the cluttered hallway. Cujo revels in the kill, barking, growling, snarling and biting into Gary's throat and chest.

Shot with stark realism that captures the severity of the sequence, Gary's death is edited with such outstanding precision by Neil Travis that it accents the unsettling and viciously violent nature of the event: a close up of Gary's face as his throat is torn out, an image of the dog's back and hind legs swinging around as Cujo throws Gary across the room like a ragdoll, a startling image of Gary's arm quivering in pain and in the throes of being killed and so forth. This is a masterfully handled sequence made all the more intense and terrifying by the sound design which marries dog growling and barking with human screams and guttural convulsing. On top of all this are the superlative musical choices by Charles Bernstein who introduces brand new accompaniments to the very fabric of *Cujo*'s score including low end piano work, synthesizer elements, strings that stab, jarring discordant notes and carefully plotted musical stings that are bloodcurdling.

Gary's death sequence is drawn out and offers gorehounds and splatter fans a fantastic moment of absolute primal visceral pleasure, which was something eighties horror movie audiences cherished and longed for. During this period, films would be encouraged to have hard R ratings and amp up the on-screen violence, and for the most part this heightening of visceral nastiness helped ensure the film's box office success. This is definitely the case in *Cujo*, where the violence is cemented in grounded realism, as opposed to the grandiose operatics of the slasher boom which would introduce audiences to visually stunning and vividly stylized ways to off horny teenagers. What rings similar to Gary's death in *Cujo* and the multiple deaths of teens in many slasher films (but not all) is the fact that this kind of on-screen death and fixed violence is all the more exciting and exhilarating to watch because the character of Gary Pervier (as well as the countless non-descript teens in many (but not all) slasher films) is someone set up to be fodder for the bloodthirsty killer (in *Cujo's* case, a two hundred pound hydrophobic dog).

Much like director Lewis Teague's previous film *Alligator*, *Cujo* examines class distinction through the victims it presents. In *Alligator*, screenwriter John Sayles has his mutant reptile start off causing havoc in the Chicago ghettos, then moving to working class families, then to the middle classes and then finally crashing the wedding of some of the city's wealthiest social elite. Teague would tap into this notion of climbing the social ladder of destruction in *Cujo*. Essentially, the dog kills three men: the first victim is Gary Pervier, as discussed, the second will be Joe Camber (his owner) and the third will be Sheriff George Bannerman, played by character actor Sandy Ward. Cujo's victims come to represent three variants of class, social standing and vocational uphold. Gary is a drunk – his work is not mentioned, left unclear and unstated – and therefore belongs to the lowest grounding of blue collar Maine. Joe Camber is a mechanic – an honest trade and a profession catering to the service of other people. Bannerman, being a police official, comes to represent the highest order of working class men in rural Maine; that of a sheriff who has been summoned to address a situation and is sacrificed for it. Sheriff Bannerman would be the fundamental link in the Stephen King universe that connects his books "Cujo" to "The Dead Zone" (something that will be discussed in a later chapter), but he would be the last of Cujo's victims in the film adaptation.

A split diameter vision of Cujo. (photo courtesy of Gale A. Adler).

JOHN SAYLES (screenwriter, *Alligator*, *The Howling*): Kurt Vonnegut once said that science fiction was the most philosophical genre and monster movies may be the most allegorical. This goes back to the cautionary fables they most closely resemble. I was a big fan of the Japanese and American nuclear mutant movies like *Them!* (1954), *Mothra* (1961), *Attack of the Mushroom People* (1963) (aka *Mantango*) and felt like *Alligator* was a perfect opportunity to explore environmental poisoning and media culture. Since the movie is set in the U.S. and gators don't move very fast, Ramón couldn't get all the way to Tokyo to wreak havoc, so I decided his journey would be through the class structure – he eats his way up from the ghetto to the centre of power. As with *The Howling*, I thought about what would really happen if one of these things hit the news – they are so starved for sensation that it would create a feeding frenzy. Unfortunately, I didn't also think of the obvious sequel, *Gatornado*. The basic idea for *Alligator* that I kept is that social problems are easy to ignore until they come to your neighbourhood. FDR was trying to coax the U.S. populace into fighting Hitler and not doing too well until Pearl Harbor then everybody wanted to sign up. Also, animal experimentation is something most people don't want to think about. It has been vital to many important discoveries, saved lives etc, but it isn't pretty. We had a mayor in Hoboken a couple years back indicted in a scheme that included kickbacks, rabbis and human organ peddling – I imagine all the participants felt like it was a "nobody gets hurt" crime. Chemical and medical waste dumping is often done by corporations and their subcontractors with an attitude that the problem won't show up for a long time and isn't worth the expense to do safely. Stephen King is a master at this kind of scenario, where human evil and weakness is manifest in some sort of revengeful creature or force. We all think we'll never have to go down in the sewer, and are really pissed when what goes on there comes into our backyard. The scientists in the movie have that blinkered vision so typical of intense experimentation – and what white-coated lab rat has not longed to shout "Bring me more puppies!"

245

MARCIA ROSS: Mills Watson who played the drunk was a lovely actor, and he was from Los Angeles.

TERESA ANN MILLER: Some dogs you can get to snarl depending on the response from their lip – some dogs are more sensitive to moving their lip, being able to curl it to snarl and the one's that can't; that just don't have that reaction to their lip would have wear a "snarling device". That was kind of a retainer that we would put up underneath his lips – above his canines – and it would just raise his lip up to show his teeth. In certain circumstances where the dog really didn't have a good natural snarl on him, or, if they wanted to see the dog running and looking vicious – which the dog doesn't do: generally run with his lips raised – it's usually a threat when he is standing still – so that is another case when they would use the 'snarling device' to enhance that vicious look in action, because it doesn't happen naturally.

Eggwhites were used for the froth and usually lapped right up by the hungry canine stars of the film.

ALEXANDER WITT: Jan de Bont was not an easy man to work with in the beginning. Especially because I was already operating cameras, I had to go back and pull focus. *Cujo* was one of the toughest jobs I've done and most of it involved me pulling back focus, and at the start I was told that Jan could do this himself and that he didn't need an operator. But I needed a job here in America, so I fought to remain camera operator and do the pull focus work for the piece. Jan used to operate with a mini-jeep so the camera was on the mini-jeep that he could move up and down. And shooting with the dog he always wanted to zoom in and out from the dog and that was very difficult because when you're shooting with dogs, they never stay still or in the same position, so pull focus is essential. A lot of the filming involved zooming in and out and upward and down and forward and back, so it was a tough job for me as the camera assistant.

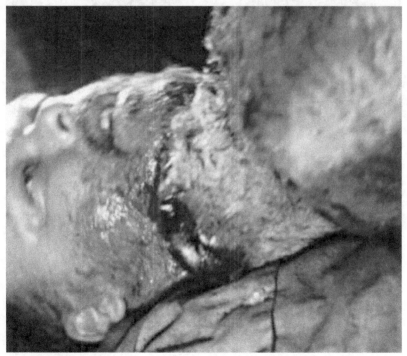

Gary Pervier (Mills Watson) is killed by Cujo. Here, the puppet head is used.

First assistant camera operator Alexander Witt snaps the clapboard into "action".

PATRUSHKHA MIERZWA: It was extremely difficult working with a non-communicative DP who constantly changed the frame. Well, that's not completely true – Jan was verbal about expressing his displeasure. The Dee-and-Danny-stuck-in-the-car sequence was probably heaven for me; the mics were planted in the car and all I had to do for a few days was mic the slate and get ambience. By then it was Moe working and I was so happy to be farther away. It was just Mark and me on the set. About week 7 we thought we were going to be fired – we heard the newly hired replacement editor had said the sound was horrible. It didn't come to us from the editor (Mark always introduces himself and invites direct communication ASAP if there are any concerns or questions). It came from production and we worried all day. After work, Mark and I met Lewis at the editor's room. There was a Movieola and Mark was invited to listen on the pair of cheap $8.00 Radio Shack headphones plugged in – it sounded like crap. In his world-class style, Mark had brought his headphones from set. He plugged in the $250 pair of Beyer-DT48s and handed them to the editor. The editor exclaimed that the sound was great! He was surprised. After that week, we came to be at peace about the possibility of getting fired – we knew it had nothing to do with the quality of the work. But my nature is still to worry. Working with Jan de Bont was a crash course in learning to split focus and multi-tasking; I became an ace boom operator quickly. And I learned to look at things from a 180 degree viewpoint, so I'll credit him for that. Danny, at his early age, designed a really nice shot with his fire truck that Jan ran with. I remember in the barn there was a meeting to discuss Cubby's death and Jan threw a hissy fit-and a baling hook (oblivious to others around him) which just missed hitting me.

Alexander Witt and Jan de Bont on set.

249

GARY MORGAN: I felt that Jan de Bont was very calm and very creative. It wasn't until they started letting him direct that he was a maniac! You know, when he did *Twister* (1996), I knew guys who were on it and he was a monster! He has this reputation for yelling and screaming and getting what he wants and stomping around! But on *Cujo* he wasn't like that at all. He was not the director, so maybe, when he got the power to be one is when he went into who he really is. But on *Cujo*, he was a really nice, calm professional and none of the things that he has a reputation for being.

CHARLES BERNSTEIN: The menacing electronic sound that marks Cujo's appearance was an ARP 2600 synthesizer, which was a monophonic early synthesizer that came after the MOOG synthesizer, and I fashioned a pulse-like sound by manipulating what they call the ADSR which is the attack-releases. The attack became release-sustained where you can shake musical sounds in the synthesis world and I created a clicky and thunky sound, then I ran it through another instrument called the Echoplex which was a way for creating an echo-effect. This was meant to mirror this rural terrain. I wanted that sound to reflect that desolate, isolated feeling that these people endured. The notion that the redneck being killed by the dog is completely surrounded by ugly emptiness.

TERESA ANN MILLER: I love this scene because you see the dog's tail wag. The tail is very much used as a rudder. Like a rudder on a boat, and the dog uses it for balance as well as emitting emotion. So when they're running, when they're attacking, when they're mad, their tail is going to move and that is in balance with the body. It appears to be a wag but it doesn't mean he's happy to be killing them. That's just part of the dog's natural body. It is very common that we teach the dog to wear his tail tied down between his legs, because in general, you know, the director will see it as well he looks too friendly, but in reality it is just his natural balance. If you've seen wolves attacking something in the wild, the tail is wagging, and it is not because it is fun, it is just the natural balance, and his natural reaction of the tail to move with the body.

GARY MORGAN: First of all, I'm a little guy. I'm like five foot four. The first job that I got in Hollywood was playing a monkey! My parents were in the circus so I have an acrobatic background and I am also a dancer and a mime, plus I have always been doubling for animals such as bears. When *Cujo* came up, they needed an animal double, of course, so it was kind of a shoe-in. I had a lot of experience with it. It's kind of interesting, the dog trainer and the dog were both trying to treat me like the dog, which was kind of funny. I would give a demonstration to the director as to what the dog could do and for the most part what I did was not exactly what the dog would do or wanted to do. You see, the St. Bernard is not an attack dog. If you want a St. Bernard to be an attack dog, you have to manipulate them. You see, a German Shepherd is an attack dog and will follow orders to attack, but with St. Bernards you need to apply training and toys. When I was at the audition the trainer Karl Lewis Miller was showing me what the dog could do at the back of this car and I was helping him put on his attack suit. He had an attack suit that was all padded. Then he put on this horrible Halloween mask, and he says to me "You won't recognize me in this!" They had the dog leashed up to a fence waiting for Karl to get into his get up. This dog was really tough and he hated this Halloween mask! Now from across the yard, Karl jumps up from behind the car and starts going like "Yaaaaaaaaa!" jumping around with this dog and the dog is freaking out! This dog is so excited! The chain link fence he is leashed to started bending and this overexcited dog is trying to get to this mask! Karl goes to the other trainer "Turn him loose!" and they undid the leash! This dog runs across the yard and takes Karl down so hard and starts mauling at his suit and throwing him around like a ragdoll! I'm standing there with my mouth open. The director and the producer are just kind of nodding like "Oh yes, that is very interesting" and I'm like "What the hell?!" They finally call out "Get him off!" and Karl's assistants pull this St. Bernard off of him. All the while I'm thinking what am I getting myself into?!

TERESA ANN MILLER: I was still in high school when my father worked with the dogs on *Cujo*. I was seventeen, I think and I remember him doing a casting for the St. Bernards, of course, and trying to find a nice team of dogs who could portray that role. I think the biggest challenge that I remember him having was getting a St. Bernard to show that many expressions, to show that terror, and yet that friendliness, because in general they are just a non-emotive animal. You know what I mean? St. Bernards are not the most expressive to emote, let's say. So that was quite the challenge for him... to be able to portray the whole character with that type of dog.

MICHAEL HILKENE: Cujo's vocals were critical to the believability of the picture and were extremely important to Lewis. When working on films that have animals as characters, it's important to be able to control the volume of the animal's voice separately from all other voices or sounds. From that standpoint, because of all the overlapping voices during the attacks, it became clear that we needed to replace the set recordings of Cujo. This meant cutting in all new material for his breathing, growling, barking and vicious snarling with high quality recordings. This was the same criteria that was used for the actors. The initial problem was whether there was a sound effects library in existence that had a matched set of recordings of a vicious, rabid, 250 pound St. Bernard. As you might guess, there wasn't one. As I recall, there were four different St. Bernards that were used during the filming of *Cujo* and, unfortunately, one of the dogs had died during the filming. We decided that we should have the trainer, the late Karl Miller, bring the three trained St. Bernards to an ADR (Automated Dialogue Replacement) Stage to record them, just like we would actors who need to redo portions of their performance due to technical reasons. This was going to be the best and most controllable way

252

to create the library that was needed. At the time, I was not convinced that a St. Bernard's vocals were going to be as terrifying as the visuals. This opinion was based on the barking that I was hearing on the work tracks. I expressed my concern to Lewis. I don't think he was too happy about my concern or about the way we were going to have to go about this, but he understood the importance of Cujo's voice being consistent. I remember that Lewis made a point of assuring me that St. Bernards can be extremely ferocious and that once I heard them first hand, I'd be impressed. It wasn't long until the day for recording the St. Bernards arrived. In addition to bringing three St. Bernards, Bernie, Daddy and Moe, Karl said that he was also bringing in a Doberman named Sampson to do the howling and whining-type sounds that we needed. This was because, he apparently couldn't get the St. Bernards to whine. If the Doberman recordings worked, we were going to pitch them down to match Cujo's pitch range. Lewis arrived to direct the session and word came in that the trainer was running late. So, we're in the back room talking, waiting for the trainer and the St. Bernards to show. The mikes were set up on the stage and happened to be live because the mixer had inadvertently left his volume controls turned up after testing his setup. This particular stage, at the old Glen Glenn Sound Company, had a side entry as well as one that led directly into the booth. Even though Lewis had made it clear to me that St. Bernards were capable of being extremely vicious, I couldn't help but wonder, "how was I going to create Cujo's frenzied attacks if the St. Bernard vocals were not scary enough?" Would I use what we recorded and sweeten it with tiger growls, or something like that? Suddenly, the most chilling GROWL blasted out of the speakers in the recording booth. It really scared the hell out of me. Karl had entered the side door with Bernie, the scariest of the three St. Bernards, held on a leash by his assistant, who looked to be the size of a tight end for the Chicago Bears. Bernie had stopped inches from the mike, didn't like something… growled… and in that fraction of a second, I was convinced that Lewis was right. That was just for starters. Karl came into the booth and asked,

"So, what do you need?" Karl wasn't exactly the biggest guy. My guest was that he weighed between 150 and 160 pounds. Since I was going to be the one cutting Cujo's vocals, Teague was nice enough to let me tell Karl the kind of sounds I was going to need. For the attack scenes, that boiled down to: slow breathing, intensified breathing, growling, snarling, attack-type barking, and then some die-down panting. Karl told us that "Bernie happens to be the perfect dog for that." At the time, I thought that we'd have to record each one separately, but Karl had a better idea. He asked us to turn the lights down on the stage and in the booth. Karl had a duffle bag with him. He pulled out a padded-flack-type jacket along with a couple arm guards and put them on. Then he pulled out this thick rubber Samurai-style mask, and donned it. All the time, Karl was staying low so that Bernie couldn't see him through the windows in the booth. To top it off, Karl pulled a solid looking rubber bat. The mixer told Karl's assistant to try and keep Bernie in the proximity of the mike and Karl gave us the sign that he was ready. Just like that, they were set to go. Bernie was already breathing slowly. We started recording. Karl opened the door of the booth. The moment Bernie spotted Karl, he stopped breathing for a second. That pause of silence was freaky in itself. Things were about to change. As Karl approached, Bernie's breathing intensified and he started to growl in a very low pitch. The growling intensified with every step Karl took. When Karl was about 10 feet from Bernie he started to raise the bat as if he was going to hit Bernie in the head. You could feel the tension build as Bernie started to snarl and bare his teeth. The trainer was starting to strain to hold him back. The intensity kept building until Karl was five feet from Bernie. I'm telling you, this was incredibly scary. At this point, Karl's assistant was doing everything he could to keep Bernie from attacking Karl. Karl lunged at Bernie with the bat. In a split second, all hell broke loose. Bernie rose up and locked onto Karl's arm with a vicious bite, causing him to drop the bat. The sound was horrific as Bernie took control, dragging the assistant forward, as he mercilessly threw Karl back and forth and onto the floor. The sounds ramped even further and became so vicious and the movements were so violent that it appeared and sounded like Bernie was killing Karl right before our eyes. It was horrific! The temptation was to stop recording and try to help Karl. On any set, the director is the person who says "cut", and Teague was the guy. Karl finally broke free from Bernie and slowly made his way back to the booth, limping all the way. He entered and dropped into the corner by the door. Karl sat there for a moment, out of the sight of Bernie and slowly removed the mask. He said in an exhausted, trembling voice, "Is that what you wanted?" It was unbelievable; I will never, ever forget that. It was something spectacular. That was the key material that I edited into every attack scene in *Cujo*.

CONRAD E. PALMISANO (stunt coordinator): Chris Howell doubled Ed Lauter. Chris Howell is 6 feet tall and 180 pounds. Bob Herron did Mills Watson, because he did Mills way back on other films. Mostly Disney pictures. Now, the dog has to lead because he is trained to do what the dog does. Then Bobby Herron, bless his heart, said "What do you want me to do?" and I said, "Well, the dog has to attack you, and there you go" so he did that a little bit. We had a training time before each sequence, where we would go and work with the dog, so the dog got to know you and know where to call and what to do. So you have to do that stuff in advance of shooting the scene, you know what I mean? So out behind the set we would go out there and say "Okay this dog is gonna jump and grab your arm and you do this. He is going to break your neck. And we have this little thing for him to bite on there". So we'd do that and rehearse. And you have to rehearse the dog with the person so that both people know exactly what is supposed to happen and the dog knows what it is supposed to do. And Karl Miller trained them wonderfully... so if by accident your hand went into the dog's mouth, he wouldn't bite you. He is not trained to do that. Right, so the dog knows you are playing with dogs – but it is meant to look vicious with the makeup on and so forth. If you're really playing with the dog and the dog is playing with you, and you're supposed to be having fun with them, because you don't want to abuse the dog and you don't want them to abuse the person – so when the dog attacks you, you're playing "Oh baby, baby, come on, up here! Ohhh, nibble on my neck". You don't say all of that, but that's what's happening – you're playing with the dog at the time to make sure it doesn't get violent. Plus St. Bernards aren't frightening to begin with.

The rabid Cujo is a product of primal horror born from tragic circumstance.

"CUJO. OH MY GOD, YOU'RE RABID…": Joe is killed by Cujo

In an original cut of the film, director Lewis Teague kept in a lot of the domestic violence that erupted at the Camber household between Joe and Charity. Built from Barbara Turner's masterful writing, this relentless bullying from Joe who would browbeat and antagonize his long suffering wife would become something that not only their son Brett would internalize, but Cujo himself. In a scene penned by Turner, Cujo – who by this point was slowly disappearing into the horrific vortex of the rabies spell – sits in the hall watching his master be rough with his mistress. Tilting his head in confusion and suppressed rage, Cujo would take this all in and bury it deep within his failing conscientiousness which will eventually die when the rabies disease takes over.

Cujo runs at full speed at the concept and ideology of "being good" and "being devoted". A dog – the epitome of loyalty – becomes the representative monster of the piece, who will kill his master. In this sequence, which closes with Joe killed off-screen, the family pet will be an instrument of retribution for domestic disturbance.

Joe Camber has failed his family in that his abusive nature, gruff stance and disconnect from Charity and Brett, will eventually lead to his demise. *Cujo* examines the sanctity of marriage, but it also exposes the ugliness

257

of matrimonial disharmony as well – silent wives with secrets, crabby mechanics with a temper, depressed farm wives who want something better for their children, little boys with monsters in their closets and so forth.

In classic horror movie mounting, the victim (here in this case Ed Lauter as Joe Camber) enters the scene puzzled and confused. He calls out to Gary, hears nothing and decides to explore. Finding the flywire door completely mangled, Joe carefully walks inside the dishevelled shack only to find his best friend dead on the floor with his body completely torn apart. Blood gushes everywhere, flesh is ripped to pieces and Joe's expression of horror says everything that is not depicted on-screen. Terrified and perplexed by the situation at hand (and also teary and for the first time showing any sign of emotion that isn't gruff coldness), Joe fumbles in fear and gathers the telephone directory book, determined to find someone to help. Joe's friendship with Gary is clearly an important centre of the film in that he emotes to his death in a sensitive way. In many regards, Joe and Gary's relationship rings similar to the brotherly companionships shared by men in westerns; that the most important unions in many westerns and action movies (the descendent of the western) are those shared by men – and this is a rare occurrence in horror, especially during the early eighties where teenage girls and their friendships would sing as fundamental to the narrative core and function.

When Joe calls out for Cujo on his farm, he gives up quite quickly, and then dumps a bag of kibble into a large trough. When he pulls up to Gary's abode, the angle is low, once again evoking the notion of Cujo being consistently there and watching. When Cujo finally does appear, he is a horrific sight to behold. His face is coated with Gary's fresh blood, his eyes stinging with burning hatred and disdain, his teeth bared, his stance ready to lunge and his deep guttural growling an insight into the warning of his intentions. Joe comes face to face with his punishment – he has been a complete monster to his wife and son, and now he will pay. Joe's last words are "Cujo. Oh my God, you're rabid…" This is the only time the term "rabid" or any mention of rabies is spoken of throughout the film (interestingly enough, Donna never tells Tad that the dog has rabies which would help her argument that Cujo is in fact a dog and not a "monster from Tad's closet"). In the closing moments of the scene in question, Cujo lunges at Joe and kills him. However, it is an interesting choice from director Lewis Teague to not give Joe a violent on-screen ending – instead, he chooses to have his editor Neil Travis cut to an exterior shot of Gary's house while Cujo slays the terrified and screaming Joe.

The rabid Cujo sets out to kill his master.

CONRAD E. PALMISANO: Chris Howell was there to double Ed Lauter but his work isn't even in the final film! Sometimes all the stuff we do doesn't always necessarily make the final cut.

MARCIA ROSS: Ed Lauter was a great actor and we cast him in L.A. He had been around a long time, and he was just a wonderful character actor that we brought in. Ed was one of a kind and an amazing man. Judith and I were big fans of his, and he had a great work ethic. An excellent face, and very believable in this environment. He didn't feel like an actor in *Cujo*, he was so grounded and real.

TERESA ANN MILLER: My dad was doubling Ed Lauter, when Ed Lauter gets attacked and killed. He was doubling him and even shaved his head to look like him. He was doing the wrestling match and he was covered in mud and blood and everything and at one point I don't know if he had got bit or scratched. He was bleeding, but they didn't know from where because of all the mud and blood. The hospital didn't know what to do with him because he was a mess! All that movie makeup and blood and what have you and they finally found out what it was. I think it was close by his neck but it wasn't something they needed to clean up or what have you. He just remembered the reaction of the hospital, seeing him come in and he's covered in mud and blood and anything else and they didn't know what the heck happened to him.

ROBIN LUCE: There was a double for Ed Lauter who was meant to be hit by the dog. The stunt man that they provided had a full head of hair, and being new in the field I was worried about the bald scalp that I provided for him. I applied the bald scalp and I hoped for the best. I just remember the dog jumping on him and my greatest hope and fear was that that bald cap would not knock off. That was one of the most daunting things I went through on the film. But otherwise, I purely enjoyed that production, it was such a landmark in my career. I mean it was the first time I headed the department and it was a great start. Ed Lauter's character doesn't get killed on camera, and I am not sure if it had anything to do with the stunt man and the bald scalp, which did by the way, stay on!

ALEXANDER WITT: The easiest footage to shoot was the stuff with the actors. The difficult stuff was with the dogs, I mean they were pretty good with their marks, but for the most part they would keep running or moving in the wrong direction, so focus wise it was very difficult to make sure they stayed in clear view.

TERESA ANN MILLER: My father worked at an air force base in California and he was so bored by himself that he requested a dog from a dog training program so that he had the companionship, while guarding his missiles and such, and what he ended up doing during his shift was teaching his dog tricks. That was how he ended up getting started with training – simply from long nights on the air force base; and he would teach his sentry dog to push a baby carriage and to stand up and salute. He would cover his face and salute to the soldiers. He did all kinds of tricks. You know, that was his early start before going to work with Frank Inn in 1966, when he first came to Hollywood. The very first Benji dog he worked with was Higgins from *Petticoat Junction* (1963-1970). That was the first Benji dog before that series of movies came out. He even did one of the Benji TV specials with Frank. He helped Frank quite a bit, even after he went off and started his own business. They remained really close friends.

GARY MORGAN: I adored Ed Lauter. He did a lot of the stunts himself. Ed is the funniest guy, and for being one of the meanest looking villains in movies, in real life he was the sweetest guy ever. He also was a dedicated performer and wanted to learn everything. He wanted me to teach him how to tap dance. All aspects of the craft were important to him. He was just this big, goofy, lovely man. In all of his roles he always played the mean guy but in his heart, he always wanted to do comedy. I spent a lot of time with Ed, but I don't really remember attacking him or anything because I don't think he is attacked by the dog – they went for his death being off camera.

TERESA ANN MILLER: It's funny that my father suggested they use a Doberman instead of a St. Bernard because I could just see the producers' reaction! That is really what the work was written for, it was written for a St. Bernard. Stephen King portrayed it in his story; it's another thing to create this vicious mentality and be able to see it in that type of normally docile dog; the reality of bringing out such rage in a St. Bernard. That's typically the type of stuff you do with Dobermans and Rottweilers and German Shepherds. So it was really a challenge to get and sell that fierceness in a St. Bernard.

CHARLES BERNSTEIN: I never worked with the sound team, but we're out in these rural areas and their contribution was invaluable because they built a sense of menace just from the desolate wastelands the film takes place in. There is an isolation and a kind of grim quality that is represented by pulsations. The environment becomes complicit in the monsters or in the dog's world and you feel there is no help nearby, and the people are not particularly going to be safe. Joe Camber is also just as monstrous, so there is a bad element in this thing too. You've got the wholesome family who are not always wholesome. So these characters also informed the music to a great degree – a dark, sort of struggling, lower middle class existence, and a rural world that is unsupported and kind of abandoned in a way. It has a very abandoned feeling. All of these aspects are rich in *Cujo*. I feel that there is nothing missing. I think each scene serves a great purpose. I have worked on films like *White Lightning* (1973), where I actually said to the producers and the director, "God, I wish there was a scene here. It feels like something is missing!" This is when Burt Reynolds is running through the field. He was escaping from prison. The producers looked at each other kind of guilty, and apparently they had had a fight about the scene they had taken out, but the director had wished it was left in. They put it back in for me so I could develop Burt Reynolds' attempt to escape from the prison! I've had that experience, but *Cujo* was pretty much in one piece.

CUJO
(a) May 23 2:00 p.m.
(b) May 24 7:00 p.m. Burbank #1 (4 HR Call)
(c) May 26 2:00 p.m. " " (4 HR Call)

Title	M#	Time	clix	orch.	Key I	II	Harp	Perc	Fen.
Title	11	:50	20-1 (A)	(H) WW III	PNO OB-3X	Em-U (Timp)	X	Crm	X
Rabbit Chase	12-A	1:51⅓	23-3 (4) 10-0	(A)	PNO PACK PNO	'OB-3X PNO	X	VFG-BELLTRE Bells, Vibs	X
Bat Cave	[13]	:55	2TOK HH3	(track?)					
Bedroom I	14	2:05	19-7 (4)	(B)					
Bedroom II	15	1:00	22-6 (4)	(C) NO BR					
Kemp/Dinner Table	23	:53	24-0 (4)	(B)	PNO	—	X	VJBS	X
Chopin piano	23A			PNO only	PNO	—			
Cujo - at Camber's	31	1:16	21-6 (4)	(A)	PNO	—	X	VIBS	X
Vic - Monster Woods	3-2	1:50	20-0 (4)	(B) 47	PNO	F.R.	X	VIBS	X
Game Drops Dish	33	1:32	21-6 (4)	3X	PNO	F.R.	X	VIBS	
Lottery Ticket	35	:34	15-6 (6)	(A) 52	PNO	F.R.	X	VIBS	X
"Oh, The Usual"	42	1:05	20-7 (4)	(C) HOWW HOBA	PNO	F.R.	X	VIBS	
Horst Delivery	43	1:12	18-7 (4)	(A) NO WW	PNO	SYNTH	X	"Temp TAMPS"	X
Donna Startled	44	:35	19-0 (4)	(B) NO WW	PNO	F.R.	X	VIBS	—
Spilt Milk	45	1:05	5=15-0 (4)	(C) NO WW	PNO	—	—	Em-U "VIBS"	—
Vic & Tad at Pinto	51	:58	20-0 (4)	(B) Timp STR	PNO	F.R.	X	VIBS	X
TV Source	52	:53							
Monster Woods	53	:24	(22-7)	PNO, HO UIB FL (B)	PNO	—	(OPT.)	"VJMS"	—
Cujo, in Fog	54/60	1:52	22-7 (4)	(A)	PNO	F.R.	X	VIBS	X
Vic & Donna at Gun	61	:52	17-1 (8)	(A)	PNO	F.R.	X	VIBS	X
Cujo Kills Gary	62-A	1:03.5	18-0 (8)	(A) HO WW II/III	—	SYNTH	—	Crm	—
" " II	62-B	:37.6	5=4-6 (16)	(A)	PNO	—	X	Crm	X
" " III	62-C	1:04	overlay POSAT	(B)	PNO	SYNTH	—	Crm	X
Cujo Kills Camber	71-A	:50	17-2	(C)	PNO	—	—	—	—
" " II	71-B	1:08	11-3 (RISE) 22	(A) III WW	PNO	—	—	Crm	—
Drive to Siege	72	1:33	20-0 (7)	(B) 1 WW	PNO	F.R.	X	VIBS	X
1st Siege Attack	73	(1:32)	WILD ARMS TRACK point	(C)	PNO	—	—	TB EQ WW	—
Franc To Cujo	75	:52	24-0 (4)	(A) 2 WW	PNO	SYNTH	X	VIBS	X
Car Stalls	76	1:22	21-6 (4)	(B) WW	PNO	F.R.	X	VIBS	X
Camper Arrives	43 Rev		(Track)	Track from 43					
Jingle Music	23 B	:10	(Improvised)						

Charles Bernstein's musical cues. (courtesy of Charles Bernstein).

263

M U S I C   C U E   S H E E T   ...   L I C E N S I N G

Following is a list of the music used in __SUNN CLASSIC PICTURES'__ _____ production of
                                         (TITLE OF CORPORATION)
_____"CUJO" (DOMESTIC VERSION ONLY)_____
                    (TITLE OF PICTURE)

Description of Picture __FEATURE FILM_____ Produced by __DAN BLATT_____

Studio __WARNER BROTHERS_____ Recorded at: ___BURBANK STUDIOS___

Music Editor __RICHARD STONE_____ Date __July 20, 1983_____

REEL CUE
REEL 1

M11	TITLE:	"MAIN TITLE PART I"	TIME :39
	COMPOSER:	CHARLES BERNSTEIN (ASCAP)	SCORE X SOURCE
			INSTRUMENTAL
	PUBLISHER:	THE TAFT ENTERTAINMENT COMPANY (ASCAP)	INSTR. VISUAL
			VOCAL
	RIGHTS SECURED FROM: PUBLISHER		VOCAL VISUAL

M12A	TITLE:	"RABBIT CHASE I"	TIME 1:00
	COMPOSER:	CHARLES BERNSTEIN (ASCAP)	SCORE X SOURCE
			INSTRUMENTAL
	PUBLISHER:	THE TAFT ENTERTAINMENT COMPANY (ASCAP)	INSTR. VISUAL
			VOCAL
	RIGHTS SECURED FROM: PUBLISHER		VOCAL VISUAL

M12B	TITLE:	"RABBIT CHASE II"	TIME 1:07
	COMPOSER:	CHARLES BERNSTEIN (ASCAP)	SCORE X SOURCE
			INSTRUMENTAL
	PUBLISHER:	THE TAFT ENTERTAINMENT COMPANY (ASCAP)	INSTR. VISUAL
			VOCAL
	RIGHTS SECURED FROM: PUBLISHER		VOCAL VISUAL

143	TITLE:	"HOIST DELIVERY"	TIME :36
	COMPOSER:	CHARLES BERNSTEIN (ASCAP)	SCORE X SOURCE
			INSTRUMENTAL
	PUBLISHER:	THE TAFT ENTERTAINMENT COMPANY (ASCAP)	INSTR. VISUAL
			VOCAL
	RIGHTS SECURED FROM: PUBLISHER		VOCAL VISUAL

264

"I SEE HEINIE, NICE AND SHINY": Donna and Tad drive up to the Camber farm

Now we enter the third and final act of *Cujo*. This would be the beginning of the phenomenally executed, magically performed and supremely iconic siege sequence that would have Donna Trenton and her little boy Tad trapped in the beat up Pinto under attack by the crazed and manic rabid St. Bernard. After cutting from the death of Joe Camber, we find the struggling Pinto hit the rural roads of back wood Castle Rock, Maine. Acting as this fictional New England town is Santa Rosa, California which is painted in brown, golden and earthy tones reflecting an intensity of heat in the dead of summer. Interestingly enough, production was stunted by heavy rains (a dramatic polar opposite as to what was supposed to be captured on screen) and cast and crew were subjected to the extreme cold, however, the film is set during "one of the harshest summers in Castle Rock history" and director Lewis Teague and his company do a brilliant job at capturing the sweltering heat and relentless summertime oppression.

Donna leads the same children's song from earlier in the film, singing along with Tad as they drive towards the Camber farm to get the car fixed. She sings "I see your heinie, it's nice and shiny, if you don't hide it, I think

265

I'll bite it!" and on the "bite it" she playfully bites at the air in what is a nice little touch foreshadowing something that will eventually terrify both her and her son – a savage monstrous dog biting at them as they fight for their lives. Following this moment Donna begins to sing about "Alice in Wonderland" with: "Alice stepped in the bathtub, pulled out the plug and then oh my goodness, oh my soul, there goes Alice down the hole!" This poignant bookending of reference to Lewis Carroll's young heroine is an inspired choice seeing that the film opens with Cujo chasing after a rabbit and following said rabbit down a hole, only to meet his unfortunate fate (being bitten by a rabid bat which would send him into the "wonderland" of rabies incubation). Donna and Tad make vocal recognition to the point of Alice falling down a hole (here she descends into the plughole of her bathtub) and even sing out "Oh my soul!" marking a spiritual connection to fate – a transitional deterrence from sanctity and normalcy to otherness and illusion.

Donna Trenton (Dee Wallace) and her son Tad (Danny Pintauro) drive up the dirt track towards the Camber farm.

266

Turning down Maple Sugar Rd (the address of the Camber farm), the decaying and completely dying Pinto sputters and jolts towards the rustic shade tree garage kicking up dirt behind it. A large oak tree welcomes the bomb of a car, extending its large leafy branches towards it, as if beckoning it to enter. This is classic horror movie fare – the heroine entering a dark terrain to come face to face with the monster. Here, *Cujo* embraces the full blown aesthetic and intention of the classic American Gothic, where even in sunkissed rural Maine, darkness will prevail and consume.

DEE WALLACE: The "I see your heinie, it's nice and shiny" song was something that I used to sing with my mom when I was little. I can't remember if I taught it to Danny or if he already knew it. I don't know if it was in the script, but we always sang in the car when I was little. It always seemed to be such a great juxtaposition from singing to screaming.

LEWIS TEAGUE: Producer Robert Singer was a silent partner. He and Dan Blatt had a partnership, but he was off doing his partnerships. He and Dan were partners in a production company, but we saw very little of him. Dan Blatt would be on the set, a very nuts and bolts producer. And Neil Machlis was the production manager. So Dan was the producer and he was a great producer. Another story – this will illustrate what a good producer – things that have made him a terrific producer… we were on the set one morning, and we were actually driving to set one morning, and it was about an hour drive. And we were going to have a very busy day. We had scheduled three separate makeup changes for Dee Wallace that day. So I asked the makeup gal to get in the car with me and Dan to discuss her work on the way to the set, because I knew if we couldn't get Dee in and out of makeup rapidly, that day, I would never finish the day. And so I'm in the car discussing with her how she was going to do the makeup, and what she could do to be quicker and more efficient. Basically what I wanted to do was intimidate her so that she'd work faster. She was not

267

very experienced. We worked with a really low budget film crew a lot who didn't have a lot of experience who had come out of Salt Lake City, and she hadn't of had a lot of experience; she had been slow up until that point, in my estimation. So I think I scared her a little bit in the car and when we got out of the car, at the set, and she ran off to the makeup trailer, Dan came over to me and said, "You know Lewis, I think we might be better off if we just did two scenes today and did them well then try to do three scenes and not do them that well". That was the exact opposite of what Roger Corman was in that kind of situation! It really impressed me that Dan was that interested in quality. So I said, "You're absolutely right, Dan. Thanks!" With the makeup lady, we talked to Dee and the production manager and said, "When are we going to do those two scenes, we want to drop one." The production manager in those days, tried to squeeze another scene in. And we had a great day! But that is just one example of the many ways Dan would approach the filmmaking process and place really high emphasis on quality.

ROBIN LUCE: Dee and Danny were both in the car and she looked like her beautiful self, and then as we get into it, she would pale down and then get splotchy from the heat and then finally into the dehydration, the lips would dry out. We wanted to point out that it was getting very hot and balmy in the car. A huge point was the sweat factor which depicted the idea of Dee and Danny getting heated up in the car, and that was all to do with how much sweat and moisture we would add to their faces. In the scheme of things it was such a small factor because you're dealing with things in such a tight tiny space, and a small time capsule, and those small details really lasted a lot longer.

With his camera crew, DOP Jan de Bont (on far right) take some time
out in between takes.

"IT'S NOT A MONSTER, IT'S JUST A DOGGY!": The siege begins

Here the film enters its final blood drenched, frenzied act, and hence the iconic siege begins. Opening with an extreme low angle as if to evoke the feeling of Cujo's P.O.V. peering underneath the shabby barn door, this first segment in what would become the film's fundamental primary goal – that is to have Donna Trenton and her son trapped in a broken down car under attack by a killer dog – is set up with an underlying intensity and unnerving undercurrent. Beautifully marrying the P.O.V. angle is Charles Bernstein's musical sting that sings out the domestic motif in his score, but here it is played with sustained and stressed notes that will eventually transition into a thunderous menace. Director Lewis Teague's handling of this opening to the lengthy "cat and mouse" horror show is sublime and perfectly executed – what he manages to do is bring all the imagined horror home and he lays down an attack of such self-concocted fears with a tangible ferocity that is embodied by the rabid two hundred pound manic dog.

As the decrepit Pinto pulls up, Donna remarks "I think we've arrived Tadder" to which the intelligent boy replies "Yeah, but is anybody home?" Donna steps outside of her car and scrutinizes the scene calling out "Hello?" Not only is Donna channelling traditional horror movie heroine

271

tropes such as being isolated and calling out for "help" or "assistance", she is also the epitome of a woman consumed by loneliness as the visual landscape created here suggests and commands. Donna stands in the middle of a vast wasteland which is empty, desolate and devoid of any contact. Here shines Lewis Teague's masterful handling and depiction of a "woman in the storm" as a primary character principle and narrative crux. Jan de Bont's story-centred and story-serving camera makes a full circle around Donna as she calls out for at least one of the Cambers to respond, giving the isolation an overriding and uncontrollable intensity, and this is mirrored later in the film when de Bont will spin Donna and her son out of control during a harrowing ordeal through the siege.

Donna is left alone with her boy, stranded on the farm. Obviously no one is around – Charity and Brett are on their way to Connecticut, Joe is dead and their closest neighbour, being Gary Pervier, has also been killed. Before Donna can react to the lack of human life on the farm, Tad calls out to her, struggling to get his seatbelt off. The seatbelt struggle becomes a symbol of the illusion of safety; Tad is stuck in what would be a "concept" of safety; however this would be completely jeopardized when Cujo attacks. Donna remarks "Everything in this car is broken!" while Tad "wishes daddy'd get a new car".

Stephen King's writing on cars is something to take note of here: obviously his most memorable and iconic of literary vehicles would be his monstrous, she-demon Christine from his novel of the same name (which would get its film adaptation the same year as *Cujo* from horror maestro John Carpenter) but instead of a vindictive lover in the guise of a possessive Plymouth Fury, here in *Cujo*, the car is an unreliable trap and overheated dead-end. In King's novel and in the film adaptation of *Cujo*, the Pinto acts as a double edged sword – it is something that may suffocate our heroine and her child, but it is also something that acts as a fortress keeping the monster at bay. The Ford Pinto would be a staple choice for movie cars during the late seventies and early eighties, most notably for families trekking across country. Variants of the Ford Pinto station wagon would be found in multiple dramas (*3 Women* (1977), *Silkwood* (1983)) and comedies such as the stylized variant like the Ford Country Squire which would come to know pop-cultural iconography from films such as *National Lampoon's Vacation* (released the same year as *Cujo*, 1983). However, much like King's choice of making Christine a Plymouth Fury – which was the only classic American muscle car not to be recognized or celebrated in the same vein as the Mustang or the Corvette (rendering "her" as an ignored underdog) – the Ford Pinto would undergo a systematic scrutiny come the late seventies when Ford would recall 1.5 million of these cars from production lines due to failing basic safety requirements.

Cutting back to the assumed P.O.V. shot from underneath the barn door which suggests the notion that Donna and Tad are being watched by Cujo, we gradually shift to another beautifully conceived angle where the camera stalks Donna from behind, as she bends into the car trying to free Tad from the seatbelt. Manipulating the audience is exactly what horror film directors aim to do, and here Lewis Teague visually closes in on Donna who has her back turned to us, the viewer. Establishing the shot as Cujo's P.O.V. is what is intended, but the payoff is even more inspired. As the camera creeps up behind Donna, it comes to a halt, and there is an expectation of Cujo lunging from that perspective, however the monstrous dog will appear at the opposite front seat window, surprising the audience who were expecting him to own that established P.O.V. The "boo" moment is born from an element of not giving what the audience expects, and as Cujo powers through the gap of the window just above Tad, unrelenting terror ensues. The image of this now unrecognizable rabid dog thrusting his bloodied head into the car window, barking, growling and snapping at Donna's hand as she tries to wind up the window is horror movie magic – the violent thrusting, the aggression, the frenzied menace and the brutality of Cujo's first attack on Donna and Tad is a horrific and harrowing example of wonderfully weaved together cinematic fear. The sound design is exhilarating and heightens the ferocity of the piece using

Tad's screaming and hollering to match the bloodcurdling barking and growling from the dog, while the sharp edits made up of extreme close-ups of Cujo as well as the screaming Tad and the terrified Donna are stitched together with astute meticulousness.

Cujo bolts towards the open door of the Pinto, but Donna slams it shut before he can reach her. There is a tiny moment of breath as Cujo surveys the busted up car. This is where the film brings Tad's horror right to the narrative heart when he blurts through his tears: "How did the monster get out of my closet?" Here, Tad's imagined fear of monsters in the closet have now become a menacing and vicious reality – Cujo, this malicious and mad canine hellbent on tearing little Tad to shreds, is now the lurking beast that haunted his wardrobe and caused many sleepless nights. Donna holds her petrified son close and tells him "It's not a monster, it's just a doggy!" and on that inspired line comes a jolting shot of brilliance – as soon as Donna concludes that Cujo is in fact just a "doggy" and not at all a closet-dwelling monster it is instantly matched with an enraged Cujo leaping upon the bonnet of the car clawing at the windscreen, barking angrily, snarling and determined to kill mother and son.

The intensity of this sequence is masterfully handled by everyone involved: Dee Wallace's performance is simply electrifying. She is such a naturally gifted actress that her shift from agitation ("this is great, this is just great...") to being absolutely terrified is a magnetic and dynamic example of performance. Danny Pintauro throws himself into such a concentrated state of panic and hysteria without missing a beat. His sense of precision, timing, naturalism and thorough understanding of terror is outstanding. Animal trainer Karl Lewis Miller's work with the dog used in this scene brings out an incredibly frightening performance, as the dog eagerly participates in some of the scariest onscreen animal attacks ever put to film. It must be noted that *Cujo* would certainly be the most popular film about a killer dog – fellow *dogsploitation* horror movies would deliver cinematic terror throughout the years such as *Dogs* (1976), *The Pack* and *White Dog*, but it would be *Cujo* that comes to the collective filmic mind when the discussion of destructive canines arises. In *The Pack*, a film that also had Karl Lewis Miller train a group of dogs to do some violent stunts, actress Hope Alexander-Willis would find herself in a similar predicament as Dee Wallace in *Cujo* – that of being trapped inside a car while – not one – but a whole pack of dogs would attack (Willis recollects working with the dogs and Karl Lewis Miller further on at the tail end of the quotes for this chapter).

With the emotional stress levels soaring high, Donna presses down on the car horn in an attempt to scare Cujo away, leading into a series of frenzied images locked together in a patchwork of sheer *cinema par excellence*: the low angle looking up at the steering wheel as Donna tries to start the car, the extreme close-ups of the panicked Donna and Tad who are already wet with sweat from the sweltering heat, the image of Cujo clawing at the windscreen barking angrily – all of this makes for a dynamic introduction to what the rest of the film will fundamentally become: a woman determined to save her child from a savage beast. Lewis Teague decides to close this opening to the siege with a sublime crane overhead shot that drifts from the car and closes in on Cujo. In doing this, Teague creates a poetic reflection of the rabid dog as fear realized.

Cujo in essence becomes a punishment for adultery, a tangible leviathan from a child's closet, God's judgement, the devil hound of retribution, an unstoppable force of justice, the reminder of domestic harmony and the mythical dragon who stands in for a violent backlash against familial dishonour. The image of Cujo, completely covered in dry foam and saliva, eyes oozing yellow puss, blood smeared upon his muzzle, his lips quivering with fury, his eyes fixed on the Pinto waiting for movement and sound, bears semblance to that of the possessed Regan MacNeil (Linda Blair) in *The Exorcist* who patiently waits for Father Karras (Jason Miller) – the Jesuit priest sent to exorcise her – to enter her bedroom. The demonic energy of Cujo patiently waiting to strike again matches the burning intelligence and ancient malevolence embodied by the twisted and disfigured little girl strapped to her bed in Georgetown, Washington.

275

Keeping with religious terms in reference to *Cujo*, Donna Trenton will now face the Three Days of Darkness which is an eschatological prophecy from Roman Catholicism where the "faithful" are advised to stay close to their homes and families in order to survive these dreaded days. Of course, "staying close to home and family" is something that Donna has completely betrayed and her "punishment" is to spend three days of prescribed "darkness" locked in her busted up car facing a relentlessly bloodthirsty, very sick and very large dog. In Stephen King's novel, Donna has a self-reflective moment while stuck in the car contemplating her next move. Here she questions whether or not Cujo has been sent to her as an angel of death, set to punish her for her moral sins. She poo-poos it in the novel and it is never bought up in the film (as it shouldn't be, in fear of being a sore thumb). *Cujo* is a testament to morality, and ultimately the test of a mother's love. Donna Trenton will forget that she is alone, bored, alienated, longing for affection, someone's wife, someone's lover and at a character deciphering turning point, she will only know and understand that she is a mother, and in this and through this she will gradually become a warrior, fighting to save her son's life. The counter to this is the innocent Tad who is trapped in the hellish cesspool of depravity, depression, decay and immorality. In King's novel, Donna in essence fails to save her child, for Tad dies of overexposure, however in the film, he is permitted to live rendering Donna heroic, resourceful, a success and most importantly, warranted and validated as a human being. "I want to go home!" screams the wailing Tad as he clings to Donna's chest, while her terror manifests into mournful tears ("Ok...we're gonna go home..."). The concept of mother as nurturer and protector turning into mother as bloodied and soiled warrior is something that becomes the overriding character arc for the protagonist of *Cujo*, and it works beautifully – fundamentally thanks to the majestic handling of the material by the supremely talented Dee Wallace – and by the end of the film, Donna will be as ferocious and as bloodthirsty as Cujo himself.

Director Lewis Teague talks the beginning of the siege through to actors Dee Wallace and Danny Pintauro, while "Cubby" one of the St. Bernards playing Cujo stands alert on the Pinto bonnet.

DEE WALLACE: Danny was brilliant, period. He was wise beyond his years and still a little kid. He just knew. He was an old soul and he just knew. For me it was like working with another adult actor and sometimes even better. He didn't come in with any preconceived notions, he was always right there with me, and we worked off of a script but often improvisation came around for both of us. We would go with it. We earned each other's trust, and I would always say to him "Now the dog is just acting, the dog is not really gonna hurt us" and after the scene I would go through it with him and tell him "See? We did some great acting there and your scream was excellent, but now we're all fine, right?" Because when children are that little they cannot distinguish between fantasy and reality. It was always important to me for me to be that role model for him. A voice of reason I guess. And maybe I was doing it for myself. Danny's mother was there, but Danny was pretty self-sufficient. I mean his mother was there to take care of him, to look over him, to make sure he wasn't being abused, but Danny was an old soul. Many child actors are like that. The kids in *E.T.* were old souls in little bodies, and that is always amazing to bounce off.

GARY MORGAN: I didn't know anything about the novel. I knew that it was about a rabid St. Bernard, so they told me the basic background. They have this woman and a child kind of held hostage in a car and there were some attacks that they needed to stage. Now, whenever you double an animal, the more they can have the animal do the better, of course. A lot of times your insurance is when an animal won't do what they need or won't perform, then they have to do the animal suit. Also, whenever you see a star being attacked – for instance in *Back to the Future Part III* (1990), I was the bear double. Whenever you see the bear it was chasing the trainer. Whenever you saw Michael J. Fox's close-up and the bear stands up in front of him – over the bear's shoulder – that was me. When they shoot between the bear's legs to get a shot of Michael J. Fox, it was me and if it was a real bear, it was a real bear chasing the trainer – just like the St. Bernard. When you saw the real St. Bernard, it was attacking a stunt person or another stunt guy, then when you saw Dee Wallace's face it was me over the shoulder.

The frenzied siege becomes the third act of the film.

DANIEL HUGH KELLY: As far as the novel went, I really liked that the dog was unstoppable – and to me the dog represented retribution from God, if you believe in God, or from a higher force or being. This dog represented what will happen to you if you screw up! And that is a very simplified view point on it, but to me that made the dog much more terrifying and unstoppable and something beyond something to be able to deal with. And yeah sure, a rabid dog and a rabid dog as big as Cubby was, that is just as intimidating just on that alone, but to me if you didn't have that element of unstoppable retribution, you would just have a simple story about this poor dog who got bitten by a rabid bat. That's what I read into it, and I loved how Stephen King wrote that novel. He intertwined it so well, and the fact that every character in this book is guilty, severely guilty of stuff, except for Tad the little kid who isn't guilty of anything. It's God's retribution to all of us and I loved that book. I had done a series, one of the best soaps on television for years, and a lot of theatre in New York and around the country, and initially getting the role in *Cujo*, I thought, well this would be a really cool first movie experience.

Leviathan waiting.

LEWIS TEAGUE: Well, let's see. There was a time when I was planning to shoot a shot a certain way and Jan said "Why don't I put the camera down on the floor" and I thought "Why?" And he said "it'll look great" and I said "okay, go ahead and do it". It was again, it was a scene where the tennis bum is menacing Dee Wallace in the kitchen. The fact that we shot from a low angle made it more menacing. So he was right on that one. And I'm glad I let him do it his way. There was another time where I was shooting a scene and I wanted it to go quickly. A director has to budget their time on set during the day to get what's important to get the shots that are really important... the time that it takes to get them, and if there is an easier way to get a scene and it's not that important. For example, there was this one scene I wanted to shoot it all from the same direction, just change lenses, so I could get the wide shots, so to keep the scene to keep the actors moving; choose one actor with one lens, then without moving one actor shoot the other actor with the same lens. There was a lot of movement. I thought it worked out great! Jan wasn't very happy with him, but he did it, and it worked out great. There were times when I felt like we were wasting time, for example I wanted to do that shot where it goes from a real wide angle, the car and it's on a crane and the camera drops down and you see it looking over the St. Bernard, the camera keeps moving around to a front shot of the St. Bernard and then moves into a close-up of its eyes. It took a long time to get that shot and I was ready to abandon it at one point, or simplify it, and Jan kept saying "No, no, no. We can do it. We can do it" and he would be screaming and yelling at his crew, and we finally got it and I am so glad! It's such a beautiful shot! It was a great working relationship; it was very collaborative. Jan had a lot to contribute. It was a terrific relationship, because not only did he rise to the challenge to make difficult shots work, the fact that he would be ready to deal with challenges inspired me to be more challenging, and come up with more interesting shots! So it was a very wonderful working relationship!

Lewis Teague directs the action in Santa Rosa.

Lewis Teague and Dee Wallace go over a scene.

Donna Trenton (Dee Wallace) is mauled by the rabid St. Bernard. Here, stunt man Gary Morgan stands in.

DEE WALLACE: Karl was such a kind, sweet, sensitive soul. He slept in the barn with his dogs! We weren't allowed to have any relationship with the dogs, which killed me, because all I wanted to do was pet them and fawn over them. But I wasn't allowed to interact with Lassie when I did *The New Lassie* (1989-1992) either, because the dogs only have to have the relationship with the trainer. But Karl was so dear. The first big attack scene was probably the first day of shooting the entire dog siege. This is the first time the dog comes up to the window, and we're rehearsing all this stuff and Lewis Teague comes over to me. Now, because we had rehearsed it with the dog and it's terrifying with all the sound and having him right there, we needed to rest the dog and then Lewis comes over and says "Dee, um, this is going to be really hard on the dog, so do you think after we shoot the dog, somebody can stand in for the dog?" I say, "I don't know, Lewis. Let's try it", because I am very sensitive to animals and their care. So Lewis comes up and we're rehearsing and he goes "Woof woof woof!" Danny cracks up laughing. I crack up laughing. The crew cracks up laughing. So, I said, "I don't think this is going to work! It's just so not the same!" It's terrifying to have the dog at you even though you know the dog is just going after a toy. It's the reality and the noise!

MICHAEL HILKENE: While loud bright irritating scenes raised the audience's anxiety level, the quieter scenes gave them relief. However, after Cujo's unforgettable first shock attack on Dee and Danny in the car, I felt that Lewis and Neil had set up the audience perfectly. By that, I mean the quieter scenes actually added to the tension. When we were back at the farm and everything seemed calm, the audience was always on the edge of their seats, dreading that another shock attack could happen at any moment.

CHARLES BERNSTEIN: It was important to me that Cujo had a very definite and distinct theme. It was not consciously done where I didn't alter either one of them so they would be able to co-exist, so to speak, but I didn't have difficulty making that happen. The themes were already manifested, and I was simply working with them and bending and dealing with them, as needed in order to make them happen. But it wasn't part of the original choice of the themes. I would take musical notes and change the environment around them. So you can put it in a more major or minor setting and that will then make it a little happier or a little sadder or you can orchestrate it in a darker way with low strings – there is a number of techniques which will allow themes to be manipulated so that they have a different kind of effect on the listener. So that was more the way that this worked.

TERESA ANN MILLER: Every day my dad would go to work and they would have full jumpers on to protect their clothing because it was such a mess! By the time you get into the full character of Cujo and his baddest element; it was full of earth wet down and put onto the dog as well as movie blood mixed into that. Then they would take an eye cream that is an antibiotic for eyes and they would drip it from his eyes to create that yellow goo coming down out of a big strip from his eyes. That was every day for a good month and a half, because he was predominately the rabid Cujo character. And yeah, you know, get up, get showered, go to work and get filthy! So, it didn't make much sense! But boy, it was just a mess to make him look worn and vicious as well as the sickness, you know from the dog being seen, so you could really see this deterioration of the character.

DON CARLOS DUNAWAY: I have enjoyed a few horror movies in my life but I'm not a buff. I have never read Stephen King, except for "Cujo". The book is way too long for me, and with a lot of filler, but built around a really scary core, which he's really good at. Obviously.

The crew – including Alexander Witt and Vern Nobles.

VERN NOBLES: The animal trainer Karl was kind of a weird dude – he only drank "near beer", because he was a recovering alcoholic. He had a little squeaker and he had three St. Bernards that would all go crazy when you got the squeaker going. We were in Petaluma, in the Spring/Summer, I guess it was. It was really hot the whole time we were doing that Pinto sequence... so we were stuck inside there, and the dog was ripping the car apart, literally – ripping windshield wipers off, ripping handlers off, you know. And we're crammed in there with Dee and the little kid... usually Jan and me. And there was a whole week's sequence that was crazy. And actually, one of the dogs bit the stunt girl's nose and he died the next day... but he actually died because St. Bernards are famous for liquid in their lungs. It's a normal thing. But it just happened after he bit the stunt girl. They used a St. Bernard in the dog suit too because the St. Bernard wouldn't jump through a window. I mean Karl the trainer was a really nice guy, really personable; hung out with everybody. He just needed his "near beer". That was the funny thing about him. He'd get really cranky if he didn't have his non-alcoholic beer – he'd get really cranky. It was actually really like family style crew, everybody was super friendly, and then there were a few people sleeping with a few people here and there. We actually had a few crew members... I was only twenty-years-old then – I wasn't even legally allowed to go to the bars when we started the movie. Yeah, we had a few [problems]. In the original town of Petaluma, they didn't like us at all, because of the crew guys going out with other people there. We actually had signs with like *Cujo* – that the town had in Mendocino – like a dog pissing on the town that they put up around. I mean, they really didn't like us there. But all the crew guys, every weekend, we all went out together, eat together, party together. It was like a real family. A lot of the guys were from Utah, because it was part of some classic deal, so all there crew was from Utah. I don't remember if we did go union at the end. But most of everybody there was L.A. crew were all union, but I think it was all non-union. Petaluma was where our hotel was.

Camera assistants Vern Nobles and Alexander Witt tend to the shot while DOP Jan de Bont looks over from the left.

Cujo sits and waits: the siege as well as the Three Days of Darkness has begun.

PATRUSHKHA MIERZWA: I remember Karl as an edgy personality. He chain-drank "near beers", smoked, and said, "Sic' em up, Cubby!!" more times than I can count. I think his nervousness contributed to the tense set on a core level. I remember *that morning* when we arrived at the farm; it was pretty early in the farm sequence and Mark and I were there early to set up and heard Cubby had died in the night. That was quite a shock. Moving cantankerous Moe to lead dog was another dreadful layer. I still get a chill remembering the scene where Dee has Moe on her. It was frightful on so many levels; the generally tense set with a (rightfully) apprehensive Dee, a young, frightened child, a very heavy, mean dog, drugged just enough to keep him malleable but not have a stroke and die. A vet and Human Society rep were there but no one could really control what would happen. I did boom that, and watched Moe struggle in bouts of waking up.

CHARLES BERNSTEIN: It's a question of energy. When we are looking from below the barn, under the car, the energy is very subtle, it's not manifested, it's not pulsation, there's no action. The music has to kind of read the energetic feel on the screen with the actors when the camera moves and so forth. You'll find that very often the music is tracking the mood, the energetic level of what's going on – on screen – and when the dog attacks, the energy level is suddenly frenetic and everybody in the car has their heart beginning to be to understand what the story was really about. In the script it is supposed to be one hundred degrees outside. When we were shooting in this place called Santa Rosa, California, which can get quite cold, the heat had to be acted out because it wasn't really there. The director of photography and Lewis built a jigsaw puzzle out of the car, so that it could be contained. What they did was they made it so that they took the roof apart, they could take the back apart, and so that they could put camera angles and things in it. I had never seen that before in a lot of movies. But I had never seen anybody put so much forethought to get all these angles in this little tiny car. We needed to have

287

this car be able to come apart, so they had it diced up so that they could pull the back section off, the front section off to get the pieces. So that was one of the things that was very unique about *Cujo*, because so much of the movie is taking place inside this little car and from two angles for an hour.

HOPE ALEXANDER-WILLIS (star of *The Pack*): Karl Lewis Miller was amazing! He's gone now. He died. He and I shared the same birthday. So, we had a bond over that. He was really funny and really, really smart! And his connection with the animals was on a very deep, deep plane – they totally trusted him! He refused to let them do anything that he didn't do first. So, if there were any stunts, he would do them before he would let his dogs do them. And they trusted him. They trusted him completely! I remember there was that dog from the start that closes the film, the lovely collie that gets to be rehabilitated, and she was meant to be quite fretful throughout the film. And Karl would have to yell at her to get her to become wary and frightened and it would kill him to have to do that! He would get so, so depressed from doing that, and as soon as they would yell "Cut!" he would race to her and make sure she was ok. And she was. Happy as a lark after that. They were all rescues. And then they became a part of his acting troupe. He was amazing. He was really amazing to watch! I watched scenes that involved the dogs. I, of course, watched them burning down the house. That was pretty spectacular! I have slides of everything somewhere – back in the day when you took slides. I have a lot of slides actually of filming. They used Vaseline to make the dogs look shiny and scary as well as edible stage blood, but these dogs were having fun. I love the way Karl and all of his trainers took such great care of the dogs! They didn't over-work them. I mean, they treated them like children, it was beautiful. The leader of the pack, Josh and I bonded. I'm telling you, I really felt like he was my leading man as much as Joe Don Baker was! I hung out with them (the dogs) and the trainer a lot. I don't really remember how long the shoot was. Probably a month or maybe longer. But the dogs were great – they were brilliant "actors". I have a wall of photographs from my career, and people. I have Michael Redgrave and I have Tom Stoppard and I have this person and that person and then Josh from *The Pack*. Yes, he was a fabulous leading man! He was everything you would look for in a leading man.

Two of the dogs from *The Pack* (1977). Trained by Karl Lewis Miller. (photo courtesy of Hope Alexander-Willis).

"FUCK YOU, DOG": The Pinto fails for good and Vic checks in on Donna

With the summer's sweltering heat burning intensely, young Tad Trenton distracts himself from the dire situation and isolation by drawing. He hums to himself, busily sketching away with his crayons, while his mother Donna sits in sweaty contemplation, watching the steering wheel, fixed with a deep building distress. The perspiration on her lip and nose glistens as the oppressive heat envelops her and her son in the decrepit Ford Pinto. Deep in thought and facing something tumultuous and terrifying, Donna is "woken up" by Tad who calls out to her, begging her to try and start the car again. In a sense, Tad shakes her alive – something that will become a thematic outpost for the film, where this woman stunted by loneliness and boredom will be forced to "become alive and aware" in order to save her child.

With Tad bolting up and asking "Mom, aren't we going?", Donna is forced to act on the situation at hand, rather than internalize it and meditate on it. Taking Tad's advice into consideration, Donna flicks the key around in the ignition and the Pinto starts to purr. Dee Wallace's expression here is the personification of great relief under disabling stress; she closes her eyes as if to say "Thank you, God" and then continues to rev up the wreck of a car. The sound of the engine startles Cujo, who bounds towards them, leaping into action, letting out some warning barks and then finally stopping in his tracks to watch them. His face is completely coated in white foam, his eyes soiled with grotesque goo and fresh blood oozes from the top of his snout. He locks gazes with Donna who warms up the car and makes a turn, ready to leave the farm. In a moment of pure disdain and as an extension of her crippling frustration (as well as a wonderful descendent of some inspired infamous movie lines such as "Smile you son of a bitch!" from *Jaws*), Donna looks into Cujo's direction and snarls "Fuck you, dog". Cutting back to Cujo there is a quiet understanding that will develop as the siege continues; that this dog will not surrender and not give up, just as much as Donna will not surrender or give up. The film will pit these two characters against one another – one wanting to kill and the other simply wanting to survive and more importantly, protect her child.

However, on "Fuck you, dog", Donna's car stalls once more, and the alternator light flashes indicating the car is now well and truly dead. Donna panics and starts to get increasingly frustrated, while Tad sits in the passenger seat taking in all of this anger and being all the more fragile and vulnerable. Donna struggles to get the car moving, but nothing happens. She howls in anguish and gets angry at the situation she has put herself and Tad in. Tad asks "I thought you were mad at me…", confusing self-inflicted torture with contempt for behaviour. Donna's reply is insightful to her character, she replies "Never at you, baby". Donna's fury and painful realisation that she may be stuck out on Camber's farm for a very long time, becomes a response to her frustration with her situation and also with her strained relationship to her husband. She screams at the car's dysfunction whilst also voicing her infuriation directed at Vic ("Why didn't you get this car fixed?"). The musical shift here is also an interesting choice in that it goes back to the family theme, prompting a sombre moodiness and bleakness to Donna and Tad's position.

Childlike query also comes into play here when Tad asks "Can he get us in here?" and "Can he eat his way in here?" adding to the film's fairy tale allegory and its dealing with imagined and tangible monsters. While Tad asks these innocent and delicately phrased questions, Donna watches Cujo swagger back to the barn, escaping the blistering heat. The perplexed and troubled maiden watches the dragon descend back into his deep dark cave, while the babe in the woods frets for his safety. Danny Pintauro handles these quiet moments within the frenzied and extremely gritty, grim and violent siege sequence with a resourceful control that taps into solemn despair, fragile hope and exhausted confusion. His co-star Dee Wallace counters these moments with a hushed strength that will gradually evolve into something all-empowering and brutal. Wallace's emotional responses to young Pintauro are born from a sense of vulnerability and deep compassion, and as she struggles to find a way out of dangers reach, her character's arc will suddenly be given room enough to stretch out and flex its well-rested muscles.

Cutting to sundown, the Camber farm is lit as though it is on fire – Jan de Bont's camera paints a picture of a hell on earth, where the color scheme is burning with reds, oranges and thick golden hues. Donna Trenton is now experiencing her first night of the Three Days of Darkness, trapped and besieged by this two hundred pound leviathan. Cujo rests and waits on the Camber porch, watching the woman and her small child struggle in the nasty heat and being careful with their tiny offering of air. The idea of story tropes in horror fiction and film where characters are stuck in a small space under attack by something monstrous is classic monster movie fare, and here in *Cujo*, director Lewis Teague delivers a successful entry in this subgenre. Author Stephen King would go on the record at saying he wanted to create a terrifying story that took place in the constraints of a small space to evoke feelings of claustrophobia and heightened intensity – and also to give another dimension to the horror, that not only is the protagonist fighting off a monstrous entity (in this case, a rabid dog) but also battling the elements, suffocation, dehydration and violent heat.

What follows is the first in a series of quick breathers that depart from the siege sequence that help the audience take a moment's rest from the intensity of Donna's situation. With an exterior shot of the Trenton household at night, we hear a phone ringing; a spewing out of desperate and urgent rings. Cutting to a city restaurant (a long way away from the rural settings of Castle Rock, Maine) we find a suited up Vic Trenton making such an urgent phone call. He gives up and walks through the ritzy eatery and finds Roger Breakstone while classical music plays and a waiter serves up lobster (a nice tribute to New England eating). This tiny moment (as aforementioned, the first in a series of them) will also serve Lewis Teague in how to present a narrative ease and flow, where jump cuts from the Camber farm will not always be necessary and a throw to out-of-town Vic Trenton worrying about Donna will.

From the black tie business dinner where glamour runs high, we cut to Donna in the dead of night, stuck in her Pinto with Tad begging to "go pee". Terrified of opening the door to let her son urinate in case the prowling Cujo lunges and collects him into his powerful jaws, Donna poses if he "really needs to 'go'", to which Tad replies "real bad". Here we get a sense of how pathetic Donna's position is right now, that while her husband dines on lobster and drinks wine, she is stuck out in isolation, terrified of a lumbering beast that might quickly devour her tiny son.

From the corner of the frame rests the bloodthirsty Cujo, who watches Tad's urine hit the dusty plains. However, before he can pounce on the unsuspecting child who is coddled by his mother and held very close to the car seat, he hears the Camber phone ring (possibly Vic, or maybe Charity or Brett "checking in on Cujo"). Interestingly, this is the second time Tad will be urinating in the film – the first time we meet him he is using the toilet all by himself (a "big boy") and now he is assisted by his mother, which comments on this child growing up having being stunted and that he will actually regress back into infancy whilst under great stress. Later in the film, he will lie in foetal positions and gasp for air, as if a full regression has occurred, plodding him back inside the womb.

When Cujo hears the loud ringing telephone he reacts violently. He is conflicted at one point (some beautiful work here from animal trainer Karl Lewis Miller) and darts his head back and forth from Donna and Tad towards the house where the loud phone calls through. He makes his decision and decides to attack the obnoxious loud sound of ringing bells. He runs towards the house and smashes through the window snapping at the phone. Donna sits and watches, with Tad safely back inside the car. She is terrified at the thought of the dog being able to break through glass and just the extremities of his anger, rage, bloodlust and fury. Cujo lies back down on the porch, his face snarling, lifting up his chops to show his teeth, while stringy white foam spills out from the sides of his mouth.

The camera crew light the scene outside the barn door.

The crew take a much needed "chain massage".

DEE WALLACE: I don't remember Peter Medak being on the film for too long. I think he was there for like three days and it was three days of "What the fuck is going on?" I was excited because I had seen some of Peter's other work that I loved, so I was expecting this brilliant person to walk in and do this and after the second day I went to Dan and I said "What is going on? He doesn't have any of the same vision that we have!" He wanted me to be dressed down in just a bra and be in this see-through dress, and to have everything have a sexual connotation to it, and I was like "Dude, I'm a mother! I'm playing a mother, and a mother whose life and death depends on her son's life and death! No I am not wearing something see-through with my bra out!" I didn't get it, I didn't get his vision and Dan seemed to be rather surprised about this. And I was like "Weren't there any production meetings about this?" and quite frankly I don't even remember Dan's response to that. People saw two days of dailies from Peter and said "no". I went to Dan and Dan went "Holy hell!"

so Dan went to Lewis. Now Dan originally wanted Lewis on this film, but the film went to another studio and they didn't want Lewis, so Peter was brought in, and when all that went down, Lewis was approached and he took over. Whatever Peter initially shot, we just started over again. I have a faint memory of being in the car and looking up and seeing Peter, but we wouldn't have shot anything in a see-through blouse, because I wouldn't have done it. I loved Lewis straight away. He was very kind and incredibly intelligent. He is a brilliant man. For me, it was very important that I was respected and that I felt like I could trust who was looking over this project with me. I love direction if the direction made sense and excited me. If someone gave me the direction of "Put on this see-through blouse", everything in my character goes "This guy's a moron, I can't do this", then an actor bogs and pulls back and it's really hard to get things out of them because everything is screaming "Don't do this!"

Producer Dan Blatt on the farm in Santa Rosa. (courtesy of Danny and Margaret Pintauro).

TONY RICHMOND: We worked with Karl Miller and the dogs, and the dogs were great. We did some tests with one of the dogs, but we didn't shoot much at all. Karl was great, a very good dog trainer. Working with animals and kids is the worst thing in the world however. If they don't want to do something, it is time consuming and painful. It is incredibly hard. I remember hearing about someone being bitten by the dog on the nose and I thought it was Dee Wallace, and I remember laughing about it. We also did very basic makeup and wardrobe tests with Dee and the other cast members, there was nothing special, just basic test footage. Nothing to report on there.

CHRISTOPHER MEDAK: I called Jack Buehler the costume designer "Uncle Jack". He was a very vivacious gay man who loved his men and loved his drugs. He was bigger than life, he was very flamboyant and loved his weekends in San Francisco, and what blew me away was how much debauchery he got into. He was able to show up to his job in ways that none of us could have done. He would be out all night on the drugs and sleeping around and then turn up early ready to work. I remember seeing him on set with his three ring binder of Polaroids of all the continuity shots which never left his sight. He was constantly on the go. A lot of his job involved him painting. He carried around a little puff bag and he would have dirt and grime in there and he was always fucking up Dee's costume to make it look all grotty and grubby and to get it exactly it was from the last shot. He was a great artist and had a great eye for detail. I went to his funeral and miss him. Jack's assistant Nancy Fox has kind of gone off the deep end and not in a good way. She is into New Age shit that is not helping her in any way. But back then she was so awesome. She worked with Jack on this and films like *The Howling*. I dated Nancy for years. It is heartbreaking to see what she's become.

NANCY G. FOX: I actually dated Chris Medak – Peter Medak's son. He was my boyfriend for a couple years after the movie. We're friends still to this day. I remember I had my twenty-third birthday on the set, and Dee sent me a singing telegram with balloons and someone came and sang to me. They also got me a cake. Dee is like family. She is incredibly generous and lovely.

DEE WALLACE: I remember all the producers being nice and supportive. I worked mostly with Dan. Back in those days I think I was a little more challenging to take care of on the set, because I just got into the part so much! I have to tell you, *Cujo* was the hardest thing I've ever done emotionally, physically and spiritually. The hours and the emotional expense that we had to put out every day. I was working with a child and a dog, so whenever they worked they printed it, so whenever I was on, I had to be on all the time. And it became the case and question of how much do I break down, where do I break down, how do I break down, how far do I go into this, because every scene was so emotionally stirring. Even the scenes before the car siege had an emotional tension. I was so grateful that Lewis Teague and Jan de Bont worked on the film – I mean what a team they were on the film! That look and the tension and the wonderful stylisation of the film and everyone on it felt the heaviness of what we were doing on the set. I have that one picture of Lewis and myself and Gary Morgan in the dog suit and we're in the kick line. I mean there weren't many moments like that on the set, and if there were any like that, Gary created them! Because I just couldn't take myself in and out of the character and that place I was at. It was too hard for me as the kind of actress I am to go in and out of being silly and light and back into this hysterical place I had to be. Most of my work was with Dan, and Dan was a close friend of mine. He was very ingenious in how to work with me and help me and coddle me, and he and Chris, my husband, commiserated as to how to get Dee through.

TERESA ANN MILLER: In my father's manner of working with dogs and all the Jekyll and Hyde characters that's he's done in the past, everything from *White Dog* to *The Amityville Horror* (1979) to *They Only*

Kill Their Masters (1972) he was known for the Dr. Jekyll and Mr. Hyde characters in animals. He had this way of building the trust in the animal, and giving them the confidence to appear and respond in that menacing way, and yet it was a game! The animal knew not to take it too far and the animal knew it was a whole bit of confidence building in that he brings out in the animal. It had a lot to do with his tone and his mannerism. If he wanted an animal to be portrayed in a happy manner – his whole mannerism will be happy. He'll be "Good boy. Can you be happy? Good!" and see how the animal responds to that. Now, in the more serious scenes, he'd bring down his demeanour, and he'd say, "You stay right there. You watch me. Put your head down and watch. Look at me. Look at me" and the dog would just bring out a whole different emotion, you know, just watching his body language. My father was very, very physical in his working with the dogs and I mean that in a sense that he'd be hopping around on set and jumping around, getting the dog's attention. I mean, he really did put all of his physicality into it, and in return the animal gave that performance back.

DANIEL HUGH KELLY: Sadly one of the dogs died overnight. I have talked to people who have owned large breed dogs and they have all told me that dogs such as St. Bernards are susceptible to their stomach getting turned. This was definitely not because they got excited, it's just the sad truth that large dogs this big are susceptible to this kind of thing. I remember Karl was just devastated. I had a couple of drinks with him at the bar when this had happened and he was just distraught. It really made me appreciate, not only the work that this guy and these beautiful dogs did, but just the connection and friendship he had with these animals. It was so tough on him when that dog died.

CONRAD E. PALMISANO: These were Roger Corman days. It could have maybe been *Piranha* or things like that. Lewis Teague could have been there on *Piranha* doing some other little things, because people came in and did these things in the Roger Corman world, right.

The assistant camera crew adjust the Panaflex for the next shoot.

CHARLES BERNSTEIN: Well, each one of these – we can call them a monster... the villain in horror movies – it can be a dog, it can be a menacing spirit, that you mentioned, it can be nightmare monster, it can be an actual human being. I did a movie called *Love, Lies and Murder* (1991) – I think a six-hour mini-series, where the dark character was actually a very ordinary, you know, father and husband kind of guy, but he was as evil as any of these monsters. So, each one of these kinds of characters needs a musical presence that serves a number of purposes being able to represent that force, when that force isn't present on screen, much the same way John Williams famously evoked the shark in *Jaws*! Something that even when the monster isn't there reminds us of the presence of the monster... it's that function. And there is also the function of trying to

301

present an aspect of that dark force that is all that dark, you know, so that it humanizes or gives that at least dimension to the evil force that is just not 100 per cent darkness. And then that theme has to interact with the other elements of the film, so it's usually a very challenging job to come up with a representation of darkness. I think in the case of *Cujo*, the dog itself and the hunting horn idea kind of helped out, you know, so it tied more to the dog, but one tried to have a connection to the actual force.

A NEW MORNING: Vic wakes up in a hotel room, a newspaper boy delivers the world's problems and Tad shares "The Monster Words" with his mother

Opening on the hot sun rising over the mountain plains that surround the Camber farm, this next sequence begins with Donna waking up from her first night stuck out in isolation and coming face to face with a snarling Cujo. She is startled by the image of this bloodied and ravaged dog who sits at her driver's seat window, staring into her eyes and patiently waiting for an opportunity to attack. Unlike other ecologically themed horror movies involving dogs such as *Dogs* and *The Pack*, *Cujo* brings the horror home to the domestic interpersonal, rather than being about societal flaws and a response to animal neglect as seen in those two major contributions to the subgenre of not only natural horror but of *dogsploitation* horror. *Dogs* explores the notion of science infiltrating and influencing the nature of the Californian canine community whilst also commenting on student unrest and university campus politics that permeated seventies sensibilities, and *The Pack* dealt with the repercussions of abandonment and forces the natural order to take on the human populous (represented by two sets of "families") while enforcing concepts of rationalizing within the human experience. *Cujo* brings this subgenre of horror out of the social/political and dives head first into the personal, and this is something

303

that will happen within the eighties coming out of the ecologically aware seventies, where family-centric dramas will merge with horror. Films such as *Ordinary People* (1980) and *Endless Love* (1981) will deliver melodrama in dark terms, and horror movies would lead the way for these pictures to embrace such grim realisms such as *The Amityville Horror, The Shining, Poltergeist* and *Cujo*.

With the camera panning across from the front of the Pinto and landing on a sleeping Donna who wakes to confront her "monster", the new morning sequence is quiet and restful. Cutting to Vic waking up in the comfort of a hotel room to a buzzing alarm, the stress levels are building, as he once again calls through to his household, desperate to find his wife. A picturesque crane shot glides over the Trenton household and the glorious beachside view as a young newspaper boy delivers the world's problems. This lovely juxtaposition of a child bringing forth news (be it bad or good or neither) and Vic trying to call through to connect with his wife, is a poignant response to the failure to communicate which is an ongoing theme cemented within the narrative and subtextual construct of *Cujo*. The issue of miscommunication and the dangers of putting too much faith into the "signal" is a thematic element that would pierce the fibre of the previous horror outing from actress Dee Wallace in *The Howling*. The following moments of this morning sequence has Donna resting on the idea that "when the mailman comes, we'll go home", and here this dishevelled, hot and bothered woman relies on the prospect of the bringer of the world's news (amongst other things) will help bridge a gap between her predicament and a re-entry into normalcy and the centred universe. The image of the Camber's mailbox precedes Donna's promise to Tad in a perfectly established precursor to a sombre and contemplative scene.

After another failed attempt at starting the car, Donna sees Tad reading his "Monster Words" and asks what they are. Tad seems reluctant to hand them over (these are for him and his father) but Donna pleads with him. She grabs hold of the sheet of paper with only seconds later Tad asking for it back, as the water situation is remarked upon and is completely dire. The magic in this sequence is the fact that Tad reads them in a quiet whisper while we bear witness to the rabid Cujo staggering across the filthy earth. As Tad recites the mantra that keeps monsters at bay, this vicious and child-hungry ravenous dog crosses through the once familiar farm, and Donna concocts some ideas of her own. She spots Brett Camber's baseball bat and contemplates an idea – this sad image of the bat not being played with and left abandoned on the ground is a picture of despair blended with possible glimmers of hope and inspiration.

The black Labrador used in the St. Bernard costume.

DANNY PINTAURO: I think it's really interesting because in hindsight, I know the story is much more intricate than it was at the time, especially because I had no connection to the book. Now I have more of a connection to the book and I understand the layers of the book that weren't added to the movie, such as the dog being the embodiment of another character. I've never gotten around to reading the book! I should really get around to reading the friggin' book!

ROBERT CLARK (SFX): There was a point in the movie where Lewis wanted a big crane shot where the dog was stalking Dee Wallace. He wanted a long shot and the trainers had to be yards away giving the dog the gestures, and that's where they felt they could have used the costume on the Labrador. The black Labrador that was used in *Cujo* was a superstar, he had this fantastic proud attitude. I mean Kathie and I made a test suit for the Labrador that he would get used to and understand its weight and some restrictions, but I don't remember if I ever saw him in the suit! Kathie would have been there for fittings, while I was at the workshop.

KATHIE CLARK (SFX): We did a costume for a dog as well. Funnily enough I had done this before on *Deadly Eyes* (1982). It is such a crack up because there really is not a set pattern for a dog, you just have to take a quick muslin pattern to get the right sizes happening, and then where his legs would fall and then a zipper up the tummy, so that you could drop the fur suit over him and drop his legs into each hole. *Deadly Eyes* was good preparation for *Cujo*. I thought I could make one costume for *Deadly Eyes* that would fit all the dogs, but that wasn't the case. Then they had attitudes! So some of the dogs needed more gussets under their front legs so they could move better, and other dogs didn't care so they moved easily in their rat costume skins. On *Cujo*, I remember the trainer Jackie Martin was in charge of the black Labrador. She brought the dog in and showed us how well trained he was. I mean this dog would take every one of her

Animal trainer Jackie Martin with Karl Lewis Miller and Sheriff Bannerman stunt double. Along with "Daddy", one of the St. Bernards used to play Cujo.

Jackie Martin and "Daddy"

commands, if she was to say "Show teeth" he would, if she said "OK growl" he would. He was amazing. Robert and I had nothing to do with the St. Bernards however. We went to Jackie's place and I remembered how well trained this dog was, I mean he went from looking sweet and then straight into looking viscous. I have worked with a lot of animals and you don't really have an opportunity to hang out with them, they're there to do a job also – they have their focus to work on. Except on *Deadly Eyes* we did have some time to play with the Dachshunds that were playing the giant rats, I mean they were small and there were a lot of them. But I still had to do my job – one of the funniest things about that was when I put the little rat costumes on these dogs they would stand there frozen thinking they couldn't move, then they would realize that they could and they were great. They were very happy. And it was hysterical to watch these dogs run in swarms, and they would get into little rumbles and bite each other's costumes, they were very cute. I also worked on *The Island of Dr. Moreau* (1977) which featured a bear, a lion, a tiger and other wild animals, and even though they're trained, they're still wild animals. So you have to be careful and not goof around because you can get bitten. Sadly I didn't get to be on the set for *Cujo*, which is upsetting, that would have been very interesting.

TONY RICHMOND: I mean Peter was devastated, I mean you don't do things this way. You don't just fire someone because it rained, that is just insane. I mean Dan Blatt was crazy. He was not the most attractive man and he had pockmarked skin. I remember it was pouring rain one day and we were in the hotel and went up to a mirror and started picking at his scarred skin and he said "You know, I used to be very attractive before I came into this business." I just roared with laughter. It was totally insane.

CONRAD E. PALMISANO: Karl Miller had trained the dogs and they were way, way on the movie before I was invited in. The critter cage is apparently a cage that you put a toy in for the dog to attack. You can't put

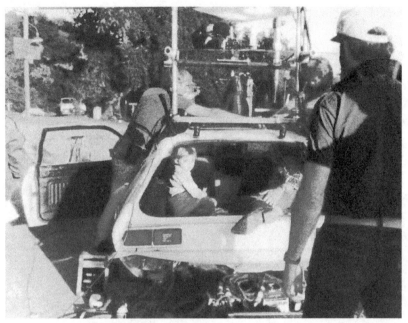

Setting up the scene with Danny Pintauro at the back of the disassembled Pinto. (courtesy of Danny and Margaret Pintauro).

a squirrel in a cage and get the animal to attack the squirrel in the cage, but something must have happened, because when we went into filming with the St. Bernards there would be a female trainer who would get into the back seat with the critter cage and show the St. Bernard the critter cage and then she would go and make noises, and that's when – whatever the dog was, and we had several to make Cujo – he'd be pawing at the windshield and going crazy, trying to get to the critter cage. So whatever they were doing they were making phoney noises and the St. Bernard would go berserk trying to get inside to where the critter cage was. And that is how they got all of those attacking scenes! The dog wanted the critter cage! They put like a little fur ball thing of something in there and the female trainer would make the noise for the critter cage and have something in there so the dog could see something, and like, she's hiding in the back seat, she would sit up and show the critter cage, so the dog who is standing up on the hood of the car, and she would duck down and make the noise "Eeeee Eeeeee Eeeee Eeee" and the dog would then paw at the windshield and fight to want to get into the car to get to the critter cage.

"HOLD MAIL 'TIL NOTIFIED": George Meara saves a trip

In Stephen King's somewhat convoluted draft of the screenplay, there are a number of scenes that precede mailman George Meara not delivering Joe Camber's goods to his farm. In the King draft, Meara is seen delivering mail to a Castle Rock local and then as he leaves, he calls her a welfare cheat and farts loudly (declaring his flatulence for her). Later, Meara does the same to his mailman base operator Rick (an off screen character) who he refers to as a "bald asshole". In King's draft, Meara is presented as a bitter and cantankerous loon who resents people and possibly hates his job which he has had for many years – in the final film, he is a minor character, completely there to serve his role as a local with an established job. What is interesting to note however, is that in King's draft, there is a major detour written that moves us away from Donna and Tad being trapped in their dead Pinto, making way for a succession of scenes that lead into Meara getting close to the "whereabouts" of the recently killed Joe Camber.

Before Meara reaches Gary Pervier's farmhouse, King writes of Steve Kemp breaking into the Trenton home and trashing it ("Go and be God's gift to women somewhere else huh?") and Vic and Roger Breakstone having yet another conversation about the Sharp account and Donna being missing in action. King has Meara reach Gary's house where he spots Joe's truck. On his transistor radio, he lets Rick know that he could leave the goods for Joe at Gary's place to save him the trip of heading out to the Camber farm, only to have Rick remind him that Joe had requested a hold on his mail anyway. This would have proved to be an interesting sequence on film, which may have had the audience yell at the screen to have the old crotchety mailman to go and explore Gary's house and therefore report the deaths of these two men. However, this would not be filmed at all, and what we are left with is a far superior and cleaner plot development.

In Barbara Turner's adaptation, the Meara the mailman sequence comes to surface in a far more swift, direct and alert method – she sets up the scene right after the weary and exhausted Donna explains to Tad that "We can go home when the mailman comes". Turner sets up, what truly is the horror of circumstance. *Cujo* is essentially a celebration of realism – a methodically plotted, melodramatic horror story that utilizes the narrative structure of circumstantial situation as its basis for its tension, mounting terror and ultimate pay off. Every story element matters in *Cujo*, and this is one of its core strengths as a sturdy and tightly constructed realist horror story; although it readily fastens itself into allegorical, folkloric and metaphoric territory. In *Cujo*, everything that is written and conceived is a stepping stone that leads up to Donna and her little boy being trapped and under siege by the rabid St. Bernard – and this scene with George Meara is one of those stepping stones. It is a brief moment, but a swift sidebar and an incredibly reasonable example of carefully plotted exposition. The Castle Rock mail department has been told to "Hold mail 'til notified" by the Cambers, and therefore no one, not even weedy, ageing little George Meara will head out to that farm to find the mother and son held captive by the bloodthirsty rabid dog.

Opening on a large car part – which looks to be a blue bumper – we see Joe Camber's address: "Joe Camber Maple Sugar Rd Castle Rock ME 04017" on a United States postal service notice. It is collected by George Meara who heads out to tend his delivery route. He is however stopped in his tracks by Roger (an uncredited actor) who reminds him that the Cambers have asked to have their mail put on hold since they are away from Castle Rock (Charity and Brett in Connecticut and Joe, supposedly in Boston, but of course dead). Meara replies "My mind's going..." and thanks him for saving him a trip. The loaded line of "My mind's going" is a nice play on people who have worked for far too long in the same public service role, such as mail delivery. Stephen King revels in writing these small town characters who seem to live for their servitude and are stuck in permanent ruts – George Meara is no exception. He is getting old and starting to forget simple instructions, and this is something that the realism of *Cujo* serves; the concept of small town innocuousness slipping away into the vast void and recessions of forgetfulness.

Lewis Teague chooses to shoot the scene from a low angle, starting with Meara collecting the bumper and walking over to the door before he is stopped. The angle is reflective of the point of view of the St. Bernard (as if this monstrous beast is always watching). It is interesting to note that the mail serviceman that reminds Meara about the hold on the Camber mail is named Roger – he would share his name with Roger Breakstone. The concept of realism is centred in *Cujo* even to the point where characters that populate a story can share the same name (that in the "real" world, more than one man can be called Roger). Another factor here is the film's invested interest in the play on class; Roger Breakstone is a white collar worker, and here we have a literal blue collared worker in the mail serviceman: a division and polar opposite in two men who share only their namesake, and nothing more.

TERRY DONOVAN-SMITH: Robert Elross was the man who played the postal guy and he was a great character actor. I think his voice was also looped, so perhaps, much like me, they may have gotten the wrong guy from the audition! He was a wonderful presence and even though he does the scene with me and the garage and this one here, he leaves a wonderful impression.

FOR WHOM THE BELL TOLLS: A daytime call sends Cujo into a foaming frenzy

From an air-conditioned inner-city office to the thick blistering heat at the Camber farm, we cut back to the intensity and sheer terror of the siege. Waves of roasting warmth swim upward (an incredibly effective use of flames sitting under the camera's lens to evoke such sizzling scorch) and dance upon the image of the decrepit farm, made all the more ugly with a rabid St. Bernard marauding the premises. An extreme close up of Donna's weary eyes brings the terror directly home as she looks over to the Camber residence and then over at the sick Cujo who finds some refuge from the horrendous heat; his body racked with rabies and his mouth spewing out saliva by the gallon – the hydrophobia completely full blown and sending him into a vortex of dizzying madness. Donna prays "Get back in that barn, damn you..." but the dog sits and waits for some movement or noise to come from the dead Pinto. Startling these quiet images comes the ringing of the Camber telephone which pierces the sound design and ushers in a cacophony of high voltage sounds and musical accompaniment. Cujo darts his head up in an instant as he hears the deafening bell and we go straight into an incredibly well conceived and frightening moment of monstrous dog attacking mother and son.

315

Cujo gallops towards the ringing phone but stops in his tracks, not at all interested in chasing up the inanimate nuisance like last time, instead he decides to react violently against Donna and Tad in the Pinto. With masterfully controlled animal action from Karl Lewis Miller, the dog looks conflicted as to where to drive his fury (the phone or the car) and his mind is made up when he sprints towards the busted up Pinto driving all of his energy and powerful force towards the car's door. He tears through the plains and rams his head right into the car, smashing the panel and dinting the metal with sheer determination and vicious zeal. Shaking the car like a demonic force, Donna and Tad cower in the corner of the car trembling with absolute fear. Tad screams in horror, but Donna covers his mouth to stop him from making loud sounds that will add to Cujo's rage ("it makes him angry!") but the dog is relentless in his attack. He thrashes the car about like it was an oversized toy, he throws his body up from the ground and lunges at the window placing his large paws within the tiny gap of the window that once let in air and plods down to bring him closer to the flesh, he leaps upon the roof of the car and pushes down onto the windscreen clawing at it and jumps down off the car to survey the petrified woman and her child. The image of Cujo's bloody snout pushing through the window and snapping at the tormented Tad is a wonderful nightmare-inducing picture of monster personified and a child in the most vulnerable state. Dee Wallace's performance is electrifying: her expressions, physicality and honest take on a woman under siege by a two hundred pound killer screams out a thousand emotions running wild at once – when she cowers as Cujo runs up the top of the car causing the shambolic wreck to quiver, it is sheer cinematic magic.

Cujo bringing himself to his feet and charging once again at the car knocking off the door handle from the inside is a magnificent multi-edged tribute to brilliant editing skill and storytelling as well as insight into the character of this crazed dog. Cujo will stop at nothing. He will even crash his own skull into a hard metallic car in order to kill this woman and her child. His care for his own personal safety is out the door – something that is completely driven by the disease of rabies, as healthy dogs would never jeopardize their own personal safety. Cujo will then rip off the other door handle from the outside, causing two doors to be jarred and enforcing this woman and her small boy to be trapped for even longer. Cujo's reign of terror is a phenomenally conceived piece of horror cinema – not only does the sequence here terrify, but it pushes its human characters and its canine killer to the limit, giving Cujo a permanent place at the table of fellow movie monsters and Donna Trenton and Tad iconography just as much.

Dee Wallace and Danny Pintauro play off one another's tremendous fear in vivid honesty. Pintauro twists and turns in absolute terror, now stripped down to simply his shorts and rolled around in Wallace's nurturing but shaking arms, the image of mother and child thrown about and turned into a sweaty mess is confronting and harrowing. The film is a visceral and challenging film to endure, and this is its sublime power – it startles and forces its audience to be in there with Donna/Dee Wallace and Tad/ Danny Pintauro as they struggle to not only stay safe, but to remain sane. The nastiness of the sequence is nothing short of brilliant: the visions of blood smeared upon the car's doors, the grottiness of the paw prints on the windscreen, the foam and goo flicking around from the dog's snapping and snarling mouth, the high intensity of Donna and Tad covered in sweat and exhausted from the heat falling into suffocation and dehydration as well as exposure to the elements and their sheer terror at the thought of being mauled and killed by such a ceaselessly agitated and ferocious dog. As the monstrousness of Cujo is well blossomed and complete, so is the tragedy within the Pinto as Tad clings to dear life to his mother, contorted into a position akin to an epileptic fit. He mutters "I want to go home..." sobbing profusely, while Donna holds him tight, praying for the horror to end. This is poignant filmmaking at its best – a driven scene, a terrifying scene, a relentlessly violent and uncompromisingly mean spirited scene that is finely executed with cinematic acuteness and precision.

317

LEWIS TEAGUE: Well, I forget exactly how many dogs we had... we had nine dogs. And we also had a man in a dog suit, and a mechanical dog head. And there were scenes when we used all of the above. For example, there is a scene where the dog charges the car and smashes into the side, denting the door. We used a real St. Bernard to run at the car and then the mechanical dog head for an insert of it smashing into the door... no, then also a shot of a man in the dog suit throwing himself at the door; because you could never get the dog to run towards the car if the door was actually in place, because its natural instinct would be to slow down well before he hit the car. So we took the doors off the car, we took the front seat out, position the camera directly in front of the car so you couldn't see that the doors were missing. Then had a dog that was trained to run and jump up into the car. It was a real dog running towards the car, jumping into it. Then I could change the angle so you could see the door was actually there and had Gary in the dog suit just jumping towards the door, just for a flash cut: five or six frames. Then a close shot of the mechanical dog head smashing into the side of the door buckling the metal. And you cut inside with Dee Wallace screaming and cut back outside to a real dog which we position on the ground and then frame the shot to see him struggling back to his feet. So when you cut all those things together with the proper sound effects and flash cuts, it looked like the dog was actually hitting the car, but it was a combination. A montage of shots.

ROBERT CLARK: There was the dolly dog who crashed into the side of the car – he head butted the car. It was just a lever in its head and it rolled and slammed into the car. That puppet head was definitely used in the film, I mean the editing makes it look so great, and it works so good. I had made a hand-held head and shoulders with a full mouth piece that would snarl and bite and that was used in a lot of the over the shoulder shots and also in the attack scenes. We also did the head piece for the guy in the dog suit.

ALEXANDER WITT: For a lot of the running shots we had a St. Bernard suit that we put on a black Labrador. This was done because St. Bernards really don't run that fast, and we needed a dog with great speed. And the suit worked as far as I remember. The whole movie involved a combination of dogs, we used the St. Bernards and then the Labrador in the costume.

GARY MORGAN: It was the dog running towards the car and what they did was they dug a starting block in the dirt with a foot racer and blocks so that I had something to push off of. It was just that last couple of feet of the dog actually hitting the door. So what they did was they had me right off camera, and the camera had a close up of the door and put blood on my head, then they had a fake door that had a light metal, so that when I hit it, it crumbled. It wasn't a real car door – it was a fake skin so that when I hit it, it would just crumble, because I couldn't dent the car door with my head! I remember as soon as they gave me this starting block and got rolling, all I could think was "Here comes the pain!"

TERESA ANN MILLER: The puppet head itself was great. I know one place that it was used for sure was in the log when the dog goes chasing the rabbit and the bat lands on his nose and bites his nose – that was the dummy head, of course, with a real bat. I also know that they used another puppet head on wheels that they rammed into the car door when he was denting it. Now they also taught the dog to approach the car with its head down – because you just don't want a dog running towards the car, now cut into the dummy dog banging its head. So what they did in training was they built a type of doggy door and taught the dog to hit it with his head to open it. It was quite a heavy door. So now when they were ready to shoot that scene they could shoot the dog from front going towards camera and you see him tuck his head which cuts into the dummy dog hitting into the metal door and that was another tip that he used when training in that particular scene.

The St. Bernard puppet head as the point of discussion.

PATRUSHKHA MIERZWA: I was responsible for capturing the original production sound and getting it to the mixer. We tried to get some sessions with the dogs – I think we were allowed one. Danny Pintauro was professional and experienced and I marvelled at his knowledge and artistic talent. He was fun to be with on the set. Dee also. The farm is where the dogs worked. We were told to stay away from them because, as a breed, they are ornery, difficult to train and unpredictable. And Karl Miller didn't want anyone distracting them. I don't think he was pleased to see a boom operator on the set. There were scenes with the actors before Cujo turned ugly; Karl's way of working was to talk to the dog constantly until "Cut". Mark (mixer) conferred with Lewis about it ruining the dialogue and suggested we try a system to allow both the dog commands and lines of dialogue; Karl felt he couldn't do that and Lewis didn't even want to try.

Filming in and around the Pinto.

MARK ULANO: Dee was lovely to work with and we got together after hours.

PATRUSHKHA MIERZWA: Stephen King played the preacher in *Pet Sematary* (1989) and I have a picture of me booming him from below the frame for his eulogy. I got a kick out of him being there. He was easy-going and pleasant, not a diva, as far as I could tell. I don't believe he came to the set of *Cujo*. Each project has its own mien. *The Slumber Party Massacre* (1982) was my first feature and the crew worked as a coherent company and the director, Amy Jones, was decisive, practical and personable. She got to know the crew and kept a pleasant, focused atmosphere. She trusted everyone to do their job and appreciated input. There was humor on the set and respect for each other's work. I knew then that I wanted to stay in film. *Pet Sematary* was another odd one – does a Stephen King script pick the person or does a certain kind of person pick the Stephen King script? The camera crew was fired after a few days on this movie as well. Then a Paramount rep came and once the suits come, you know things are going to be interesting. The crew had bonded by the time the new cameraman came so that was not as disruptive to the set.

The child actor on that Miko Hughes and I were very close; I was his first three syllable word (Pa-trush-kha); he called me Pa-chook-a. The *Cujo* and *Pet Semtary* directors were similar in their mental state and attitude towards the crew. I remember booming Stephen on *Pet Sematary* because he played the priest, giving a prayer at the cemetery. I spent a minute radio mic'ing him but we didn't really talk. He didn't chat with the crew.

JEAN COULTER (stunts): The makeup girl dressed me with blood and some makeup, but it wasn't a lot. It was time consuming to have to stop shooting and go in and put the blood on and all that, it wasn't that necessary because it was so frantic and quick. My leg needed the most dressing of blood because that is the close-up where the dog bites into my thigh.

TERESA ANN MILLER: I think the biggest challenge was for Dee Wallace. Also the rain kept crashing down on set and that would have been hellish just from the makeup aspect of it because that is the big distraction for the animal as well that people don't realise. Just the fact that the dogs want to go roll on the grass and get rid of the makeup – they don't like to stay dirty. That is the whole other training aspect of it, that you don't think of – that teaching a dog to wear all this makeup without taking it all off. When you put goop on his eyes and make it run, and you have all this stuff on his face, typically a dog wants to take it off. And that is just another whole aspect of this show that there is just so many different things that made it such a challenge; not only did you have to work the dog and get that performance from him, but now you have to give him a distraction of the blood, the makeup, the stuff in his eyes, everything else that he has to forget about in order to portray that character. So, I mean, it is just such a challenge, let alone the crew and camera and the lights and the distractions and all the microphones and everything else. I mean, when you take out all the opticals that we have to work with, an animal has to be taught to ignore the rest of the cast, let alone him looking at the trainer, mind that he is not looking at all these other things. The typical animal on the set is going to look and think what's that microphone above my head? And what's that camera movement behind me? Who is the person in the shadows with the lights on? And who's this? And what's this noise over here? And what's this sound effect? And when you think of all those things and think of the work we do, allows the animal to confidently stand in the middle of all this activity and ignore it, and perform and relay our emotions for that character – that's amazing in itself! I am a huge fan of movies. And I'm a huge fan of animals in movies. I love being on set. I laugh, you know. It's funny. I laugh. I enjoy it so much – including the work that I do.

Animal trainer Karl Lewis Miller has his dog look ferocious, however, the St. Bernard would simply be barking and clawing for his toy which would be hidden inside the Pinto.

Mother and child terrified and trapped by a rabid St. Bernard.

DANNY PINTAURO: I remember working with the trainers a lot, but it was this weird backwards relationship where I was not allowed to talk to the dog, and in turn I never really talked to the trainers. The trainers were trying to focus on the dog. So there was this whole level of the movie happening around me, but I was literally not permitted to interact with them. It doesn't make any sense! So, you know, there is this intense thing happening with the trainers while they are trying to get the dogs to do what they want to, and I'm not a part of that at all. I remember the dog got into the car in one take and they had always set it up where you can't see both of the car doors. One of them is always open, and there are people at the other end ready to pull Dee and I out of the car if the dog actually grabbed hold of us. So that happened and they pulled us out and it was this huge scary moment for the crew, but I was laughing hysterically because the dog was chewing on the little mouse in the cage thing in the car. I was like, "He doesn't care about us! He just wanted the toy!" I just couldn't stop laughing. I was like, "You guys, I am fine! Dee is fine! The doggy doesn't want to bite us! Look! He just wants his toy!" It made me laugh, because they were all so freaked out, but I was in hysterics! Those dogs were so sweet. I loved them. But like a Seeing Eye dog, you weren't allowed to play with them, so that was frustrating!

MICHAEL HILKENE: Because of overlaps in the car attacks, portions of Dee Wallace and Danny Pintauro's performances also had to be ADR'd. We came up with an intricate plan designed to be able to utilize as much of the original performances as possible by dovetailing in and out the production tracks and the ADR. The key, as with most ADR, is matching pitch and intensity. Good sync on the ADR was a bit more important in those days than today, where computer programs give us the tools and the latitude to put most ADR recordings in sync. Most of the ADR that we used for Dee Wallace was in the scenes when Cujo attacked her and Danny Pintauro in the car. Teague directed her performance on the stage and she was absolutely spectacular, matching her performance to a T. On the other hand, we were faced with a problem when it came to ADR'ing sections of Danny Pintauro's performance because of overlaps and clip-offs during the attacks. As it turned out, Danny, who was six or seven at the time, had become somewhat traumatized by St. Bernards during filming. The word was that we needed to avoid Danny having to look at Cujo on the screen during the ADR session. So, we came up with a great plan for recording sections of his screaming and whimpering. There were three baffles on the stage. On ADR stages, baffles are small walls normally used to isolate voices. They were approximately 8' tall and 4' wide and were on rollers. One of the baffles had a small window in it so that an actor could watch the screen. We made a small booth using the baffle with the window facing the screen and the other two baffles as sides. The rear of the booth was open to the back of the room. The sound inside the three-sided enclosure replicated to a good degree the resonant sound inside the Ford Pinto. The plan was for Dee to hold Danny in her arms with his head over her right shoulder, facing away from the screen. He was miked in that position. She would watch the action on the screen and, depending on how hard she squeezed Danny, he would vary the intensity

325

of his screams. Even though the goal was to get a take that matched up perfectly, there was no way that was going to happen. Fortunately, Lewis made sure that we had plenty of takes where Danny had matched his intensity and tone. The problem with the recordings was that they still weren't in sync. From there, my job was to put together a number of options of Danny's performance for Lewis to select from. Because screams are like musical notes, changing in volume and sometimes in pitch, they were often tricky to edit. In the eighties, we didn't have the tools available in most of today's professional sound editing programs that simplify shortening and lengthening sound. So, even though the pitch and the intensity of Danny's performance was great, finding spots to edit the screams so that they would match the visuals of his mouth without creating noticeable sound edits was a tedious task. I put together three options for Lewis. If memory serves me correctly, when it came to mixing Danny's ADR into the Cujo attacks, Lewis ended up using different parts of the three options. At any rate, when it was all said and done, where we transitioned in and out of production sound and ADR throughout the picture is barely perceptible. In the eighties there were normally three mixers on a dubbing stage. Ray West was the Dialogue Mixer, Bob Glass handled the music, and the late David Hudson mixed the sound effects, backgrounds and foley. To be safe, we decided to keep all of Cujo's vocals separated from the sound effects, so we mixed his tracks onto their own channel. It wasn't until we made the Printmaster that we combined the Cujo vocals with the rest of the sound effects.

PATRUSHKHA MIERZWA: It was bloody difficult working with Jan de Bont. Jan kept an auto zoom in one hand and he didn't share information; I watched the zoom as we dollied and moved in and out if I could see the focal length. Jan changed the zoom every take. It seemed no one near me was really getting valid information, so I just imagined the shots for most of the movie.

MARK ULANO: It was my fourth or fifth time working with Jan. He worked in a European fashion, always fluid, shots were always floating or adjusting which created a documentary style environment.

ALEXANDER WITT: The makeup was part of it and it was hot during the day. Because it was all desert land it gets very cold at night. The camera would do a lot of the work, there would be lighting to make it look hot. There would orange filters and filters used to make the scenes look hot. In those days you did a lot of on-camera and we used 85D filters and changed them to be warmer and added a little more orange and then in the final print you could make it even warmer than that.

MARGARET PINTAURO: They made Danny look a lot whiter but I remember there being very little makeup used. The mornings were very cold. But of course they had to make Danny and Dee look like they were sweating in the car.

ALEXANDER WITT: There was one episode with Jan where he got very angry. I couldn't see the way he was holding the camera, which was a Panaflex, and he started shouting at me "Turn it on! Turn it on!" because the dog was charging at us. And I started yelling back at him, and in all honesty, that's where some kind of respect was given to me from Jan. He liked the fact that I screamed back at him. He was tough and very tough with the crew. He was always yelling and getting angry with them. His brother Peter de Bont who worked with me and Lewis on *The Jewel of the Nile* (1985) was on the set of *Cujo* and the two of them would get into fights. But Jan got along very well with Lewis who was a very calm man, a very mannered director. Their working relationship was excellent.

MICHAEL HILKENE: Later on, we recorded some subtler sounds and breathing from Daddy and Moe. Those recordings came in handy for some of Cujo's lower key stuff. I've got to hand it to Lewis Teague. He was absolutely right about the St. Bernard vocals. Thanks to him, Karl Lewis Miller, and of course Bernie, Daddy and Moe, I had a phenomenal Cujo library that worked for 95 per cent of the picture.

KATHIE CLARK: What I remember most was that we built a dog head that was stuck onto a rolling cart so he could smash into the side of the car. He was just a head, but I built a partial body just in case the camera got back a little bit and the audience would see the cart. That way they could really push this dog head very hard into the car. That head was fibreglass. We had at least three big St. Bernard heads – one was built for the Labrador.

NANCY G. FOX: I remember the St. Bernard costume, it worked very well. The costume was designed to be shot in flashes so the audience couldn't tell where the real dog started and ended and where the man in the costume started and ended. I thought the end result was incredibly well done.

TERESA ANN MILLER: My father showed up in Santa Rosa and I wasn't on set at all, so it wasn't something we did local in town that we could see for ourselves. I'm not familiar with stuff on the set at all. The car gags, the bat and the rabbits… he was just so grateful to have had Dee Wallace to work with and to trust and she had a lot of faith in him to try everything safely as well. Ed Lauter – and that whole cast – had faith in my dad. Lewis Teague was amazing. His vision and his cooperation was the inspiration for the whole project. He really brought the team together and it's really something that his proudest moment was *Cujo* – it was such a great accomplishment, in so many ways. Dad always joked about how he gave the breed such a bad name and then redeemed himself with *Beethoven*. He always thought that was funny. He said, "I finally redeemed myself in everything I did for the breed back in the eighties! I finally made it okay to have St. Bernard's again, in *Beethoven!*"

DANIEL HUGH KELLY: Karl was very quiet and very professional. Since *Cujo* I had done a lot of movies and TV shows that involved animals and I have never worked with a trainer as amazing as Karl. This guy cared about his animals, and he knew them intimately. At that kind of knowledge and that kind of experience is incredibly vital for what Lewis wanted to do. Lewis and Karl became very close and that was another ingredient that was incredibly interesting to watch. I mean, Lewis was directing this film and he had to truly trust Karl and Karl has to trust him, and fundamentally the trust rested on the dogs being looked after and not at all abused. And it was such an interesting dynamic to watch play out. It is so close to the way in which a director would work with a choreographer. If one of them is wrong then you have your leading lady there holding a child, so this could go south really quickly! I mean you think of St. Bernards and you think of them with a barrel around their necks trekking the Alps helping people, but they can also be pretty frickin' mean!

TERESA ANN MILLER: I would say most of what I learned from my father was shown in my experience with *Inspector Rex*. In those fifteen years I taught things that had never been done and shown on TV. A lot of people in the U.S.A. don't know the show, it wasn't popular like it was in Europe. Rex was a very emotional character. So that is where I really got the opportunity to do a lot of the emotion emitting in the work with the German Shepherd and anything from the police officer being killed and showing that sad emotion and the anger emotion and what have you. I was never in the position to bring it out in that way in *White God*. I mean, for me, that was a level of Karl Miller, you know what I mean? That was very typical of his type of working I had been able to portray that level of Jekyll and Hyde character in a show. I took from and referred to him – I mean, I still do, all the time, you know – and I work animals in a way in the same sense that he did and that is because from what I learned.

JEAN COULTER: For the most part it was a matter of playing with the dog, and the audience would have no idea that this dog was just playing and looking for his toy which was hanging around my neck. So when I was working with the dog outside the car, he would run at me and play with me. But on film with the editing and sound and camera angles, it looks terrifying, and looks as though he is attacking me. It was all playing for the dogs on set, they were having a great time.

KATHIE CLARK: Bob and I worked with Peter Knowlton who rented an apartment and laid cardboard all over the floor. We set up our shop at this apartment. We had his kitchen which was very convenient to use as well as a small garage that we could use for all our chemicals. This is where we built the dogs. There is an inkling of a memory about Rob Bottin being approached to work on *Cujo*, but I don't really remember.

ROBERT CLARK: I don't remember Rob Bottin being approached for *Cujo*. But in conversation with Peter, who was closer to production, he would have had more knowledge on that. It was a very tight knit industry at that time. It was brand new. As far as being acknowledged it started being a separate department. It was a lot of fun back then.

CHRISTOPHER MEDAK: The prosthetic dogs were incredible. The layers that were available to us were minimal but we made it work. Bob and Kathie Clark were great, they had built a dog that would lunge at the car. And also a suit for a black Labrador who was used for leaping, because St. Bernards can't leap. This dog was used to leap through doors and windows.

ROBERT CLARK: I definitely read the book before the movie came out, but I only read the book because we did the film. I never read it before we got the job. Peter Knowlton called and said that he had this job happening and that was the first time I had heard of *Cujo*. I don't recall if he mentioned that it was a Stephen King story, but I really don't think I was familiar with it beforehand.

VERN NOBLES: It's incredibly dark – the movie. That just has to do with the director and how they direct… and Dee was really good! When she was in the car and she was so hot and miserable – she really was miserable. So that helped, but we had a really big rainstorm and all the trucks got stuck and we couldn't move them for two days. There were a lot of problems on the movie. Being low-budget, it had its issues like when all of our trucks got stuck and we couldn't move them. When we were trying to move from the house to the hill to the other location because they had – basically we had two days where we had no equipment. I mean, you could see that everything was stuck! Jan wanted to use all the newest, coolest lights, and they didn't have the money for it. Peter really had an image for the movie and an idea of how he was going to go. I mean, it was just the first few days that went way over and production freaked out. He would have been a better director. Peter Medak actually did a lot of the camera moving and things that Jan later introduced… but with him, there was lot of not defined scenes, it was kind of strange, like he couldn't understand how the audience was going to understand it, but he saw the bigger picture… when it's all together you will. He made it more like a Stephen King mystery than just a hardcore horror movie, you know. When Lewis came in it turned into more of a horror movie.

TONY RICHMOND: Peter Medak and Dan Blatt didn't get along, they clashed. Peter is amazing, and even though many producers have told him in the past that there wasn't enough time to do what he initially set out to do, he always managed. We both did. Peter is an incredible director and so good with actors, and actors love him. It's all about story and performance, and when you get actors who adore the director it is wonderful. And he has a great eye and a great story sense. He and Dan Blatt were just not meant to be together. Peter has a sense of humor, and

Dan didn't have one at all. There wasn't enough time to do *Cujo* properly and when Peter mentioned that, that totally upset Dan. Peter was correct here, and Dan wasn't the sort of producer that could sit down and work things out – he wasn't resourceful enough to manage his time. Dan would get hysterical; there were a lot of triggers there.

ALEXANDER WITT: *Cujo* was not storyboarded. It was mostly thinking on our feet as far as how the shots went. In those days, most people didn't use storyboards, they were mostly used in commercials.

TERESA ANN MILLER: Gary Morgan would stand in for the dog and do the dog stunts so that the actors could know kind of what the actions were and how to interact with the animals, sure.

GARY MORGAN: I spent a lot of time with the dogs of course. They didn't like the suit. There were about three dogs. The main dog was Cubby. Then they had a dog named Daddy and another one. Now, Karl's dog was Cubby. But what a lot of trainers do is they contract others trainers to get what they need. Karl trained Cubby, and he was the number one dog. Cubby was great! Daddy was a little mean. If you got up close to Daddy, he might bite you. They had another one that was a good jumper. Also, sadly, Cubby passed away, right after he bit Jean Coulter's nose, the next day he died! Sadly, what happened was something that large breed dogs like St. Bernards suffer from on occasion, and basically what it is is a twisted gut, where the stomach flips over and you can't really tell what it's doing or when it is happening. But healthy active large breed dogs can have this happen and it's tragic. So Karl just came to the kennels the next morning and the dog was dead. A lot of large dogs can get this even in the best of health, like Cubby was and Karl was an absolute mess. He loved these dogs so much. Also, he was on the wagon before that and hadn't been drinking, so he couldn't even numb his pain with booze. Well, after the dog died, I remember seeing dailies – we all went in – and Karl

Karl Lewis Miller pays with "Cubby" – one of the St. Bernards used to play Cujo - on location.

was just a wreck, that was his number one dog, it was his dog. So he was sobbing and he was really upset. After that we had to deal with Daddy. Now, Danny Pintauro was a sweet little kid, but he was really young! I think he was like six or seven! There were some scenes that were harrowing. They had a thing called the critter cage and it was like a little hamster cage where they would piece a piece of fur in it – they would shake it and the dog would go bananas trying to get this little "critter"! So they would like lay down in the car and the dog was outside and to try and get the dog agitated they would shake this little cage and the dog would go crazy! So they were like laying on the floor of the car and shaking the critter cage and the dog would try to get through the windshield, and they would go "Dig it up! Dig it up!" and the dog would be on the hood, and he would be like digging at the windshield, scratching the windshield, getting on the roof and just thinking of how to get to this critter cage. They got this dog

Daddy later on in the movie, when the dog is supposed to be really rabid, and they had him covered in blood. He had this weird stuff that was made out of egg whites – like froth that they were putting in his mouth – it was all edible stuff – to make him look like he was foaming at the mouth! Then they had this dog eye medicine that was yellow and they would put that down by his eyes so that it would look like his eyes were pussy. That dog would be going crazy! At one point the kid would like freak out and start crying, I mean this kid was hysterical. The producer wraps the kid in a blanket because it was freezing cold, even though it was supposed to be set in summer time. It was winter time however and it was cold and raining. It was pouring rain for weeks at a time, so there was a muddy yard, and the kid was cold and tired. The kid was supposed to wear like a pair of shorts. So the kid is crying and freaking out, and the producer grabs the kid, puts him in a blanket and takes him into the house and was calming him down and saying "Danny, you're safe in the car. The dog cannot get in the car. As long as you are in the car, you are safe. I promise you!" The kid calms down. They get the kid back into the car and the next take they had the window cracked open a little, like a story point, because they were trying to get air and it was supposed to be sweltering hot – so, it is the back window and they had it open a little bit. The dog is on the roof of the car and the very next take the dog looks down and he sees that the window is open, so he puts his paw in the window and slips and falls off the car; as he falls off the car his paw opens the window, the dog jumps in the car and is sitting in the back seat with the kid. The kid is clinging onto the roof like a cat! Okay, now the dog is sitting in the back seat wagging his tail like "Yay! Let's go for a ride!" The dog was not aggressive or scary at all, but scared Danny regardless!

TERESA ANN MILLER: The film was brilliant! I mean, it was terrifying! It was so believable and… oh my gosh, the adrenaline – watching them go through this, watching them suffer in that car and the torment by the dog, and such a massive dog which is what made it even more frightening! He could dent the car. He could try to get towards them. I mean it was such a brilliant film!

"Cubby" the dog is petted by trainer/owner Karl Lewis Miller in between takes.

"I NEED SOME SUGAR": Vic is distracted

The cityscape that can be seen through the advertising agency office window is not clarified; however it is a vast polar opposite to the rural terrain that traps Donna and Tad. Vic anxiously calls through in an attempt to find his wife, but there is no answer anywhere. He is distracted and nervous, riddled with anxiety and tension. He crosses through to his peers and sits down at the board table, completely lost in thought and concern. Headed by Roger Breakstone, the agents watch multiple TV sets with the Sharp Cereal Professor continually reassuring his viewers that there is "nothing wrong here". Roger breaks the tedium of this repetitive adage and calls out that the team is going to need an entirely new campaign. When he asks Vic what he thinks, Vic is lost in runaway thoughts about the whereabouts of Donna, and doesn't even respond. The world of business and economic stability is rendered meaningless and unimportant now in the faraway eyes of Vic Trenton, who will eventually abandon Roger and the Sharp account in order to reunite with his wife.

Cujo presents the world of advertising as a distraction and as a distancing device. It is not a tool that brings people together, instead it is an industry that provides a diversion and fuels the agitation and irritation in its characters. The closing moment of this cutaway from the siege has

337

Roger remark "I need some sugar" which makes commentary on the product he and Vic and the rest of the team peddle. It is something that reinforces the fact that *Cujo* is ultimately invested in what is pure and honest (fundamentally the love shared between mother and child as well as father and child) and that the "sugary" elements that surround it are distractions, fabricated illusions and personal detachments.

Worry about the Sharp cereal account grows.

ARTHUR ROSENBERG: I recall Daniel Hugh Kelly was not a happy camper but none of that was my business. I am not sure he and I would be the kind to "talk craft" together. Dee Wallace was terrific. I thought she was always professional, always nice and did a hell of a job with a very hard part. I had a lot of respect for her. She carried a reassuring calm as I recall. She impressed me. But, frankly my role was small and supporting so I don't recall very much. There was a nice wrap party in Santa Rosa and a good omelette restaurant. So many of the roles I did bring specific memories like *Coming Home* (1978) or *Being There* (1979) or *Footloose* (1984). *Cujo* to me was really a job. The part was not big enough to merit much and the shooting was not particularly eventful for me. I came, did my job, went home and looked for the next job. And was very

338

surprised to see what a hit it was. Interestingly enough my cousin, the rocker/songwriter/icon Al Kooper was and still is very close friends with Stephen King. For me, though, this was the next job really.

GARY MORGAN: I was on set before day one until the end of the movie. I was around for all of it. I'd been contracted for all pictures, so I was there for all the stuff. After that movie, I bought a house in Laurel Canyon and all of a sudden Daniel Hugh Kelly shows up at my door and he goes "I want to rent your guest house." He said "I just got a TV show called *Hardcastle and McCormick* and I'm moving here. When will the guest house be ready?" At this point the guest house wasn't even finished yet! Daniel goes "I'm checking into a hotel. I want to live in your guest house." He was determined to! So he lived in my house for two or three years after *Cujo*. We became friends on the movie and then he lived in my guest house for like a couple of years! I finally said, "You are making so much money on this series. Go buy yourself a house!" And he did!

WOMAN IN THE STORM: Donna and Cujo's confrontation leads to her being bitten

Stephen King would go on the record to say that the seed of inspiration that sparked his writing of "Cujo" was during a period he was having issues with his motorcycle and was advised to see a rural dwelling mechanic. This mechanic had a large breed dog that wasn't friendly and approached King baring teeth and growling, prompting the mechanic to warn him about the nature of the beast. King would then set out to write the novel (right off the point he had completed "The Dead Zone" and "Firestarter" (1980)) which would be one of his most bleak, claustrophobic and the first of which would not have a supernatural element – there was no psychic ability as seen in "The Dead Zone" or pyrokinetic little girls as featured in "Firsestarter". Here the book would open with "Once upon a time…" but it would betray the traditions of fairy tales by bringing the closing moments of the story to a dark and depressing finale, where Tad Trenton dies of dehydration and exposure.

In his novel of "Pet Sematary" (1983), Cujo would be referred to as a "dog that went rabid and killed four people" (the fourth being an inadvertent kill meaning Tad's tragic demise). The novel and film would become a referential point for many years to come and become part of the pop-cultural landscape popping up in reference everywhere from

TV sitcoms such as *Designing Women* (1986-1993) and *Mr. Belvedere* (1985-1990) and varied motion pictures from comedies such as *Moving Violations* (1985) to dramatic pieces such as the reimagining of King's *Salem's Lot* (2004). Funnily enough, in "On Writing: A Memoir of the Craft" (2000) (King's wonderful memoir and personal accounts on his craft) the author would make mention that he didn't remember writing "Cujo"; that the novel was conceived and delivered during a period he was drinking heavily. However, the book is one of his best and a poignant, personal, intelligent, terrifying and also moving piece that encapsulates not only the human condition, but the world of animals in relation to the world around them. In the novel, the scene here in question reads out like a power play tossed about between a mother trying to fend for herself and protect her child, and a St. Bernard lost in the misery of rabies and driven by an uncontrollable desire to kill.

Opening on a close-up of Donna Trenton's withered and weather-worn face – her eyes bearing black rings, her lip wet with sweat, her skin dry and sun damaged – this electrifying and horrific sequence begins quietly and builds up to a screaming frenzy where the "woman in the storm" is punished, marked by the devil and driven to insanity. Dee Wallace wears her passionate and sturdy heart on her sleeve here, as she goes through the sequence showcasing an array of intuitive emotional range. Here is an actress that delivers gold through a higher plain, working beyond the simple knowing the mark and knowing what to bring to the character. Her acting ability is supernatural, and from a plateau of otherworldliness and clairvoyance – with Dee Wallace there is a deep rooted spiritual grasp at in conception and delivery of her characters, and Donna Trenton is her finest moment among many.

Checking on the exhausted and overheated Tad, Donna decides to make an attempt at getting out of the car and making her way to the Camber household. The door handle is of course broken, but Donna turns into a resourceful heroine and remounts the gadget and pries the door open. She slowly creeps out of the car, closes the door behind her tight shut and scrutinizes the scene with careful intensity. Cujo lies behind the other side of the car, hot and bothered but determined to strike. Donna checks that the car door is secured to protect her sleeping boy and then drifts around the car, fighting the heat and scoping the surroundings, careful not to make a sound that would attract the ravenous and deadly two hundred pound dog that prowls the area.

Donna drops to the ground to check under the car, and as she does this we notice coming into frame behind her the bloodied and foam soaked snout of Cujo leading the front half of his body into frame. A horrifying close-up of the dog's face follows, baring teeth, glistening with fresh blood and eyes burning with hatred, fury, determination and bloodlust. Letting out a guttural growl, Jan de Bont's camera zooms in on the terrified Donna and the dog leaps into action attacking her. Here the film jumps right into what it does most magnificently, it delivers truly frightening moments of violence; visceral, bloody, ruthless, angry, loud, aggressive, brutal and relentless.

Now completely ravaged by the disease of rabies, Cujo sets out to terrorize mother and son trapped in the Pinto.

Cujo uses his great force to lunge at Donna, taking her down and tearing into her flesh. She pushes him back, hollering and fighting him off, as Tad – now woken with fright – peers over the car seat screaming in terror. Donna screams and kicks at the dog, while the frenzied animal rips through her pink blouse, mauls at her skirt and claws his way through her skin drawing blood. In a response to the concept of women taking self-defence lessons during the early eighties (something that would become increasingly more prevalent during the time), Donna brings her knee up to Cujo's penis and testicles and turns his angry barking and snapping into a quick yelp. During the period, the rape revenge subgenre of the action film would become a massively successful and prominent film choice with movies such as *Rape Squad* (1974), *Lipstick* (1976) and *Ms. 45* (1981) (aka *Angel of Vengeance*) becoming incredibly popular cinema going excursions, and here in *Cujo*, a film that truly has a woman being victimized and forced to fight back, employs this kind of "female empowerment".

From a gender politics perspective during the early eighties and coming from a branch of seventies second wave feminism, *Cujo* is fundamentally a rich case study of a woman reclaiming her turf and position of power as protector, nurturer and earth mother. Donna Trenton may be "trapped" by men and boys (and most vividly a male dog), but she grows from this and becomes just as primal and just as bloodthirsty as the killer canine that wants to tear her apart.

Attempting to race back inside the car, Donna is met with a ferocious canine desperate to kill her. She is pushed into the car by the aggressive rabid dog and bitten. When Cujo's fangs sink into her leg, director Lewis Teague chooses to use jump cuts in her scream – a scream of pain, despair, anguish and what ultimately is the cry of the lonely and isolated "woman in the storm". She is now infected by the horrendous disease of rabies and essentially now "at one with the dog" – these two antagonists are one in the same: polluted and driven to kill. The frenzy and stress-inducing intensity of the scene is masterfully concocted: Cujo buries himself into Donna, shredding her flesh, biting and snarling, barking loudly and violently and

344

vigorously shaking her around. Donna screams and hollers fighting him off while her son cowers in the back of the car screaming and crying. It is truly a harrowing and viscous image, and as Donna brings the water bottle up and crashes it into Cujo's head, smacking his skull with violent repetition, the dog soon backs off but not without pulling at her skirt, ripping it and turning it into a set of rags. Donna manages to slam the car door shut and the unstoppable force that is Cujo rises from the ground and claws at the window barking and desperate to get back inside.

Filming the siege. (courtesy of Danny and Margaret Pintauro).

Tad crawls over to his mother calling out "Let me see!" in reference to her massive bite wound which bleeds profusely. Tad's desire to see his mother's blood is an interesting choice here – possibly an insight into the child learning to be nurturing himself or perhaps a morbid fascination with gore. Donna cries out in pain when he touches her leg and he is scared off, bunching up into the corner of the backseat. Donna falls

345

into a dizzy spell and Jan de Bont's camera begins to circle mother and son who are lost in the vortex of terror and despair. Much like Brian De Palma had his cinematographer Mario Tosi spin his camera around a dancing Sissy Spacek and William Katt in *Carrie* (romantically at first and then spinning out of control), here de Bont (under the astute direction of Lewis Teague) pans across from Donna to Tad to evoke a feeling of loss, building madness, frenzy, instability, terror and above all the loss of control. This visceral effect builds and builds until it spirals out of focus and closes with Vic Trenton waking out of a nightmare.

DEE WALLACE: *Cujo* is my favourite film I have ever been a part of. I really appreciate it when people suggest that I should have been nominated for an Academy Award for that performance. Stephen King is very giving about that in all his interviews; he is a big champion of that idea. You know, it all came together when I read the script and I went "Oh, fuck! This is awesome! What an arc! What a tour de force! You know, I am going to get to do everything! Oh fuck! And it's with a kid!" I met Danny and I just knew it was going to be special. I just thanked God every day that I got that kid. Because if the kid didn't work the movie didn't work. Oh and Karl Miller – you know, there were thirteen dogs, and they were all trained to go after different toys so that they could get their different shots. Then, of course there was Gary Morgan in a dog suit with myself and the director. He did two tiny little shots in the movie. He did do the big attack scene in *Cujo*. I had talked Dan Blatt into letting me do it, and at the last minute, he said, "You know, if something happens to you – you're the money and we're all dead!" So, the big attack scene is the stunt woman with a real dog, and me with a stunt man, all intercut. I swear to God, if you go frame by frame you can't tell! The editing is so brilliant in this film! That stunt woman had this toy around her neck, and when she leaned forward the dog was supposed to go in to attack her, and as soon as she leaned back, the dog stopped. That is how well trained these dogs were! So, they got in and they did it – they got it in one take, right? Lewis said, "Print! We got it!" and the stunt woman said "Yes!!" – before somebody had their hand on the dog and the dog came in and bit her nose off. Now, it was not the dog's fault, it was the stunt woman's fault. They picked it up and put it back on, it was fine. But Dan said, "See Dee, this is why we don't like the actor to do it!" you know, and she was trained, but you forget until the guy has a hand on the dog... the dog thinks he is supposed to attack when you come forward, you know? Oh, so many things happened on *Cujo*!

Director Lewis Teague guides his stars Dee Wallace and Danny Pintauro, while "Daddy" does his thin on the Pinto bonnet.

DANNY PINTAURO: The funny thing is people were always so worried about me in terms of taking the stuff that was happening and turning it into a real emotional scar. Everyone thought that the movie was just going to scar me as a child! That was funny to me! So what the crew would do is lighten the mood after intense scenes, especially in the car sequences. Also, after every take Dee would say, "Now remember it is not real!" Everyone was constantly doing that. I would look at them and I would be like "Yeah, I know! I'm okay!" I kind of got to the point

Producer Dan Blatt and star Dee Wallace take time out during the intense shoot.

where I was like, "You guys, stop! I'm okay!" But they were so worried about me because I was so emotionally distraught – like more distraught than any child should ever feel. Then I would stop the scene and be like, "You guys, I'm fine!" I was just acting! "I'm good. I'm good!" I think that is why it happened – that is why they would stop and make sure I was not traumatized. It was so real and so scary to watch me go through that for all of them and then the camera turned off and I would be like, "Where's the dog? I want to go play with the dog!"

PETER MEDAK: I remember using the stunt guy and him trying on the dog costumes.

GARY MORGAN: The dog suit didn't belong to me. I forgot the person's name who controlled the action of the suit, but they were kind of a prima donna – they often are. It's interesting, because I was in the stunt department but every other department was trying to take control of me. The trainer wanted me to be in his thing so I could help him do stuff with the dogs and the guy that was in charge of the dog suit on the

348

Danny Pintauro keeps warm with his mother Margaret by his side.

set was trying to get me in his department. But I was in stunts, so I was under the stunt coordinator's dominion. I mean the suit itself was great! Whoever made it did a really great job! Inside the dog's head was a hockey helmet. They bent it around like a hockey helmet, so that I could have it on and that so my movement would translate because my head was sort of back in the head, because it was probably six or eight inches between my nose and the dog's mouth in order to see out of. I was also in black face – they painted my face black so that if you caught a glimpse inside the dog's mouth, even a flash, you wouldn't see because it was just black! This was kind of funny because I was walking around the set in black face! It was like Al Jolson! One day they had visitors to the set and I remember someone being absolutely shocked saying, "Someone is doing black face in this movie?"

IAN KINCAID: We were doing a shot at one point where we were on top of the Pinto looking down into the car and panning around. While we were setting it up, Jan was leaning in through the back hatch window and he had it held open with a clamp on the window holding the glass up. So Jan was waving in and someone bumped the hatch and it removed

349

Gary Morgan poses in the dog suit.

the clamp and the thing came slamming down on his head and it tagged him! He screamed in pain and he goes "That fucking hurt worse than the fucking lion!" because as we know Jan was scalped by a lion on the set of the movie *Roar* (1981)!

GARY MORGAN: A couple of times I cut my nose from the hockey helmet in all the attack scenes just bouncing around. I think I cut it when I hit my head against the car door. These were just little injuries. I mean I did movies where I got injured really bad. This wasn't one of those occasions.

ALEXANDER WITT: We made a hole in the car and put the camera inside it where we were able to shoot at 360 degrees without seeing anything around. I don't know if that was done before, but from there David Pringle was a master technician and he came up with different ideas to make that shot work. Jan in general wasn't an easy person himself, he wasn't easy to work with, and he expected everyone to be as ready as he was. I see it myself now, when I set up a scene, a lot of people don't pay attention. Jan wasn't a guy of many words, in those days. I did eight films with him.

From top to bottom: 1. Gary Morgan does a jump stunt in dog suit. 2. Gary gets into dog sitting pose. 3. Gary goofs around on set.

Gary Morgan in the dog suit, and at the bottom, with his family.

Gary Morgan on set, just casually strolling around as a biped rabid St. Bernard!

Gary Morgan on set in the dog suit with Dee Wallace – prepping for
their on-camera confrontation.

Gary Morgan and family.

From Gary Morgan's photo collection: the final moments of the film.

From top to bottom: 1. Filming the dog attack on Ed Lauter.
2. Ed Lauter and his stunt double. 3. Mills Watson, Gary Morgan in
blackface and Ed Lauter.

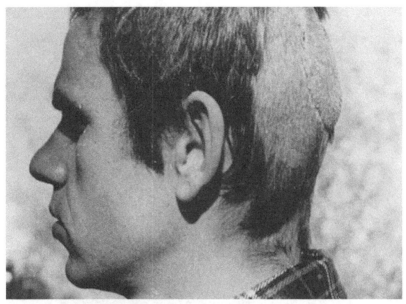

Jan de Bont, after being scalped by a lion on location for *Roar (1981)*.

Jan de Bont on the set, working with his crew.

Jan de Bont at camera, with Lewis Teague looking on.

Jan de Bont planning a shot.

Jan de Bont surveying the scene. Gary Morgan to the far left in dog suit.

Washed out by the rain.

Gary Morgan takes a breather from the confides of the dog suit.

Alexander Witt (in flannelette shirt) surveys the scene.

Filming the 360.

KATHIE CLARK: I build costumes for a living now and back then I was in between constructing costumes and working as a sculptor, so it was my job to create the dog suit for the stunt man. The main purpose of the suit was to be shot in a frenzy, so it would be more a case of flashes of fur in the car when he was attacking the mother and child. So it was to stand in for the dog, because obviously you can't put the dog in there. At that time my career had gone from being hired as a sculptor and fabricator, and then I got involved as a costumer and costume designer, and then after I went back to sculpting and fabricating which is what I still do today. But I was never at all hired as costume designer on *Cujo*, that was already set in stone with the producers with their set designers on the film.

GARY MORGAN: Danny was acting but occasionally he would slip into real hysterics. The same thing happened with Dee Wallace. There is a scene where Dee Wallace is sitting at the driver's seat and on "action", I leap on her, knock her on her back and I'm on top of her, in the front seat of the car. She has the thermos bottle and she's beating me with the thermos bottle – anytime you saw the dog on Dee, it was me. So during the attack she said to me "It would help if you bark!" So I'm growling and barking and all that and Dee slips from acting into real hysterics – I mean she is sobbing and crying. Now, I am down and out of the car, and her legs are open and her skirt is climbing up and I'm down there between her legs! After the shoot was filmed, the crew are waiting for her to calm down and to pull it back together, because she is crying and sobbing and being a method actress, taking a little time to come back down from all that heightened performance. So, I start to sniff her in the dog suit! Now Dee is an old friend of mine so I knew her before making the movie. She used to be a dancer, I knew a show she was in with my little sister, before that. So I'm like sniffing her and she's going "Gary, stop it!" and she is like pushing me away "Gary, stop it!" and I'm like sniffing and sneezing and now she slips from hysterically crying to hysterically laughing and she's trying to push me, and the director is going "Gary, stop that! Now! Knock it off!" Now Dee is laughing "Gary, stop that!" I'm like sniffing her leg and trying to hump her and the director grabs me by the collar and jerks me out of the car at which point I grab the director by the leg and start humping him! The crew was hysterical! Now, I picked up a spritz bottle that the makeup girl was using to make it look like Dee and Danny were sweating, and I start spraying the director on the leg as if I was pissing on him! It was just one of those moments that broke the mood – it was necessary for such an intense shoot!

Dee Wallace gets mauled by Gary Morgan in his Cujo costume.

CONRAD E. PALMISANO: Gary Morgan is a little acrobatic guy, so he is very agile and like that. It was the first time having had him in the dog suit. When the dog head was on him, his face was maybe four or five inches back from the nostril of the dog. So when you would talk to him, you could look past the snout and you could see his face back in there, his ears were where the St. Bernard ears were and not where the mouth was. So the dog suit was believable and they shot everything when the dog was attacking Dee Wallace over Gary, and there was one scene – and mind you we set this up for weeks – and again, because it was supposed to be very, very hot and it was cold, after the scene they would have to wrap a blanket around Dee Wallace and calm her down for four or five minutes… you know, for the scene and for the character, she would get very upset, so they wrapped things around, they guarded her very carefully. So on this one particular day – this was after weeks after shooting, mind you – in the scene, Dee had tried to get out of the car and then the dog attacked her. So she is sitting in the driver's seat, her head is in the passenger seat, her feet are outside on the ground and Gary is between her legs and leaning over the top of her as he is trying to bite her throat or whatever in the scene. Mind you, I didn't know that Dee and Gary were long-time friends before this movie. I had no idea that they had this long-time friendship. At the moment when they holler "cut!" – and Gary again, is standing between her legs. They holler "Cut! Cut! Cut!" and she starts hitting him with the thermos. He starts sniffing his way down between her breasts and down her stomach and to her crotch. Now mind you, his face is four or five or six inches away from where the nose is that is actually facing her crotch – but he is sniffing her, you know how dog's do? He's pretending to be a dog sniffing her crotch and she starts hitting him with the thermos and then eventually her brain starts to come back and she starts go "Gary! Gary, stop it! Stop it, Gary!" And her hands are on the forehead of the dog, but he is still sniffing her crotch, with the nose of this phoney dog head. Everyone on the set is freaking out in dead silence, and then all of a sudden, Lewis Teague the director, come up and grabs Gary by the shoulders and he pulls him back away from Dee, and Gary who is on his knees, looks up at Lewis. Lewis says "Gary, stop it!!" Gary jumps up and grabs Lewis Teague's leg and he starts humping him like a dog would! Lewis starts screaming and trying to pull away from Gary, but he is still humping the director's leg and the crew went into hysterics! It took fifteen minutes to restore order – it was so funny! It was one of the funniest moments I have ever had on a movie set! It's who Gary is – he's a comic!

He's a clown. He's a comedian. And from that moment on, I fell in love with Gary; he's one of my dearest friends ever since from that moment to this moment. If I had done it they probably would have put me in jail. And his attitude and everything like that – everybody just laughed! Dee started laughing, Lewis started laughing, the entire crew was laughing. I say it took fifteen minutes to restore order. Gary was enthusiastic as a puppy was to a new roast beef bone! He was happy to do it, he was excited, he was energetic and a pure professional besides all the antics!

Dee Wallace hides the fact that she is freezing cold with a huge grin on the set of *Cujo*.

JEAN COULTER: My husband was taking the pictures on set. I never used to take pictures on films, and for the most part you're not allowed to have a camera on set, but we got away with it on *Cujo*. I started working in this business when I was five years old, so I knew what the rules were.

ROBIN LUCE: In regards to the gore and the bite marks, now, as I work, we have these beautiful silicon pieces that have the pre-bites in them. Our technology as makeup artists has really transpired a lot and has become incredibly realistic looking. Back then, at that point, it was kind of out

367

of kit. I did the bite marks and wounds with mortician's wax, and a little tissue, and some blood and you had to really keep your eye on it because it was never just one piece that you laid on – I never ordered one piece for that film, whether it was latex and they never had silicone back then. I never ordered one piece, it was all done freehand. It was all done with mortician's wax, gel blood and tissue, and we never had the illustrator palettes back then.

CHRISTOPHER MEDAK: The production designer was Guy J. Comtois, and I loved him. He was an incredible artist and he stayed on board after my dad was fired. He was very passionate and very dedicated to his work. He was also a delight to work with and like Jack Buehler, he loved life and living to the fullest. He loved his men and was very proud about his promiscuity. He met his assistant, the art director on *Cujo*, on the streets of Paris. This guy was a prostitute that Guy met and bought back to L.A.! This is the beauty of these things, it's always interesting to see how people come to be and how people have such bizarre backgrounds and fates. You know, Nancy and I looked after a place that Guy and his prostitute lover had while they worked on *Fanny and Alexander* (1982), they were lovely, but it always cracked me up that that's the way they met.

JEAN COULTER: I had to do a fight with the dog and for that fight I was in high heels and by the side of the car. It took a long time shooting, that's for sure! I had this strap of thick leather around my leg when the dog had to grab hold of my leg and chew my leg. The leather piece was worn underneath my skirt. I never saw the other stunt women on the set. I think they were hired after I left. I was the one called to work with the dogs. The only time I knew that they had someone else was when they called me to come back.

CONRAD E. PALMISANO: Well, Jeannie Coulter was there and the dog bit her nose, and separated her nostril from her face... and it was

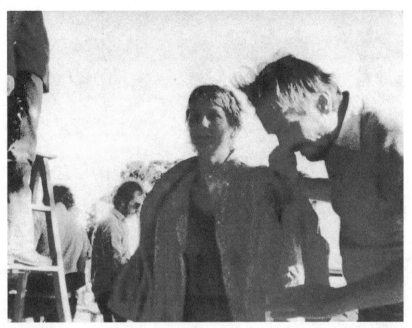

Dee Wallace is tended to by costume designer Jack Buehler.

Dee Wallace, in a dressing gown, prepares to do a scene.

Dee Wallace, in a dressing gown, prepares to do a scene.

just like a mishap, because again, the dog was playing and so forth, but that is the life of a stunt person. We were shooting over Jeannie's back, as if she is Dee Wallace, shooting at the dog attacking her. So when we did over the dog to Dee – it was Jeannie. When we did over her to the dog it was... so it bit her and she had to have four or five stitches put there to reattach her nostril to her face. And then we brought in the others girls after this. So Roxana Whitfield was a lion tamer, and so she came in to fill in after Jeannie got bit. Roxana Whitfield worked in an animal park in San Francisco. She did very, very little on the film.

ROBERT CLARK: During that period, that era of the late seventies and early eighties there was a definite shift in makeup effects and creature effects, which we never called it in those days. I mean if you look at movies like *An American Werewolf in London* (1981) and *The Howling* there was a kind of shift from B-list to A-list sensibility. So when a film like *Cujo* came along, which was an A-list film, then there was a major concern about how we can really do this and how can we really do it up. Before that they may not have even decided on using creature effects. So Kathie and I were working with Peter on a film that was called *Rats* and then was released as *Deadly Eyes*, and with that film we had a lot of control in that we had to make thirty or so costumes for Dachshunds, dressing them as rats. So Peter saw us doing that and pinched the idea for *Cujo*, to dress up dogs in costumes. There was a St. Bernard costume for this Labrador which I know was Peter's idea for sure, and I don't really think that that costume made it into the film. It is very common, I mean you shoot a lot more than what is used. But the theory behind using the dog in the dog suit was that the St. Bernards were completely trainable but the trainer had to be very close and they would control them by hand signs, which was fascinating to me, because they can't of course be making noise, but some actions St. Bernards just aren't able to do – such as jumping swiftly and quickly. So we had this Labrador and he was beautiful and loved being in that costume, he would prance around proud as punch and look incredibly happy in it!

KATHIE CLARK: The film being a non-union movie didn't matter for me and Bob. We can still get away with it, I mean I worked on *The Grinch* (2000) and made a giant monkey for the Grinch's cave and I built it right on Universal Studios and it was non-union, but they kind of look at you and think of you as a kind of specialty, and when I invoice them, it's like they purchased this creature from me, so that's how you deal with it when you're non-union. I don't remember the production of *Cujo* being under Peter Medak's direction, and also when you work in a shop – your own personal space – it doesn't matter really who you are working for because you are so focused on what it is you're doing, and here Bob and I were required to build St. Bernards. It was strange with *Cujo* however, because usually when it's a case of working with special effects that are going to be used practically on location we would go out on set, but we didn't on this one. Peter Knowlton must have done all that grounds work, maybe he wanted all the credit for it! I mean no one else showed up on set!

ROBERT CLARK: I would say making up aliens or monsters in comparison to realistic creatures like dogs such as the St. Bernard in *Cujo* are both challenges. The challenge to make an animal that is convincing is great, and the main part that was hard was getting the right fur. Working on *The People Under the Stairs* (1991) was very much inspired by *Cujo*, because I had to sculpt Rottweilers. It is so much easier creating long haired dogs, because the shaggier they are you can get away with things. I was getting calls to make dogs after *Cujo*.

KATHIE CLARK: Robert and I work together beautifully. We started with Sid and Marty Kroft in the seventies and we were eighteen. Eventually in the eighties we had our own special effects studio. Even though he is an ex-husband now, we still work together. Robert is one of the biggest names in sculpting in films, he does all the big movies and we have a son together who also does the same job. My current husband "Fireball" Tim is a car designer and he works with me, dealing with the client. I mean back in the *Cujo* days, I was the same – I didn't like dealing with outside people such as actors or anyone, I just wanted to stay focused on my sculpting and fabricating work.

JEAN COULTER: I was very popular in the stunt business and I doubled a lot of girls. My size was right, I was thin and small and I was blonde, so there was never ever any issue with my hair color, no one wanted me to wear a brunette wig, I was blonde and that was perfect for the role. Plus I had worked with animals in the past, and someone called me and asked me to do this film and I said yes. I used to double for *Charlie's Angels* (1976-1981), I doubled all of the girls – I had a great size for this work and a great face for this work, because the cameraman could shoot me from one side and then from another and no one would be able to tell the difference.

MARGARET PINTAURO: I was initially worried about Danny working with the dogs, but they were all very well trained and there was nothing to worry about. Most of the dogs were taken away from the car after they did their job and it was left to Dee and Danny to do the rest of the work, screaming and acting out the terror. There was also a guy in a dog suit, a mechanical dog head and other things used to make up the dog, but as far as the real life dogs, there were five of them. Danny wasn't frightened of the dogs, but he wasn't allowed to touch them. The owner of the dogs felt that the dogs shouldn't interact with Danny, for both their own protection.

JEAN COULTER: People had heard about my talents and they would just call me up and ask if I could do certain stunts and I would be doing things on the spot. I had worked with animals before and people knew that, so that was helpful. I had a great rapport with the dogs, even though there was one dog who was trained to do all the "mean" things, and he was hard to get along with; plus I wasn't allowed to get along with him. All the other dogs on set were lovely, and I was able to play with them. I always have had a thing for animals, I love them, I have trained them and I have a special bond with them and you can read their thoughts. They love you and they're loyal, I just love them to bits.

DEE WALLACE: Donna is a strong, incredible, courageous and loving woman. For me, *Cujo* was all about the length a mother will go to defend and protect her child and I had a great mother who would go to great lengths to defend and take care of me, so it was a subject that was close to my heart. I had no children at the time, but now that I do and I watch *Cujo*, I think I wouldn't do anything differently and not make any other choices with that child, knowing what I know about motherhood now.

Dee Wallace, the star of *Cujo*.

JEAN COULTER: Every film has its dangers and everything is so different. I loved working with animals, so *Cujo* was fun. When I was doing the part in *Jaws 2* (1978), I had to play a character, an onscreen character, so I wasn't hiding behind the fact that I was standing in for an actress, as I did on *Cujo*. In *Jaws 2* there was a lot of fireworks in the boat, and I had my eyebrows and eyelashes burnt off, so even there, without working with animals there is danger. It's totally different and a different kind of danger. *Jaws 2* was a six month job – there was a lot of boat work, a lot of driving the boat, I had a dying scene in the movie which the producers thought was far too morbid to show. So that was cut. We also had to deal with the weather conditions – I mean, I remember it dropped to thirty degrees and was snowing on the water in *Jaws 2*, and it's harder to shoot on the water and dealing with the weather concerns. On *Cujo*, it was a quick shoot, and mostly because I was injured. But what I loved about both movies is the fact that the filmmakers have to make these creatures look real – I mean on *Cujo* there were real life dogs, but there were also mechanical dogs used and puppet heads of St. Bernards, and on *Jaws 2*, it was a fully articulated mechanical shark – and the beautiful thing about these things is that they have to look real. That was a major challenge for both directors of both movies.

KATHIE CLARK: We used taxidermist eyes and from memory I think we used bear teeth for the teeth. We would go to the taxidermist and buy all these plastic pieces for the mouth, and you could choose as to what would suit the St. Bernard – we could have used a wolf, but we went with the bear because that was more of the size of the St. Bernard head. It was cost effective, because you could buy a whole set of teeth for like twenty dollars instead of setting the teeth or sculpting the teeth and making them from scratch. You have to have a steady hand especially when you're dealing with the eyes and all the very intricate stuff.

ROBERT CLARK: You always do as much research as you can, in those days it wasn't as easy as it is now with the internet. Back then you used books and you would be stressed for time so you would have to jump right in. We would get a lot of anatomy references as possible, and something that I have always found useful in sculpting animals was found in drawing books and "how to draw" books and I remember getting a book all about drawing St. Bernards, and it covered the skeletal structure and the shape of the skull which was very helpful. And we would buy jaws and teeth and eyes from taxidermists and I am pretty sure the teeth for Cujo were bear teeth that we would alter, and cut them back and make them a little bit more narrow. We found stuff that we could used for the sculpt for the Cujo head.

JEAN COULTER: Karl was such a nice man. He would explain what we were going to do and he was very laid back. I loved working with him because he wasn't a pressured guy, he just let me work with the dogs and it was great. Also, I remember the dog parts that Gary Morgan used – he had a St. Bernard head that he would wear and then use as a puppet. He of course also was in the dog suit. But I don't remember any of the other parts or animatronic dogs used at all. Gary suited playing the dog! He is such a clown. In fact, he does live performances all around the world. He was so agile and athletic and really got into playing the role of Cujo in that dog suit. I hired him on a show that I coordinated and got him to do a high fall. He was a fun guy! He is small and was perfect for playing a dog! If you have some time to laugh on set, that was usually with Gary. When you work long hours, you need people like Gary on set.

KATHIE CLARK: I never saw Peter Knowlton after *Cujo*. Bob had a falling out with a major company that he originally met Peter through. We worked for him for makeup and special effects labs, but then later met him at an established company, but after *Cujo*, directly after, we never saw him. He was a big, big drinker, so I fear that he might not be alive.

SFX artist Peter Knowlton holds the animatronic dog head.

DANIEL HUGH KELLY: I met Gary Morgan out on set and talk about gregarious! He was very outgoing, non-stop talk, and he was an amazing stunt man. He was very consciences and very religious I might add, I mean he was a very sweet man. I was on Broadway doing *Cat on a Hot Tin Roof*, and he and his wife came along and that was probably the last time I saw Gary. He was just a great guy. I mean him and his whole family are incredible. He would send me these Christmas cards of him and his family and they would be pictures of them doing these outrageous stunts. Every time I think of Gary Morgan I smile.

JEAN COULTER: I got into stunt work through acting. You see, I was acting, and I realized I just couldn't make a living doing acting. My sister was a big child star, and that's what I thought I wanted to do, but I was very physical and I loved the idea of doing stunts, so I started working on shows and it just snowballed. I had dance and gymnastic backgrounds, and I was a swimmer and a snow skier and I took car work at the LAPD where they train officers by the beach doing car work. I took Judo and Karate, all sorts of things, so I knew a bit about everything, I never wanted to be a pro, I just wanted to know enough so I could do the work.

ROBERT CLARK: There was a driver who was very young that Peter hired, he was our runner. We would say we needed stuff and he would go out and look for it. And one of the hardest things to find was fur! You could go to a fabric store and find fake fur for coats or that gorilla style fur that was long and shaggy. But a lot of that fur looked like the fur you would see on a toy. We needed fur that looked like a real animal's fur. At one point, we really needed the white part of the fur to be perfect and it was really hard to find this. The young kid went downtown and came back with this semi-wavy, white perfect fur! We were shocked and he told us that he met some guy that took him into some attic and pointed out a roll that looked good enough for white fur. He bought eight dollars worth and it came back perfect. Kathie and I had developed a method that once you get the whole animal made, you start shaving different parts of the animal. In the case of Cujo, we started shaving his snout and around his eyes, so we could sculpt where the coat would be shorter. It makes it so much more realistic and not at all like a stuffed animal.

KATHIE CLARK: Robert and I had no idea about the project, and all we understood was that Peter Knowlton approached us to work on it and hired us. Peter needed some sculptors and fabricators, so Robert, who was my husband at the time, came in as just that. A whole bunch of materials were used to sculpt the prosthetic dogs, and firstly the head had to be sculpted with clay. We had to take a mould off of that and then cast a few different heads, one of those was done in fibreglass, and one was done in rubber and then we made a hollow one that could be worn by an actor as part of the St. Bernard costume. Once we pulled the material out of the mould, my job was to dress it with fur to make it look as realistic as possible. It's strange when you're working on a costume for someone – I get very nervous around actors and stunt people, and I just need to remain focused on my work at hand. I want to get it completely right and perfect what it looks like and feels like and how it will work on camera. I don't want to answer too many questions from actors or stunt people, however they're usually very quiet too, getting into character or working themselves into the job. In Gary's case, he had to be on his hands and knees to take the pattern, because the suit would sit so much more differently if he just stood up. He had to be in the position that a dog would be in, so I could mark the prototype for the pattern and then build it from the mannequin I had which was positioned in a dog position. It had to fall correctly, in the way how a dog would physically stand. Gary's comfort was totally taken into consideration. But first and foremost it was all about the look. Firstly, you make an under-suit and if the animal has haunches than that would act as the internal pad that you would sculpt, and then would lay it with extra padding at certain points so it's relatively comfortable. It's hot however. It gets really hot in those costumes. Even though he's meant to look like a dog in this car he has to have breathing holes and vision, unless he is only going to be used for two seconds. He could have gotten in there and done the job quickly, but for *Cujo*, Gary was in that suit a lot and for long periods of time. I do remember that the producers were not completely concerned with how the suit looked – they just wanted Gary to get in there and do scenes that the real dog couldn't do and to showcase some friction and frantic activity – a flurry of fur and action. It is amazing when I hear special effects people talk about *Cujo* and they are always stumped as to when the film features a real life dog and when it features one of the dogs I worked on or Gary in the costume! It is so well done!

ROBERT CLARK: Kathie and I had worked with Tom Burman for a while and he was the only guy who had his own shop and his own special effects makeup lab, and this was before people like Rick Baker and Rob Bottin were starting to spring up and more workshops started popping up and getting into action. Tom used a material for making moulds called tool stone which is what you would cast on latex, and that is what people used. It was a dental material and it was quite expensive. I mean if you wanted twenty two pounds of it or something it was like sixty dollars. We had made plaster moulds with casts, and they were very cheap, and there's hydrocal and ultracal which was very dense and very strong material, and I thought "Well, why can't we mould latex in this?" and people looked at me as if I were stoned, but I thought "Fuck it, I'm tryin' it!" so I grabbed some ultracal and Rob Burman actually cast the rubber for us, and he was Tom Burman's son, so he cast the Cujo heads in the foam latex and it worked famously. Ultracal was fourteen dollars for one hundred pounds compared to the dental material which was so expensive. So *Cujo* was the turning point for that, because everyone started using ultracal for latex moulds after that. Another thing was we would have a cast of someone and sculpt over that, that was the standard way of course, but on *Cujo* of course we didn't have a cast of the dog – I mean there had been casts done of animals before. Tom Burman worked on *Altered States* (1980) and in that he had to make a cast of a goat, and the goat got so excited it fainted. So when the goat fainted they put the cast on it and when it came out of being unconscious it was all done, so the goat was fine and the sculpt was done. For *Cujo* there was never, ever any thought on sculpting from the dog's head, so what we did was make the sculpture from the mould which came from designs of the St. Bernard's head, and then I had to sculpt the face and do all the articulation. Once I had the mould, I had to strip it out and reseal the mould with the latex and filled it in with clay and then touch it up with the open parts which are the eyes and mouth. Then once the clay was removed the articulated heads would take shape.

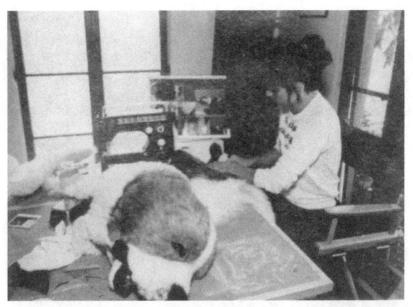

SFX artist Kathie Clark builds the Cujo costume for stunt man Gary Morgan.

JEAN COULTER: The dogs had this drool that would hang off their mouths, and I am sure the dogs didn't like it, and they would try to wipe it off. I mean this was a two to three foot long drooling. Gary Morgan would say "Now do I have enough drool?" There was always a lot of fun on set when we stunt people got together. We had a stunt coordinator there and of course Lewis was there, and we all had a great time. When you do a film like *Cujo*, you need to have a bunch of people who bounce off each other and run smoothly. There is no room for egos. I mean, Lewis was lovely, he was always calm and he never was screaming at me or at other people, like John Landis who on *The Blues Brothers* (1980) was just angry and always yelling, but here on *Cujo*, everyone had time for one another.

MARGARET PINTAURO: Danny and Dee stayed in character in between takes. That was interesting to watch. And that was Danny's choice entirely. Danny thought of Dee as his mom, and that's how he

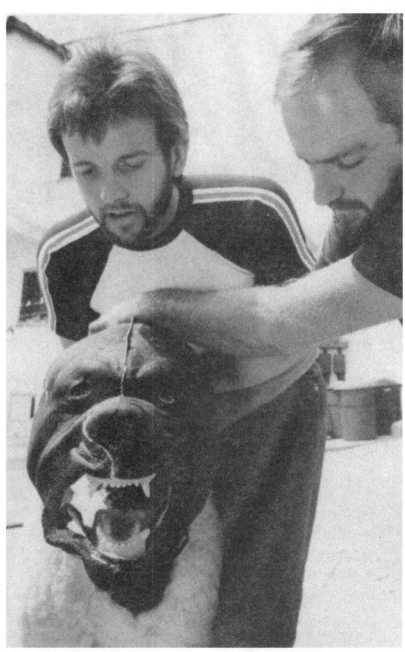

SFX artists David Nelson and Peter Knowlton fitting the head sculpt of the animatronic St. Bernard onto the dressed fibreglass body.

The animatronic dog team! Included here are artists Larry Carr, Jean Cherie, Robert Clark, David Nelson, Peter Knowlton and Kathie Clark.

portrayed it. He thought that it was play acting mom and son, and that was fine with me, it was amazing to see. He was an in the moment actor, so that made him very similar to Dee as an actress.

ROBERT CLARK: Karl Lewis Miller was a big Elvis fan, and he kind of had his hair styled like Elvis. He even had this big picture of Elvis hanging on his wall, and Kathie and I commented on that. He was a cool guy and he knew his stuff. He had all these animals and he could get them to do anything, and it was just beautiful to see his connection with all these animals.

JEAN COULTER: You know the dog I worked with died right after my nose was taken off. After I got bit, a day or two later they called me and told me that the dog had died. I was shocked. I was like "Ummm, did he have rabies? How did he die?" Then they told me that his stomach had flipped which is something that large breed dogs such as St. Bernards are prone to, which is very sad. It had nothing whatsoever to do with the shoot, it's just something that happens to this kind of dog. A perfectly healthy St. Bernard can flip its stomach, it's a breed issue. When that dog died it really, really upset me. I was recovering in hospital and just thinking about the dog and crying and was very sad about it. Cubby was one of the dogs used to play Cujo and he was such a sweet dog – he wasn't mean at all. Karl Lewis Miller loved him so much and he was so well trained and well looked after. We just teased him for so long and I knew it was too long and by the time I called them to get him off me, it was too late – he bit my nose off! We were working in the car and I was laying down between the two seats in the front, and he was on top of me and he weighed like one hundred and ten pounds and I weighed like one hundred and four, and he was crawling on my chest and he was trying to get at his little toy that was tied around my neck. I would tease him with it and he would try and take it off me. Lewis kept saying "This is perfect! Keep it going! Keep it going!" and this dog lunged at me and clawed really fast to get his toy, and you know how fast a dog claws at something to get a toy or food or whatever it is they're after. So he did this, clawing at me and chomping at my chest to get the toy. Then I lifted my head and he took a massive bite at my nose! He tore my nose right off. I was lucky though, I could have lost my eye, I could have lost half of my face, I was very lucky. To think that I lost most of my nose was intense, I mean he had torn off the flesh and ripped off the entire nose, it was just a piece of bloodied skin that held my nose together. There was so much blood flow, and if there was none of that tiny bit of skin that dangled off and held my nose together than I would have had no nose whatsoever. I was rushed to the hospital, and the doctors there wanted to sew my nose up right away

384

and I said "No, I won't let you touch it, unless there is a plastic surgeon here." Because I knew that they would sew it up any old way. So, it took two hours for a plastic surgeon to come to the hospital, and he did a great job. I had forty seven stiches and it worked out great because you couldn't tell where the tear in my nose was. I mean you could if you looked really, really close, but he did a good job. The producers called me to come back to do another stunt, because another girl they had had to fall on her back when the dog lunges on Dee Wallace, but this stunt girl couldn't do it, but I couldn't go back to work. I couldn't come back, because I couldn't take the chance of my nose not healing properly.

Stunt woman Jean Coulter prepares to take on "Cubby". (courtesy of Jean Coulter).

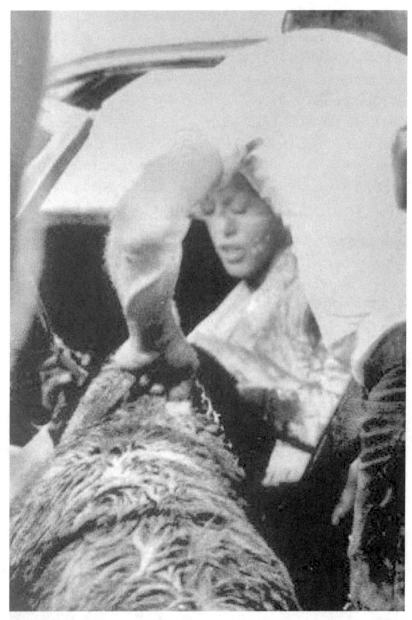

Animal trainer Karl Lewis Miller leads "Cubby" into the dissembled
Pinto to "terrorise" stunt woman Jean Coulter. (courtesy of Jean
Coulter).

An off-camera shot of one of the St. Bernards in heavy makeup.

TERESA ANN MILLER: My father remembers the stunt woman wrestling, and although it is play and although it is reasonably safe – they still have teeth and they still have nails – so at any point, the foot can rip the nose or the lip – I mean, you never know. That is why you have stunt people to protect against that. It is still an animal and it can actually happen. Now it didn't happen viciously, but accidents do happen.

GARY MORGAN: The woman who replaced Jean Coulter was Roxana Whitfield and she wasn't really a stunt woman, she was an animal trainer and she had a lion and tiger act. She was a great girl. I really liked her. She was used to working with big animals. She had long blonde hair almost to her mid back and they cut it all off for that. She was great because she was used to working with animals – she wasn't afraid of the dog and then they had another double but he was never filmed.

TERESA ANN MILLER: When you have a dog that has to do a leaping attack and a knock down and wrestling and what have you, and now maybe sometimes you'll use a second dog for stuff like that. But keep in mind it's also not to tire your lead dog out while you are working, because you've got to really balance the day's work of filming, so that the animal doesn't get tired and burnt out. And so that is the importance of having three to four dogs is so that you can balance the workload, because you've got to be able to accomplish a day's work, you know. And we can't tell when the dog is tired, we're done for the day, so we'll really focus on, usually, letting the lead dog do his character work and then you bring in the other dog to help with the physical work so that he doesn't get too tired.

ROBIN LUCE: My father was an architect and he was the president of the AIA, he owned his own firm. I was training through my father to be an architect and I was doing the math, the calculus, I mean I did it all and he wanted me to take over his firm. I had no idea that the industry of makeup artistry existed, I had no idea that there was such a thing as the makeup field. I just graduated from high school and I had a job in a hair salon and my boss just got a makeup artistry class in the only makeup academy in Los Angeles back in 1978, that place was called the Elegance Academy. And it was the visitors' night and he took me there, and he thought that I would really like it, and I just fell in love with it automatically, so I went back to my dad and I told him that makeup is really want I want to do. My father always lived by the rule of doing what you love and that you should love what you do every day. Then it is not just your job, it's your passion. So my dad supported me in that, and so I went to the Elegance Academy, and when I got out, I got married. I got married at a very young age, for the first time. My husband at the time was great friends with Ve Neill, and so he introduced me to her and we got along smashingly. She bought me on *Sword and the Sorcerer* and also on that project was Greg Cannom and ever since then I have loved makeup work. Ve was one of the first women that got into the union, and I banged on their doors for ages to get into the field, but no one would open the doors to me. My training field was all of those great horror movies which were not union films, I mean most of those films were Roger Corman movies, and Frank Mancuso Jr. who did all the *Friday the 13th* films.

MARK ULANO: *The Slumber Party Massacre* was a classic Roger Corman film – contained locations, minimal resources, a lot of ingenuity and a very warm team spirit above and below line. *Pet Sematary* had some terrific people but a real diversity in experience levels in the leadership of the project. *Cujo* always had a broad sense of career move for everyone involved versus a passion for the work for its own sake.

PATRUSHKHA MIERZWA: If I'm going to be honest, the transition from being costuming and working as a seamstress to doing sound came down to the medium, respect, and money. I started in theatre and actually continued in costuming when I came to L.A.. (A Norman Lear pilot, Michelle Pfeiffer's first film, Ray Milland's last). I was used to being part

389

of the company in theatre, and found I was relegated to a workroom off the set in film. I sadly found that theatre was not at all as financially viable here in L.A., and pursued the film business. I worked on a Movie of the Week about Chippendale's (the premiere strip club) and had a lot of time on my hands as the guys had their own outfits. I asked everyone about their jobs and that's where I remembered Mark Ulano from an earlier job. He offered to teach me sound; I wanted to have a job in the middle of the creative process and it paid twice what I was making in wardrobe. Most importantly, I wanted a job where I was paid for my mind. That's booming! There wasn't the camaraderie that usually happens on the set of *Cujo*: it was emotionally expensive to get to know people as someone was getting fired nearly every week. We had just come off a shoot in Salt Lake City with Sun Classic, and stayed close with the electric dept. In fact, I wrote an Ode to them in our newspaper. At some point I need to release the tension and started a crew newspaper; it had stories about people involved in the movie, the location, any elements that seemed appropriate. Chris Medak had stayed on and was a delight. He was a young Brit, with black spiky hair, blue eye shadow and, I think, black leather and chains (at least that's the way I like to remember him). I asked him to write the lifestyle column and we got the scoop on clubbing in San Francisco on our days off. He also gave makeup tips. A fond memory comes from early on when we shot the bucolic scene at the beginning. The St. Bernard was supposed to bound through the meadow until he finds the hole, gets bitten, and its downhill from there. Well, it turns out that St. Bernards don't bound – it's physically impossible. So they got a Labrador to do it. Someone made him a St. Bernard costume... but failed to allow for the difference in body volume by building padding into it. We're out in a meadow, here comes the Labrador and when he runs through the grass, his "St. Bernard skin" is so much bigger than his own, that it hangs off him like a malting buffalo. We had cows grazing and they weren't in the frame so Chris Medak was sent to corral them. There he was, in blue eye shadow and black boots, 6 feet tall, flapping his arms to appear larger, and calling to them, as he bounded through the hillside. We had a song; I don't remember when, but sometime during the middle of the film, with Cubby bloodied and slimed, Mark started singing "Besame, besame Cujo". It wasn't an official song – just something to be silly about.

GARY MORGAN: I wanted to really get into being a dog. It is always a tendency for a human being to always put your elbows out when you're on all fours. I remember the producers were constantly saying "Keep your elbows in!" They could tell they were out from across the ground as I was running on all fours before jumping – so for most of those shots they used a real dog. They shot me doing a lot of it but I was very conscientious about keeping my elbows in and keeping dog-like movements. Because that minute you go "Ugh, that is a guy in a suit!" then it is no good and you lose the audience. I watched that St. Bernard a lot, and spent most of my time constantly watching his movements and then doing those attack scenes. When the dog bit Jean's nose, what happened was they had this leather piece on the dog's neck like an extension of a collar, and then they had this rag on her. They would take this rag and then get the dog all agitated: "Get it! Get it! Get it! Get it!" Then they would hold the dog back and show them the rag and then they would have it on Jean's neck. Then they would let the dog go and he would leap on her and grab that rag, take it down and shake it, trying to get that rag and shaking it to attack her. Then they would reach in the car, get the dog by the collar and get him off of her. Sometimes they had to give him the rag too. It was like a release thing because he would not let go of the rag. They would get him out and after he was out of the car, poor Jean would sit up and they would do another take – she did this all day! She was getting battered! In one of the takes as they were pulling the dog off of her, she sat up before the dog was fully out of the car, and the dog saw the rag and the dog grabbed for the rag again as she was sitting up and that is how he grabbed her nose. He was trying to reattach to the rag. As she was sitting up, he grabbed for the rag, she sat right up into it, and it took the edge of her nose off. The dog took her nose off! Her nose was hanging from where the nostril was! He took that right off! We got her to a plastic surgeon and she was back at her hotel room. The stunt coordinator, Conrad and a few other people all put tape on our noses, and visited her. We got band-aids and all put band-aids on our noses and went in. She started to laugh so hard that her husband goes "Come on guys!" He wasn't in the mood because he was obviously depressed. Jean is a pretty girl, and before you know what it is going to look like, all you can think is, "Oh no. I am going to live the rest of my life with this horrible scar!" But they did a great job, you couldn't even tell where it happened. You can't even tell it happened. It was insane. You see, St. Bernards have mighty jaws. I have a skull collection. I'm into skulls. I bought the skull of a St. Bernard at a store. I bought it because when you look at it the teeth are so large, without all those gums, and the crown of a St. Bernard's head is huge and it's got this big ridge and that is how you can tell how strong an animal like this bite could be! Like a hyena has a big ridge, so do St. Bernards. You look at its skull and go "What is that? A gorilla?" You can't even tell what it is. When I tell people it is a St. Bernard, it blows them away! Across the forehead, it is like two inch thick bone – you could hit it with a pipe – it is such a ferocious looking skull, that it is amazing that sense of power that they've got in their jaws! More than a bear's! I have a bear skull and the St. Bernard skull is scarier looking than that!

TERESA ANN MILLER: I never imagined that I would be doing what I'm doing and working with my dad so closely. Like I said, I helped him a lot of the time as a child, and I would be his so-called "stand-in actor" working with the animals and such. I remember him as a child always... he was a performer – he didn't sing, he didn't dance, but he performed with "animal action". That was his mantra. That is what he always said. I remember as a child, my first birthday party I had, he'd put on a little show with Scruffy, the dog from *The Ghost and Mrs. Muir* (1968-1970). So that was kind of fun, and all the kids knew our house and all the fun animals to come see, and what have you. So I remember having that as a child. I remember him always going off to work and such and I don't think I knew any different. And even once I was grown, and even after *Cujo*, originally, I had started working closer with him to get into meeting some people to possibly do some still photography. I wanted to maybe be a set photographer. That was one of my initial ideas. The more I worked with him the more we just fell into a groove and we worked really well together. I mean almost without words, you know what I mean? Because I knew him and I knew what he needed and how he worked. The longer I worked together with him and started doing my own shows with him it was just really obvious that this is something that I enjoy doing. I loved doing it. I completely loved the idea of doing photography and was more interested in working with the animals.

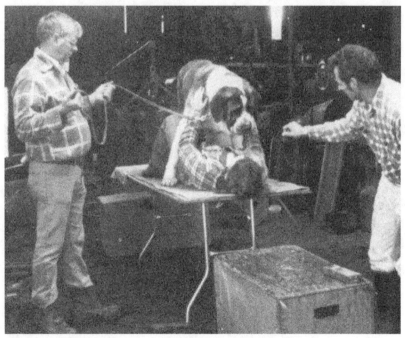

Animal trainer Karl Lewis Miller (on the right) instructs one of his St. Bernards in preparation for an attack sequence.

"PLEASE GOD, GET ME OUT OF HERE": Vic confides in Roger while the Three Days of Darkness continue

Now perhaps in need of the "Monster Words" himself, Vic Trenton wakes in fright in his hotel room, springing up from the bed and coming into a close-up staring directly into the barrel of the camera. Wet with perspiration and driven by worry, Vic is now set to act on his fears which have now transitioned from career woes to personal concern that involves his wife.

Cutting to the hallway of the inner-city hotel, Vic now carrying his suitcase and ready to leave knocks on Roger Breakstone's hotel room door. Roger insists that Vic is worried about his "creative juices" and is in a state of "panic" about the Sharp account, but Vic's tangible fear is no longer about the advertising agency. Vic confides in Roger that Donna has been having an affair and voices his concern ("Roger, she hasn't answered the phone in two days") while the darkness of the hotel hallway at night is broken up by bursts of light that deliver the revelatory news of Donna's secret. While Roger pleads with Vic to stay on board to help rescue the account, Vic steps into action as a man determined to find his wife.

The night is silent and calm back on the Camber farm. Besides the chirping of crickets and cicadas, there is mostly silence as Donna tends to her bloodied body, dressing her wounds with ripped portions of her dress and blouse. Suddenly, without warning Cujo leaps up onto the bonnet of the car and watches her. He rests his head and stares straight into her eyes. Quietly in prayer Donna utters "Please God, get me out of here..." The sentence would become the tagline for various movie posters for the film, making for an alternate choice for the commonly used "Now there's a new name for terror".

NANCY G. FOX: Danny Hugh Kelly was very nice and a very good looking man. He was easy to costume. It was a sense of making him look distressed as time goes by and he can't reach out to his wife. The police uniforms were rented, and they had to look like New England policeman attire. The director Lewis Teague was pretty quiet really, I don't remember him telling me things about the way characters looked really. Yeah, he was pretty quiet. But I was friendly with Chris Medak, and of course Jack Buehler and a lot of the electricians who I had worked with on other movies. In those days I worked with a lot of the same crews; we were all friends. I have a picture that Dee Wallace gave me of her and I, that she gave to me framed. Dee had to go through a lot in that film, and her looks was the main thing that Jack and I had to work on as far as making her look dishevelled and bloodied and dirty. We had powders and fabricated dirt for the costumes. One of my favorite memories is having a plane be sent for me to get on board and fly out to San Francisco to go to shops and buy Dee's pink blouse. Multiple pink blouses! The clothing was designed in a way to be torn apart and used as bandages and so forth. It was incredible. I did not believe that they would fly me out to San Francisco to source costumes. That was crazy!

ROBIN LUCE: Daniel Hugh Kelly's changes in skin tone was designed to be believable and to be subtle in their changes so we can go through all the emotions that this man is going through as he gets stressed about the whereabouts of his wife.

Dee Wallace's glowing beauty shining through the grime and grit.

DEE WALLACE: The clothes were designed to lose the top part over the course of the film and to be cool which was a ridiculous thought seeing that it was cold out on the farm at points, but because Danny and I were meant to be playing characters stuck in the severe heat, these clothes were meant to appear lighter or made to be cooler – the kind of summer blouse you would wear on a hot day. Originally, Jack Buehler wanted to put me in pants, but I said "As an actress I want to be in pants, but as the character

I am still much more vulnerable in a skirt." Then we talked about flats as opposed to heels and ultimately I would have preferred flats, but heels are great because they add to the femininity and the vulnerability of the character – and trying to run away in heels automatically creates so much more angst then flat shoes. I think all of that worked in her vulnerability because as strong as she was, she had to be vulnerable also which is again why I think Dan Blatt wanted me for this part, because I have that handle of playing in between quiet resilience and vulnerability – which is why Steve Spielberg liked me, he tapped into my childlike strength.

JEAN COULTER: I simply met Dee, we never got to know each other. I don't hang out with actors, only stunt people and the stunt coordinator. I'm not impressed with stars, I grew up in the business and I knew everyone and was there to do a job. I mean, I knew people like Farrah Fawcett but that never fazed me, I was a stunt woman and I was there to do my job. When I finished my job, I would leave the set, I never hung around.

ROBIN LUCE: Lewis Teague definitely had a particular look that he was looking for. Then it was going through the script and breaking it down and defining at what point their look would change, even if it was slight because it could be dramatic, and a sense of less is more. The biggest challenge would be the subtlety, that whole concern of getting the characters to look like that they were dehydrating and in such a small amount of time and space, I mean we were stuck in that car. So, I felt like I had to be conservative with the choices I made and as we went along we decided to make them look more dehydrated or add more red to the skin or paler or adding sweat, and that was a massive collaboration with Lewis Teague because he was very particular with what he wanted these two characters to look like. So it was a collaboration for sure – I would go away and come up with my ideas and bring them to him and he would have his own, and we'd go from there together.

GARY MORGAN: Dee and I got to be great friends on the movie and because I was a dancer and Dee was a dancer we knew a lot of the same people on Broadway. I was a Broadway dancer and so we were instant friends! I would be hanging out in her dressing room and she would be so upset with the way she looked during the siege sequence in the film, and she'd say "Look at me!" She looked horrible! Bloodied and bruised and her hair was all plastered down and she would get all upset. I would say, "Oh, Dee, you are still beautiful! And you're probably going to win an Oscar for this, you know?" Because she was so upset, she would have moments where she would just break down and just cry to me saying "Look at me! This is what people are going to see!"

JEAN COULTER: Danny Pintauro didn't have a stunt person, not that I remember. I never saw another child on set, and for the most part they hire small people to double for children, and there were none of those on set either. Lewis Teague was wonderful. He was very laid back and really nice to work with. He wasn't yelling or screaming, he was just a nice man. And it was so easy to work with him. Some other directors get impatient and they get excited if they don't get what they want. John Landis on the set of *The Blues Brothers* was exactly that!

LEWIS TEAGUE: Cutting back to Vic and Roger wasn't difficult, that was very useful and helpful for me to have those scenes to be able to cut to them periodically and use that as an elliptical device to cut away. Getting it to work sometimes required playing a lot around the editing room. But Neil Travis, the editor was brilliant! It was so much fun to work with him! He was a very good editor!

ARTHUR ROSENBERG: I thought the final results were really scary! I was surprised that the rest of the world was so taken by the film. One thing I do recall but I have no idea if it was true. I was told one day that one of the St. Bernards had died during the course of shooting. That they

399

are too big to do running scenes, they don't really run and that its heart had given out. Again this is a dim memory, but I recall someone telling me they had a "stunt" Cujo, like an Airedale or something, in a Cujo suit to do the running scenes.

ROBERT CLARK: Peter had a place in Silver Lake, and it was a large apartment with a garage and Kathie and I worked in the garage. It was a two story place and he had cleared it out for us to work in the living room and kitchen area. We had put protection sheets on the floor, and we had to be careful, but we also had a job to do. And it all worked out fine. There were probably six people working on prosthetic dogs. There was a guy who had never done mechanics before, but Peter knew him, Dave Nelson. He went on to start a shop on his own. Larry Carl was there, who I worked with a lot in those days.

CHARLES BERNSTEIN: You know, it's amazing how un-scary a lot of things are when you take the music away; it's kind of neutral and it's like what's scary about that? Music tells us how we need to be feeling, and horror does depend of those stings and lead ups and all of that to be effective. It's always surprising to me how empty films are without that element of being manifested, you know, in the musical sound. In any case, I think all horror movies really depend on their composer's score to carry the day. The visuals are magnificent as are the visual effects and everything that you see on the screen is fantastic, but again, it really begs for some emotional impact that only music can give.

PATRUSHKHA MIERZWA: As an example of Jan de Bont's work method: A shot in the front yard looking at the farmhouse could be anything from: big enough to see the house and walnut tree to being inside the car, and the camera could physically move 50 feet as well. To move the dolly, he would just wave his hand enough for the dolly grip to see. He changed frame sizes all through rehearsals and through every take. And I remember standing next to him, splitting my focus between trying to read the frame size and watching the action. I asked the camera guys to share info with me, but they weren't getting much. We had a Sennheiser 815, a couple 415s, some Micron radio mics, and we planted the car. We had our package set up several different ways to cover a wide range of possibilities and the mixer worked magic.

DAY THREE: Tad has a seizure and Steve Kemp pays a visit to the Trenton house

The morning is heavy with heat as the sweaty and distressed Donna Trenton slowly wakes from a pathetic unrestful sleep only to hear her worst nightmare become a horrifying reality. She turns her wet head towards Tad who lies in the middle of the car gasping for air. His eyes are rolled back showing the whites, his hands are clasping at the hot air, his body is bent backwards in agony spitting out feeble attempts at taking in oxygen and his head is flopped like a thrown out ragdoll. This would be one of the most terrifying and harrowing sequences of the film, where the thought of losing a child to dehydration and over exposure to heat and the lack of air becomes a painful truth. Donna collects her son into her arms and rocks him back and forth (once again, Tad regresses into infancy) and she desperately tries to get her boy to breath. She looks through the blood stained window of the Pinto and with a clever use of jump cuts thanks to editor Neil Travis she spots various points of hope to save her suffocating son. She spots the dishevelled Camber farm house, and then closes in on the porch, then the front door and finally the door handle which makes for a beautiful and fast moving zoom-in on a destination that is essential to her son's survival.

403

Frantic and panicked, Donna holds Tad up and begs him to breathe, Tad claws at his throat, clearly motioning to let air inside. His eyelids flutter, his mouth is dry and opened and his breathing is wheezy and distressed. Danny Pintauro's performance here is painfully real, and the actor had been quoted in saying that he had stomach issues as a baby that would cause him to have such a similar seizure – this would be something that he would refer back to in order to play out such a graphic and frightening scene. Dee Wallace matches his brilliance with her exhausted and anxious attempt at reviving him and bringing him out of his seizure. In many ways, Wallace and Pintauro are very similar actors in that they throw themselves into the reality of the piece and bring with them a finely tuned purpose and a sturdy reasoning behind their very honest, truthful and "on the mark" performances.

Donna puts her fingers into Tad's mouth, trying to ensure he doesn't swallow his tongue, and the child bites causing much pain to Donna's tender fingers. She also attempts to leave the car but is stopped by Cujo, who hears them and comes bounding toward her. The bloodied and rabid St. Bernard bolts towards the dead Pinto and crashes into the window barking angrily, clawing at the glass. The grime of the windows frame mother and child like a perverse representation of a damaged womb. In essence, the sweltering heat and oppressive and yet protective confines of the busted up Pinto reflect the security as well as the restriction of the human womb – that a birth is destined or at least necessary in order to revive life, family reconstruction, the bond between mother and child and the halcyon nature of domesticity. Cujo is that "mean, dark world" that parents teach their children and in order to survive such monstrousness, one must confront the demon and move forward. Donna and Tad remain trapped, but eventually Donna will work towards a sense of warrior woman in the closing moments of the film.

Donna sings to Tad while the dog barks at them from outside. She brings back the "I see your heinie" number that has been sung twice before however this time it is used in order to save Tad's life. When he joins in (a weak breathy voice struggling to recall lyrics) Donna is relieved and she holds him to her heart, pouring all of her love into the boy. When he finally starts breathing, he breaks into a heartbreaking cry calling out that he wants to go home.

Steve Kemp (Christopher Stone) becomes the intruder.

Cutting straight from that moment, we are back at the Trenton home, however, none of the Trenton family are there. Instead, Steve Kemp lingers outside peering in. The intruder finally is seen intruding – in the first scene at the Trentons he is welcomed, the second time he sneaks up on Donna from off screen and finally here he is seen making himself at home and opening the backdoor and coming into the kitchen. He calls out "Donna?" and casually walks through, stopping at a bowl of fruit (the red apple of temptation) and then contemplating – actor Christopher Stone showcasing some magnetic and intense facial expressions that sing with disdain, resentment, anger, jealousy and rejection. Here is a man scorned, and also a man completely not willing to take no for an answer. Finally, Steve runs his fingers across a set of kitchen knives and Charles Bernstein's music thunders in; a menacing and mean spirited motif, linking Steve to thematic elements that accompany Cujo.

The music builds and we cut to Vic Trenton finally "catching up" to what the audience already knows. He is seen driving down the same street he "found out about the affair" in his red Jaguar. The music drives him and becomes a frenzied ascension, building with tension and mania, as we cut to Vic opening the front door to his house and finding the place completely trashed. He races up the stairwell to his bedroom and finds it completely in ruins. Feathers from quilts and pillows dance about the floor while personal belongings are smashed and thrown about the place and the biggest insult is the fact that Kemp has vandalized and "spoiled/soiled" the Trenton bed. Kemp has made his mark, claimed a territory that he always saw as his own and has polluted the sanctity of Vic and Donna's marriage. Closing on the image of the Trenton bed in ruins, the sequence is a perfect summary of thematic elements that run through the makeup of *Cujo*: rescue, sacrifice, regret, desperation, alienation, suffocation, rape of the spirit, pollution and vandalism of sanctity and the moral code and the conflict that arises within the construct of staying safe as well as remaining trapped.

ROBIN LUCE: I had the issue at hand of applying makeup on a child, and the makeup set ups I had to choose had to be in making them a particular way in a toxic-free kind of way which was not so much in fashion those days. So I had to choose my products carefully because I was dealing with lips and a child. So, because these characters had to look incredibly dehydrated during the siege sequence in the car, I had chosen a medical adhesive for their lips that was used in the medical field. I don't think that they use this adhesive anymore in the medical profession, but I had to choose something that would make their lips look dry and cracked and in my research this was perfect for this effect and was the safest thing to put on their lips. If they had gotten it on their lips and it entered their system, it wouldn't be dangerous. The adhesive was sticky, but if I stretched their lips and then applied the material then powdered their inner-lips it wouldn't stick together, I mean it was a little trickier with Danny Pintauro because he was six years old. So, that was my biggest concern – to make sure that whatever I put on him would be quick and safe for him and it would give Lewis Teague the look that he wanted.

Director Lewis Teague overlooks the busted up Pinto. Makeup artist Robin Luce stands at far right, looking in on her work on Dee Wallace and Danny Pintauro.

MARGARET PINTAURO: When they started the scenes when Danny was having those convulsions, which look terrifying in the movie, and are really hard to watch, I was actually surprised. I said to Dan Blatt, "My son used to have convulsions when he was a baby, but that is not the way he used to convulse" so that was just the way Danny invented it! He came up with that on his own.

ROBERT CLARK: I was not on location, I was never on set. Peter Knowlton took care of all the work on set. I am pretty sure that he was the one responsible for making up the dogs in all their drool and getting them bloodied and dirty. There were five dogs used in *Cujo*, five different St. Bernards, and they all had different markings. So Peter had to make sure that their coats all matched up and to make them look rabid was the main concern.

JEAN COULTER: You can tell when an animal is sick with rabies. They walk differently, and hold their head differently and most certainly have foam oozing out of their mouth. My husband and I would build a fence around our house to keep bears away, and for the most part that kind of thing worked. However, there was this one time when we spotted a rabid fox approaching and this fox staggered towards the house, which is very rare for a wild animal to come close to a domestic household. That was my experience with rabies and it was a scary situation.

GARY MORGAN: We used the dog puppet head to bite the door handle, and the animatronic dog was dreadful – they never used it once in the movie! There were some tests of it and it was such a joke when they showed it on film that they never once used it. They had all these different eyes for the animatronic dog, from regular eyes to cloudier to really sick looking and I don't think that they ever used any aspect of it in the movie. They did use the puppet head once or twice. So the puppet head was occasionally used for some snapping. The dog's mouth did not work on the dog suit I had, so they used that puppet head when they wanted like a snapping effect at Dee. They intercut the real dog, the puppet head and me fiendishly and I thought it was amazing the way they edited it! I mean, I knew it was me, because I knew what I did, but for an audience, it is just a perfectly edited film.

Animal trainer Karl Lewis Miller holds the St. Bernard puppet head, while director Lewis Teague contemplates it's use.

KATHIE CLARK: We worked from pictures for the St. Bernards. We had tons and tons of references, and all these images were provided for us. They had three St. Bernards for the shoot so we had to match up our dogs as closely as possible to these dogs. So for example, if one of the dogs had a white spot on his back, we would have to replicate that. So, when I would apply the fur, I would match the dark parts to the dark parts and the light parts to the light parts – we worked with at least three colors of fur, and then we came in and air brushed it afterwards so that was a lot of blending of the colors to keep it looking from fake fur. In those days, it was store box costume fur, now there are companies that make seriously realistic hair that you can order in bulk. If you were to make *Cujo* now it would be super expensive, but the fur would be gorgeous, but back then we had to use what existed, and you would air brush it and tease and sometimes iron it out so it didn't stand straight up and remained down.

ROBERT CLARK: A lot of the scenes where Dee was being attacked used my dogs that I designed and created. When she is clubbing the dog with the water bottle, that was a puppet head that I had built and also when she is swinging the baseball bat at the dog off camera, she is using one of my dog head puppets as a guide. The dog head that was used to bite was sculpted out of fibreglass and a handle was attached that you would pull at the mouth and the other hand would operate another handle that would control the jaw. It also had a couple of finger rings that made it snarl. But it was never seen in any close-ups to show off the snarl, it was just there to help the action of the scene. That head probably got the most mileage of all the prosthetic dogs used.

GARY MORGAN: It was a difficult shoot, especially because of the rain. The dog suit would get so wet and muddy and there was one point I couldn't put the suit on because it was kind of like they put it in a garbage bag, and it was getting mouldy and wet, and disgusting! The stunt coordinator went up to the guy who looked after the suit and said "You expect my guy to put on this wet, disgusting suit?! Don't keep it in the bag. Leave it out somewhere so it will dry. Or leave the suit out for him." But the guy that looked after the suit was like "I don't want to get my hotel room all muddy!" So the stunt coordinator said "Get the suit its own hotel room then! I'm not letting my guy put this disgusting thing on!" He was all pissed off and all upset, but they dried the suit for me!

JEAN COULTER: The dog I most remember was Cubby. The other dogs I don't recall their names. I know that there were five dogs. Cubby was the dog I was going to do the fight scenes with around the car. I did get familiar with all of the dogs, but only really worked with Cubby. He was a good dog.

DON CARLOS DUNAWAY: The cutting back to Vic from Donna was not entirely successful. The structural problem was that Vic was terrified of what might have happened to Donna, but the audience was not: they knew exactly where she was, and wanted only for the good guys to rescue her as soon as possible. I think Lewis may have been trying to overcome this problem by showing the damage Kemp has done to the house. I wasn't aware that he had that in mind and for me it was over-the-top and gratuitous. It's one of the few soft spots in an otherwise amazing movie. Lewis did an extraordinary job, and I'm very happy to have been a part of it.

Director Lewis Teague – a true artist.

LEWIS TEAGUE: Christopher Stone trashing the house was a good scene. The film was just too long! We just had to take a lot of stuff out. We didn't need it. I think when I saw the film for the first time, I knew that was a good choice.

JEAN COULTER: I don't go to movie parties or premieres, I wasn't into all that stuff. So I saw it sometime later, I think I saw it on television for the first time. I enjoyed working on it, but didn't want to be involved with the partying that goes on with the world of filmmaking which at that time was heavily drug addled and booze addled. I knew there was so much work that went into it, but during production there was a lot of drug taking and alcoholism. But all through it, the animals were so well looked after, and I loved working with them.

ROBIN LUCE: I have to say that my biggest recollection was working with Lewis, not at all Peter. Peter and Anthony Richmond were on the same time and let go the same time. Then Lewis had Jan de Bont as his DOP – and he was crazy! He was a crazy man and I had heard stories about him before, but yes, he was crazy. It was my first department head job, and I had to get used to all sorts of characters, and at that point it was a good introduction to these kind of people. I mean a lot of directors of photography are crazy.

GARY MORGAN: I was an actor, and I worked as an actor and I mostly did action type acting roles such as my part in *Logan's Run* (1976), but right around the time of *Cujo*, I was thirty two and the acting roles were kind of drying up. I didn't look like a teenager anymore, and at thirty two I still didn't look like an adult. I'm a little guy, so people still don't buy me for a dad. So it was right around *Cujo* where I settled more completely into stunts. For that I wouldn't do any stunts if I could have played the role. I wouldn't double somebody, you know what I mean? I said "If you want me to do it, I'll do the role!" I'm not going to make some other guy look good! But after *Cujo*, I just need to work more! How I got *Pete's Dragon* (1977) was a similar thing. I got on that film as a dancer way in advance; they call it a "skeleton dancer". You get a small group of dancers that the choreographer works out all the choreography of the whole movie on and then you help choreograph it, and then you teach the choreography

412

to the actor or the star, or they bring in thirty dancers and the skeleton dancers will teach the routines to the others. Now I wanted to play the role of one of the brothers in *Pete's Dragon*, so I went over to the casting director who was a friend of mine and I said "Can I audition for one of the brothers?" He said, "No, Gary. They want two really big guys. They call them "Oxen of Men" in the script!" But I persisted and I got the role! Working on *Cujo* compared to *Pete's Dragon* was similar in one way but then completely different in other ways. Onna White was choreographing dancers for *Pete's Dragon* – and this woman did it all, I mean she was on *Oliver!* (1968) and she also taught non-dancers to move brilliantly, and that is shown in *Pete's Dragon* with someone like Helen Reddy. On *Cujo*, there was set choreography, it was about knowing your marks and where to begin and end. My stuff was not choreographed, it was all improvised, so that when you do a fight scene it is more frenzied.

Lewis Teague on set.

413

Dealing with the elements: notice Lewis Teague in a jacket and gloves to fend off the actual cold conditions on the Santa Rosa farm.

PETER MEDAK: At the time I was signed on for *Cujo*, I must have walked out of at least six or seven major movies. One was with Barbra Streisand which was *A Star is Born* (1976) and another one was with Sean Connery called *The Next Man* (1976) and then my second movie after *Negatives* was going to be a movie called *Figures in a Landscape* (1970) in which I cast Malcolm McDowall in and Peter O'Toole was the star of it, and that's when Peter and I really got to know each other, and then he walked out and then eventually I walked out. There were all kinds of story problems, and then Joseph Losey took over the picture just like Lewis took on *Cujo*. So by the time of *Cujo* I was used to it, it's a very rough business, and I am certain that every director has their own personal horror stories, but you have to absolutely stick up for yourself, because everybody blames you for everything. I mean I got blamed on *Cujo* – and I heard things like "Peter Medak fucked up!" and I got fired. It's the only movie I've ever been fired on in fifty years. *Cujo* was a very painful experience because I made that movie in my head and then it was gone as soon I was fired.

The makeup on the dogs cast as Cujo would be applied and then quickly photographed because the animals would roll upon the ground to get all of it off straight away.

TERESA ANN MILLER: In 1985, my dad got to do the second Stephen King film which was *Cat's Eye*. What was nice was, Stephen King of course, came to the set and again really thanked him for *Cujo* which was pretty cool! I know that meant a lot to him too. You know, on *Cat's Eye* they even gave a little cameo by the St. Bernard. He actually put Christine in the movie also! *Cat's Eye* was my first feature movie I did with my dad in 1985. Oh, wow, it was amazing! It was great! We had so many animals to work. Not only with the cats but with the pigeons that worked on the film, and the pigeon on the ledge pecking at the foot that knocked the guy off the ledge. So that was kind of cool to work with. It was just a great experience. Being on location for that one and working with a very young Drew Barrymore was fun because she loved the animals, of course! She was always hanging out with the animals while we were busy training them. It was just a great experience! It was a great place in Wilmington, North Carolina and it was funny seeing my dad go through the makeup for *Cujo* again, because he kept saying he thought he would never do it again. Yet here he is putting the mud and the makeup and the blood back up on the dog – now two years later, what have you!

MICHAEL HILKENE: *Cujo* was one of those rare pictures where the dialogue, sound effects and music seemed to naturally fall in place without having to sacrifice the level of one for another, even in the action scenes. For example, if the dialogue was getting drowned out by music and/or sound effects, usually sound effects were the first thing to be lowered. However, that rarely, if ever, happened on *Cujo*. Originally, I thought that the reason the *Cujo* soundtrack played so well was because Cujo's vocals usually needed to prevail, and dictated the levels of the dialogue, the music and all the other sound effects. However, after watching the picture recently, I feel that Charles Bernstein's score also had a lot to do with it. The music is there, driving us through the attacks, but the orchestration is not overpowering and leaves plenty of room for the dialogue, for Cujo and for the sound effects. *Cujo* is one of the films that I'm proudest of because I feel our contribution to Lewis Teague's storytelling was instrumental in the movie's success.

At the back of the Pinto, director Lewis Teague and cinematographer Jan de Bont contemplate a shot.

"WHAT ARE YOU GOING TO DO ABOUT KEMP?": Vic finds
the wreckage and the Castle Rock police get involved

Character actors Jerry Hardin and Sandy Ward are introduced to the
film in its very late moments as Detective Masen and Sheriff George
Bannerman. Hardin would feature in an incredibly harrowing cat and
mouse revenge film called *Wolf Lake* (1980) which would give him an
opportunity to play a sensitive but completely dominated "good ole boy"
damaged by the mental abuse of a terrifying Rod Steiger, while Ward
would be seen in varied small roles from playing a pawnbroker in *The
Onion Field* (1979) to Bette Midler's sombre father in *The Rose* (1979).
Here in *Cujo*, Hardin plays against the complicated role he took on in
Wolf Lake, and instead is set up as a stoic and rigid police official casually
investigating Donna Trenton's disappearance, while Ward is given a lot
more to do, most notably being mauled and brutally killed by the rabid
dog in a follow up scene.

Opening on a torn picture of Donna Trenton (a lovely studio picture
for actress Dee Wallace), the scene unfolds with steadiness and a smart
deterrence from slipping into a police procedural. Here is reality caving in
on the situation – a distraught husband and father trying to find his wife
and son and now calling upon the police to help – but never making that
stride into a subplot that will involve their examination into what caused

419

Donna and Tad to "go missing". Unlike in *The Exorcist* which heavily uses the subplot of Lt. Kinderman (Lee J. Cobb) and his investigation into Burke Dennings's (Jack MacGowran) death, *Cujo* brings this sequence out of necessity and reasonability but never lets it overstay its welcome.

The dialogue that opens the sequence is also an interesting factor to consider – Masen inquires about a woman that had been missing in another town of Maine, to which Bannerman carries through with a quick response. This is most likely a hangover from Barbara Turner's screenplay that involved elements from "The Dead Zone" as a novel and its influence on the novel for "Cujo". Here, the policemen are discussing women that have been killed by Frank Dodd (the sick officer who was the initial "monster" from "The Dead Zone") but it is treated as a throwaway and not dwelt upon. Clearly, there is a massive connection made between "The Dead Zone" and "Cujo" in the principal character of Sheriff Bannerman. In the film adaptation by David Cronenberg, Bannerman is played by accomplished and sensitive actor Tom Skerritt while here in *Cujo*, the character is given a totally new "look" and "feel"; instead of the icy-eyed, handsome and athletic Skerritt, Sandy Ward gives this doomed small town sheriff an earthy robustness that rings true to the archetypal sheriff with not much to do until some serious damage hits his home turf. The character of Bannerman in both the novel and the film of *The Dead Zone* would eventually apprehend the psychotic Frank Dodd with the help of the book/film's hero – the psychic John Smith. However, Bannerman would meet his gruesome death in both the novel and film of *Cujo* and be the core link that connects these two Stephen King works.

The photograph of Dee Wallace/Donna Trenton ripped to pieces is a startling image: here the anger of Steve Kemp is on display, sprawled out upon the torn bed sheets and covers, ready for an audience (most likely Vic Trenton himself). Christopher Stone would originally have an entire sequence depicting him trashing the Trenton home – linking him to the rabid dog that has Donna trapped in the dead Pinto – and the sequence was shot, giving a visual aide to what happened at the once picturesque

Tom Skerritt as Sheriff George Bannerman in David Cronenberg's *The Dead Zone.*

A deleted scene: Steve Kemp (Christopher Stone) would originally be seen trashing the Trenton house, and he would climax by tearing up a picture of Donna, before laying next to it in her and her husband's bed.

and lovely homestead. However, once again, time constraints got in the way, and the scene was cut. However, one still of Christopher Stone lying upon the bed caressing the ripped picture of Dee Wallace remains, a haunting and unsettling image of the deranged Steve Kemp totally at a loss in a world of rejection from a woman who has since realised that she has a "terrific husband and a terrific kid".

By the end of this scene, Vic Trenton informs Masen that Donna had set out to Joe Camber's farm to get the car fixed. Masen sends Bannerman to investigate, unbeknownst to him, that he will be sending out his sheriff to his grisly death.

Detective Masen (Jerry Hardin) and Sheriff George Bannerman (Sandy Ward) investigate the situation at hand, while Vic Trenton (Daniel Hugh Kelly) worries about the whereabouts of his wife and son.

JERRY HARDIN ("Detective Masen"): I don't remember how I got the job for *Cujo* exactly, but at that time most of the work I got came by the way of my agent. They submitted me and I went in to audition. Generally speaking, what often happens is that they would send me the scenes and I would get a chance to see what is going on and what the events are what the character is envisioned as. In *Cujo*, it was a matter of understanding that I had to help out this man who had a wife who was missing or at least not responding to his calls.

DANIEL HUGH KELLY: Sandy Ward and Jerry Hardin were two very good actors who were very good to work with. The bedroom scene, when it was all trashed, was very small and very restricting, and I remember someone from the cast or someone from the crew really stunk! I mean they really smelled bad. I have no idea if they were up all night drinking, but I remember that vividly. I don't remember who it was, but I remember wanting to leave the room every time after take.

JERRY HARDIN: Unfortunately, my recall of this whole event is miniscule, because if it had been an unpleasant event it would have stuck in my mind. But this was an uneventful movie to work on only because it was essentially a pleasant time and a good job that flowed well and had no issues. I don't remember anyone from the crew stinking, but that is hilarious!

THE DEAD ZONE: Sherriff Bannerman is killed and Tad wants his daddy

Cutting from the startling image of the torn up photograph of Donna surrounded by the disarray of feathers and ripped up bed covers, we are literally thrust back to the Camber farm where the dead Ford Pinto collects the harsh rays of the summer sun. Director Lewis Teague's choice of having this image follow up from the shambles of the Trenton bedroom is a splendid and inspired expression of the class resentment that runs through the complex bloodstream of the film. Here exists the deep rooted concept of Steve Kemp's hatred of the Trenton family unit; where this sexually free and easily agitated furniture stripper's jealousy of middle class security and comfort brings him to destruction. On top of this, his destruction seems to be on par with Cujo's violent reactions (ripping domesticity to shreds) both existing in a world that sinks into an incurable vortex (primarily established by the opening titles and the panning frenzy in the car a few scenes back et al) and is turned upside down (epitomized by Tad "falling into space" in his introductory moment).

Cujo is ultimately an intimate chamber horror film in that it utilizes a small number of principles and binds them together by circumstance and incidental crossovers. The film – both its structure as a chamber horror piece and with its theme of class resentment – bears a similarity to Peter

Weir's psychological horror film *The Plumber* (1979) which pits a "dumb labourer" against a couple of intellectual academics. But what makes *Cujo* distinct to the aforementioned Australian offering is the fact that it doesn't dwell on the monstrousness of societal trappings, instead it drives it to the background keeping it cemented as the basis of the physiological terror that unfolds – most notably in the next two major sequences involving Donna Trenton and Cujo.

With the decision to cut to a swooping shot of the Ford Pinto, this stern notion of ensuring we understand that Donna and her son are trapped inside is hammered into the collective audience eye. Donna is asleep with Tad folded up beside her inside the dead Pinto which reads as a boiling hot womb for two characters that will eventually be reborn. The image of the Ford Pinto initially is a striking image with a gleaming shine slammed upon the heavy metal and the sun bouncing off the grotty and grungy bonnet. Passing that we find the filthy glass, the blood stains upon the windows, the grime and dirt as well as the shattered glass hanging onto the frames of the cars with a smidgen of hope – all of this reflective of a ravaged womb protecting not only the delicate child, but his mother as well. This densely hot mechanical compound guarding mother and son from the world and its monsters is a double edged sword, as it also suffocates them and keeps them trapped from re-entering a world that does not necessarily have to be host to lecherous monsters – be they from a child's closet, a lover scorned or a rabid St. Bernard. Donna is seen holding her breast and it is a beautifully profound choice from actress Dee Wallace who evokes an image of maternal nourishment now dry and dead. Her pink blouse is now torn to shreds and mostly used to nurse her deep wounds. She is covered in blood, sweat and dirt while Tad is limp and lifeless. Not only are mother and child in a near-death-like state of rest under strain, Cujo also catches a quiet moment, lying upon the soil watching the Pinto, his head pressed on his long forepaws. With the oppressive heat lingering, a gentle and refreshing soft breeze kicks up, picking up dead leaves that cross past the bloodied and rabies-ravaged dog. But he is disturbed and interrupted by something approaching: it is a car, it's Sheriff Bannerman.

The grand tradition of inept/unlucky police officials: Sheriff George Bannerman (Sandy Ward) approaches the bloodied Pinto.

The sheriff's car drives towards the Camber farm and Cujo leaps up and trots away already making plans on how to deal with this situation at hand – his run is swift, agile and attentive – like a perfectly healthy dog. Animal trainer Karl Lewis Miller works wonders during this sequence with the St. Bernards playing the titular role – each dog was trained and perfected in specific courses of action: one would be excellent at long distance running, another great at lunging, another very good at snarling and looking aggressive. Much like previous dog-centric movies such as *Won Ton Ton: The Dog Who Saved Hollywood* (1976) and *C.H.O.M.P.S.* (1979), dogs in film would be versatile performers readily available to not only perform stunts that would be monitored and carefully played out, but also present a range of emotions in their expressions, mannerisms, demeanour and method. Two of the strongest animal performers to come of 1970s and 1980s film and television would be a terrier cross Higgins and his daughter Benjean who would both play the iconic role of Benji in a number of films and here in *Cujo*, the group of St. Bernards taking on the canine antagonist deliver some outstanding representations of facial rage, anger and menace.

The attack on Banneran is fierce and brutal. The image of Cujo lunging at him before he has a chance to grab hold of his gun is pure monster movie magic – the violent attack comes thick and fast as Bannerman's revolver falls to the ground lost in the foamy frenzy. Cujo dives into Bannerman's stomach and thrusts his snout inside, ripping into his flesh. It is a disorientating and distorted effect as Bannerman's car spewing out police report gibberish moments earlier. On his arrival, Bannerman scouts the area and notices the Pinto, but cannot see the sleeping Donna and Tad. Before he can make a report he hears something in the distance and decides to investigate, leading into the "boo" moment of Cujo racing towards him in a flash. Cujo's growling and snarling leads into a horrific attack and the death of hope for Donna who slowly wakes to bear witness to Bannerman's slaughter. What also happens here is a fantastic trajectory where this rabid St. Bernard has now evolved (or devolved) into an unstoppable violent monstrous entity – no longer is this creature an unfortunate victim of circumstance and bad luck, now this once docile and playful pooch is a demonic force of rage, deep hatred and unrelenting bloodlust. This is all encapsulated by the frenzied images of Cujo as an inexorable beast chasing after Bannerman, trapping him, cornering him, forcing him to climb up rafters and finally fall to his death from the scaffolding of the barn where the mighty foaming jaws of the dog will rip out vital organs from the heavyset Bannerman. All of this carnage and death would happen where Joe Camber once worked on cars – now, the place of Castle Rock's best sheriff's death.

Sheriff George Bannerman would of course be the main connection to Stephen King's previous work "The Dead Zone", and he would be integral in the chase after psychotic serial killer Frank Dodd (a policeman who went "bad"). In the novel of "Cujo", when Bannerman is pinned down by the ferocious and crazed dog, he calls out "That's you isn't it

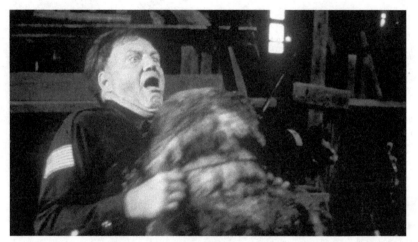

Bannerman (Sandy Ward) is killed by the rabid Cujo. Here, stunt man Gary Morgan is used to tear at the actor.

Dodd?!" looking into the dog's terrifying bloodshot eyes. The concept of Cujo being possessed by the vengeful sexually and mentally sick Frank Dodd is something that screenwriter Barbara Turner wished to employ in her adaptation, but finally follow up scribe Don Carlos Dunaway would remove all connection to Frank Dodd for the final write up.

The final blow where Cujo rips off a chunk of flesh exposing Bannerman's guts is a fantastic punch in the face for gorehounds everywhere. Actor Sandy Ward's dead expression of shock highlights the mania. In Stephen King's novel, there is wonderfully written graphic descriptions of Bannerman feeling his intestines spill out from his stomach through his fingers, and when he blocks Cujo from ripping into his face, the dog has shredded his hands to smithereens. Lewis Teague most definitely does this prose justice with his depiction of Bannerman being slain – it is a frenzied and malicious sequence, and with Neil Travis's stunning editing piecing it all together, the moment is a perfect expression of visceral horror. Adding to the sadism is Cujo racing back to Bannerman's dead body and tearing him apart, treating the corpse as a dead play thing.

Tad starts to fall into a frightening conniption again, desperate to breathe, grasping at his throat in an attempt to let air inside, with the whites of his eyes showing. Donna desperately tries to help him, crying "Not now!" and shaking him back to life. When he finally comes through, coughing and splattering and breathing again, he begins to moan repeatedly "I want my daddy!" Here, Tad expresses his most primal response to this situation – that his mother is unequipped to "deal with the monsters at large" and that his father is the one responsible for "The Monster Words" and therefore emotionally available and strong enough to take on closet dwelling cretins. The idea of comforting fathers and troubled/troubling mothers became a quiet trend in modern cinema after the critical success of *Ordinary People* where Mary Tyler Moore's cold and "turned off" mother of a tortured teen (Timothy Hutton) would inspire an examination into the complexities of family dynamics. In horror however, mothers will always continually prove to be the heart and soul of the family and driving force to bring peace and order into the situation at hand – Tobe Hooper's *Poltergeist* would force libertine parents to confront a question posed to them by a medium as to who their children "fear" the most out of them. Later the same medium would talk about the truth, purity and essentialness of a "mother's love" – sending Jo Beth Williams into a fiery stronghold defending her young from sinister ghosts ("She's just a baby!"). Dee Wallace's performance in *Cujo* as a woman whose frustration and desperation is magnified and building into a phenomenally constructed arc that will eventually bring her to warrior-woman, is a masterful handle of this feminine archetype – however, as opposed to Jo Beth Williams who starts out completely centred within the homestead without a trace of trouble in her marriage to movie husband Craig T. Nelson, Wallace is given a meatier and far more complicated role in Donna Trenton who has to reclaim her place as both mother and wife, but most importantly as a woman undisturbed by the metaphoric "storm".

Matching Wallace and young Danny Pintauro's exquisite performances is Jan de Bont's remarkable work as cinematographer here. He paints Bannerman's death in frightening realism, then brings a stylised vision of Donna and Tad huddled up in the sweaty, uncomfortable car. The glass in front of them coated in grungy filth, but adding an element of church window aesthete – adding to the religious undertones that the film somehow manages to convey; in essence the image turns from mother and child to a distorted vision of Madonna and Magi, positioned in a state of threat. When Dee Wallace screams "Alright! I'll get your daddy!" the stress levels are now at an all-time high, and Donna is now out of her wits and incredibly angry at herself for having fallen into such a dire situation. Wallace would fight to keep that moment in the film seeing that producer Dan Blatt (in fear of audiences not responding well to Wallace's anger towards her child) wanted to remove it. Thankfully, Wallace insisted that mothers everywhere would understand that frustration and rage that every parent has at their beloved kid and as a result the moment became a point in the film that critics worldwide responded to, but more importantly, mothers on an international level related in droves.

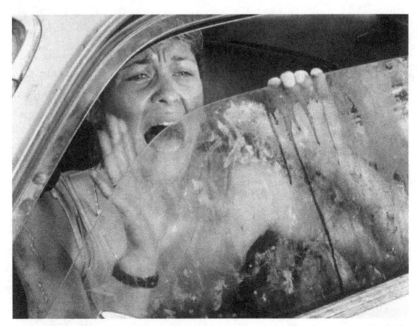

Donna Trenton (Dee Wallace) screams for Sheriff Bannerman (Sandy Ward) to help her.

431

MICHAEL HILKENE: Since we had the trainers and the dogs for the day, Lewis asked that we try and record some real St. Bernard footsteps for Cujo. So, an hour or so after the ADR session, we're setting up to record runbys and walkbys. I'm sitting on the ground in this meadow on the outskirts of Newhall, a city to the north of L.A., while Karl walks Bernie back and forth from his assistant, who's 75 feet off to my left, past me to a spot 75 feet to my right. Karl does that three or four times. I've got headphones on, a mike in my hand, and a 25 pound Nagra recorder sitting on the ground to my right. Karl says they're ready, he leaves Bernie with his assistant and walks back to his spot to my right. I have to admit that the sight of Bernie flailing Karl around is still fresh in my mind. I sure as hell wished that we could use one of the other dogs for the runbys. Too late for that now. I started recording, Karl calls to Bernie, and his assistant lets Bernie off the leash. Instead of following the path in front of me that Karl was training him to use, Bernie started running straight at me. All I could do was fall backwards and pray that Bernie didn't get his lessons mixed up with some of the ones from the set. Fortunately, I ended up getting a great angle of Bernie as he leaped over me. He must have jumped at least 10 feet. When he landed, he clipped the edge of the 25 pound Nagra and flipped it over like it was a tiddly wink. As much as I wanted to please Lewis, I was feeling like I might have to throw in the towel on this one. I recorded a couple tracks of Bernie milling and walking, one of which made it into the picture. Other than that, foley footsteps and movements were what we ended up using for Cujo. The one thing we still needed was Cujo's subtle whines and the howling for the fog scene. I can't recall if the whines and howling we had hoped to get from Samson, the Doberman, worked or not. Some of those may have been made by the famous Frank Welker, known for his many voices as well as his ability to create vocal effects for many animals. Though Frank came in to help with some of Cujo's subtler sounds, like the whines, I can't remember how much of his material was used.

CONRAD E. PALMISANO: In reality the Sheriff would have stayed up high, but in movies somebody has to read the script, right, so even though somebody would say "I'm going to climb up here and stay here"... but in the script these things have to happen, so we had to kind of work backwards and into. And even though it didn't make a lot of physical sense for a person to do, you have to work from the storyline, and the storyline is that the dog had to attack and kill the Sheriff. So you kind of have to back into that and try to make it as believable as possible. So the thing is, Karl was brave with the dogs. They were all trained to do exactly what they were supposed to do; anytime he said " Go", "Stop", "Sit", "Roll over", "Lay down", they did it. So he was brilliant with the animals with all the different dogs it took to make *Cujo*. So, Karl Miller was fantastic. And even though we didn't know each other before that film, we got in there and he said "Okay. Tell me what I need to do? How do we do this? How do we do that? He would say that and we would work with him because, you can't have a conversation with the dog, right? So the dog is trained to do A, B, C, D. So what we had to do was work the storyline into A, B, C, D, so the dog could do what was necessary to make the film work. And I think it worked brilliantly! So what the dog was trained to do we had to work the action into what the dog was trained to do. We couldn't retrain the dog on the set.

CHRISTOPHER MEDAK: Karl Lewis Miller was a gem. The dogs were great and the trainers were excellent, especially one of the ladies who was just outstanding as an animal trainer. We also had a bloke in a dog suit, a dog in a dog suit and then there were the St. Bernards. Karl was brilliant and so down to earth and hardworking.

CONRAD E. PALMISANO : To look ferocious – that was part of the makeup that they would put on them. Cubby died. They said "he twisted a gut." Apparently in large dogs, when they are doing certain things that are over the top and so on and so forth, their intestines can turn within their

433

stomach and cause them a problem. So Cubby passed away from that. And they had this very sad ceremony for him. Cubby was a wonderful dog and Karl took care of him. And that Cubby – he was so strong – we would put him strapped to a stunt person's chest – when it was the girl doubling Dee Wallace or was the stunt sheriff double, Walter Wyatt, and he had this suit that he would put on with a thing in the middle of the chest that was tried around the shoulders – that the dog could grab a hold of and bite. And if you look at the movie when the sheriff is being killed, and there is the stunt man, Walter Wyatt, this St. Bernard could pick him up – a two hundred pound stunt man! And this dog could pick him up and move him left and right and back and forth with the movement of his neck! St. Bernard's were very, very, very strong! And they were taught to attack this thing – they wouldn't go at somebody's neck, but there is this object they would put – that the dogs were trained to go for, that they could bite onto, so they wouldn't bite the person's physical body. They could bite onto this strap. And it was maybe 2 inches x 4 inches long, and 2 inches wide, and they could grab a hold of. I mean, Walter Wyatt was no small man, but he could pull Walter left and right, forward and back quite easily.

GARY MORGAN: I attacked the sheriff. This is interesting. He was a big guy too! And what they did was, he was thrashing around so much that I had a hard time staying with him, you know what I mean? So what they did was they wired the dog head, with me in it, to his chest – so I was like attached to him – they put like a harness on him, and they wired the dog's head to his chest. And he was thrashing around so much, he lifted me off the ground and he was battering me around, and I was going – I have forgotten the guy's name that played him – I was going "Come on!" and before we even did it, he was going "I was in the army and they showed us how to take a dog down, like if a Doberman was attacking you!" He says "You put your hand on the back of the dog's neck. You let him bite you, then you put the dog in a hold then you break the

434

dog's neck" But he was demonstrating it on me! I thought he'd knock me out! He did it so hard. I went "Dude! Come on!" He got into it so he was thrashing me around. It was one of those days I'm going, "Man, I'm really beat up!" That was me on his chest, but when they pulled away... I don't remember. It was probably all made up before? They also had a stunt man that doubled Sandy, in the scene where he falls. Remember when he is in the barn and he falls? That was a stunt double that did the fall.

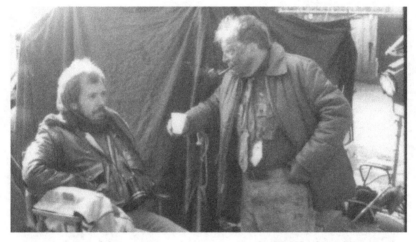

Director Lewis Teague listens to actor Sandy Ward after shooting his death scene.

"WHAT DID BANNERMAN SAY?": Vic catches on

Going through Tad's bedroom and placing clothes back into his closet, Vic Trenton's building anxiety and stress levels loom and dominate his presence. Daniel Hugh Kelly plays this out with trigger ready availability – he has a stern grasp on the maddening paranoia and the uncertainty of how things will take shape. His intelligent acting choices are met by poignant visuals that are subtle and yet so telling. Here is the first scene of the film where Tad's closet is completely wide open, in daylight and featured from the inside looking out. There are certainly no monsters here. There is light, understanding, honesty, truth and the onset of forgiveness.

Masen approaches Vic carefully. He explains that Steve Kemp has been arrested and admits to trashing the house, but that he has no idea where Donna and Tad are. Vic angrily protests this, but Masen is adamant that Kemp is telling the truth. Without arguing, Vic asks "What did Bannerman say?", to which the confused Masen throws out "Maybe he's following a lead..." which sparks something in Vic; something that needs to be thoroughly investigated. Vic steps into gear and races out of the house. Jumping into his red Jaguar, he sets out to the Camber farm.

DANIEL HUGH KELLY: Then there was the scene where I figure

437

things out and I had to get into my red Jaguar to go and find my wife. Now remember that Jaguar was a convertible, and I thought that was odd and the reason being is I thought it would be strange that I would rock up to this situation in a convertible after all this has happened with this crazed rabid dog. However, they hadn't shot the stuff with the dog yet, and I remember thinking man, I should voice my opinion here and tell them that I shouldn't have a Jaguar convertible. I thought it might look stupid. Sure enough, at the premiere, which I didn't go to, the entire theatre erupted into laughter! They had seen this monstrous dog tearing apart this car, and this guy is gonna go up there and save them in a convertible?! Crazy! I thought, Goddamnit Danny you should have said something! But in retrospect, it is refreshing and a nice humorous moment, in a film that has none. I think it's important that horror movies have some moments of relief, because that is life, we have humorous moments in life and that's what the audience responds to – the terror and the laughs. But yes, *Cujo* is most definitely a film with little to no light moments, but I think that Jaguar pulling up by the end is one. It's subtle, but it's there. Also, because Lewis, Dee and Danny did such an incredible job with that whole dog siege sequence, the audience probably needed that relief spurt of laughter when I rocked up in the convertible – it was a release I suppose. That was the last shot I worked – when I get into my car to race off to save my wife and son, and that was shot in Mendocino. We shot that in front of the big house façade.

JERRY HARDIN: I don't remember Peter Medak being attached on the film at all, I don't think I was involved when he was around. Lewis Teague was the director I remember. I vaguely knew about the novel "Cujo", but I have to say that my primary remembrance of the film was meeting one of the dogs. He was a lovely dog, as I recall I thought it was remarkable that he became the villain of the piece. This was out on location in Santa Rosa, I was lucky to go out there even though I had no scenes out there. I remember meeting the dog but have no recollection of the animal handler.

I am very good with animals, I love them, so it was lovely to meet this St. Bernard who would become so terrifying on screen. There were obviously several dogs involved, but I only met the one that was working on the day I was there on set. This dog was pleasant and approachable, and I was never warned about the animal biting anyone or being aggressive.

"I'M LOSING MY BABY": Donna takes charge

In *The Exorcist*, when actress Chris MacNeil (Ellen Burstyn) asks Jesuit Father Damien Karras (Jason Miller) if her daughter is going to die, it restores faith in the doubting priest and he goes upstairs to beat the devil out of her, ultimately sacrificing his own life to save a child he technically "has never met". In *Cujo*, when the tired and traumatized Donna Trenton drifts between consciousness and fatalistic exhaustion only to discover that her son Tad is near death, it essentially gives her the bolt of energy she needs to restore all faith in herself (much like the haunted Father Karras) and to act up and finally face the rabid dog once and for all. In essence, what Donna does is face her own personal demons, ready to confront them head on with a zealous eagerness to own her own personal victorious salvation.

The slow pan across Tad's limp, near dead body with his face pale and lips cracked with extreme dehydration, is a horrifying realisation and ugly truth: this child will die if Donna remains trapped. Donna nudges at him, wearily trying to get the boy to regain consciousness. When she fails again and again, she has the sinking realisation that he might die. She mutters "Dear God, save my baby" and then finally "I'm losing my

441

baby". The fragility of a child and his essential need to have his mother literally "bring him back to life" is what tail-ends *Cujo* and that is married to the basic truth of the piece which bridges the complexities of fear and alienation with the love and determination of a mother driven by a complete devotion to her child.

Donna's body is completely ravaged by the elements and by injury – she is bleeding profusely from her leg and arm and coated in thick sweat with a blistering combination of sunburn, fresh and dry blood as well as the repercussions of dehydration. However, these physical attributes heighten Donna Trenton turning into a warrior woman and as Charles Bernstein's outstanding music accompanies this newborn "force of nature" from finally getting out of her car for the last time and coming face to face with the hateful St. Bernard, actress Dee Wallace brings all the power, passion, devotion, dedication, experience, heightened awareness, spiritual centre, zeal, vigour and ruthlessness to this character. Wallace's performance is a truly inspired and inspirational one – she most certainly should have been nominated for an Academy Award for this performance (something that scholars of film as well as Stephen King himself have agreed upon). Sissy Spacek, Piper Laurie and Kathy Bates have all been nominated for Oscars for works based on King material (Bates winning for *Misery* (1990)) which clearly indicates King writes fantastic and complex women characters, and Donna Trenton is one of his most acutely conceived. It is a tragedy that Dee Wallace was not nominated for the coveted golden statuette that year, but ultimately a mistake by the Academy who far more often than not, snub horror as a formidable contender.

Dee Wallace's tour de force performance and her greatest creation is Donna Trenton (in a career that boasts some of the most electric performances in genre cinema) and when she finally races out of the Pinto, collects the baseball bat and swings it at the rabid St. Bernard screaming "Well come on then!", it is cinematic magic. The heroine of the piece – the perplexed and complicated fair maiden – is now confronted by the dragon.

442

The "blood drenched dragon" emerging from his cave: the rabid St. Bernard confronts the "woman in the storm" for one last showdown.

The showdown is an outstanding achievement of choreography and blocking with Dee Wallace moving back and forth as Cujo prowls and lunges. She swings the bat with ferocity and the dog leaps at her with equal rage. In what would become a mini-three act opera where Donna starts off in the wake of a realisation that her son might die and then entering the deadly terrain of confrontation, the finale brings it to this dishevelled woman smashing the back window of her car. This is pure catharsis. It is shot in slow motion and highlights her big primal scream that is primitive and explosive: a personal exorcism. Wallace's scream is similar to her letting loose in *The Howling* which unleashes the beast in her character of news anchor Karen White, moments before she transforms into a werewolf on air.

Donna Trenton in *Cujo* is the adulteress in the metaphoric "storm" forced to face her monstrous punishment – the day of judgement. Here is the last of the Three Days of Darkness which acts as a balancing point and choice maker, forcing her to regroup with her family and fall into the conventions of familial domesticity. Interestingly enough, *Cujo* copped small amounts of criticism for having a sexist undercurrent in that in its very conception there is the basic idea that a woman has to reclaim the role of "mother"; that Donna has to sacrifice her own happiness in order to be the soul mate to her husband and angel guardian to her son. This is something this scribe thoroughly disagrees with. Films of the period such as *Kramer vs. Kramer* (1979), *Mr. Mom* (1983) and *Baby Boom* (1987) are offensive in that regard, preaching the idea that when women sacrifice personal goals, men are left to take care of "women's business" with either dire or ludicrously "comic" results. The rabid Cujo is most certainly a form of punishment, there as a moral judgement and angry "hand of karma", and this now monstrous being (no longer just a dog) is to be conquered and vanquished; Donna will eventually take charge and shatter this bestial symbol of guilt and turmoil.

The threat of domesticity corrupted played out even in the film's initial ad campaign. The poster art for the film in the U.S. featured a white picket fence – a representation of the halcyon family unit and the harmonious tranquillity of suburban living – sprawled with fresh blood that read "Cujo". Both acting as a poetic illustration of thematic elements that drive the film as well as setting an ominous and ambiguous tone, the poster was part of a trend at the time for horror movie campaigns in fear of overselling the featured monster. A film such as *Nightwing* (1979) had two variant posters – one that kept it "quiet" that the film was about killer bats and one that relished in it, while films such as *The Pack* and *Day of the Animals* (1977) had alternate titles *The Long Dark Night* (for *The Pack*) and *Something Is Out There* (for *Day of the Animals*) as well as variant posters to hide the killer dog/killer animal concept.

In the showdown between Donna and Cujo, Donna uses Brett Camber's discarded baseball bat. As she swings it, the bat hits the large dog and snaps off and she falls over a tree stump, which acts as a nice call back to the damaged and fragmented tree that Brett spotted in the fog earlier in the film. She lands on her back with the broken baseball bat exposed. When Cujo lands right onto it, it pierces through his flesh and he yelps in extreme pain. Donna seems to be on her back and under attack

444

by Cujo in multiple scenes – a kind of bestial play on rape – and when she finally slays her personal demon, it is on her back. But as the film moves forward, the monster is not dead. Ultimately, Donna will kill Cujo standing up, attentive, holding Tad to her chest and empowered. In this sequence however, the frenzy leads to a semi-fatalistic coda as the large St. Bernard drops his massive head onto Donna's chest. Cujo's body slumped upon Donna will foreshadow Annie Wilkes (Kathy Bates) lying dead upon Paul Sheldon (James Caan) with her face covered in blood and ash in *Misery*, another magnificent Stephen King adaptation – and one that will also be a rarity in that it would not include supernatural horror, but horror grounded in "reality". Sobbing and without words, Donna rolls the dog off of her and makes her way to Sheriff Bannerman's revolver, she aims it at the lifeless supposedly dead St. Bernard, and has a distinct reckoning to not use it. Her refusal to shoot Cujo, mirrors virginal but resourceful Laurie Strode (Jamie Lee Curtis) in *Halloween* (1978), who seems to be offended by the concept of violence when the opportunity presents itself to her to stab the boogeyman Michael Myers. However, the Midwestern teen tosses the knife aside (afraid to be one in the same with Myers), but will bring herself to acts of defence (notably with highly feminine objects such as knitting needles and coat hangers) when there is no other resort. Here in *Cujo*, Donna will eventually take to Bannerman's gun and evolve from primal bat wielding Amazon to trigger happy modern heroine. The same gun that smashes through the glass window to break free young Tad will be used to finally severe the monster.

DANIEL HUGH KELLY: I had it kind of easy. I went down to L.A. and they were shooting it up in Northern California, and they had two weeks of dog stuff. I went to L.A. and found an agent and during the weeks they did the dog stuff, I got to know L.A. and my agent. I apologized to Dee, I mean here I was waiting around to do my scenes, and she was going through intense dramatic stuff with Lewis. Oh and Lewis looked like he aged during those two weeks during the dog shoot. He was draining on

Mother presented as warrior: the fallen woman rises to become heroic.

Fighting off the monster: Donna Trenton (Dee Wallace) is pinned under the rabid beast as the Three Days of Darkness come to a close.

him. He was such a sweet man, a really lovely guy. He was so great when the dog stuff was finished and he seemed so happy to see me.

PATRUSHKHA MIERZWA: Loved, loved, loved Dee and Chris, though I knew him less. Dee was always inclusive, she was approachable

The Pinto as an assortment of bits and pieces – a creation that would serve the camera, character, direction, editing and movement.

and likable and I remember her with a smile for everyone. Mark and I had a crew party, maybe it was the wrap party, in our hotel room; she and Chris and some crew people came. We had purchased an early 1900's phonograph and we played old records. At one point we realized we had a blank cylinder (record) and Dee sang "I'll be Home for Christmas", which we still have. I had a lot of respect and admiration for Danny – he was a prepared actor and understood camera movement and design – very impressive for such a young person. I didn't really know him well but tried to look out for him on the set. You know coming from working in costuming and being a seamstress and going into sound is not as uncommon as you might think. I started in theatre and answered an ad on a bulletin board for my first film project. It also happened to be Michelle Pfeiffer's first film and she came into the costume shop for fittings. Talk about a war story – the company had rented an office space on Hollywood Blvd for millinery and costumes as it was a 1940's flashback story. Every day I'd walk past Frederick's of Hollywood (trashy lingerie) and the big glass storefront windows filled with scantily-clad mannequins, then up some dark stairs. It looked like a time capsule from the 1940s. Many

447

wood-panelled offices were abandoned and there'd be a wino passed out or, on occasion, a man pleasuring himself. I remember during one fitting I said to Michelle, "You're going to be a star someday; remember me" and she demurely said thank you. I said, "No! You're going to be a star and I want you to remember me." She did become a star but we never had the occasion to work together again... I'd like to think she *does* remember me. I worked with her sister Deedee on *Vamp* (1986) – also very sweet with an infectious smile. Working in film and in the shop, I was even less a part of the process; I missed being with the main company. I had occasion to visit the set twice and liked the energy (and even filled in on camera for an "over-the-shoulder" piece of coverage). Lastly, there was an expectation that I would sew/alter/repair actresses' personal clothing without compensation. And I'd gotten tired of hearing, "Make me look younger/thinner". Mark was the mixer on that set and we worked together again exactly one year later. It was a smaller shoot and I had an opportunity to interview the crew about their jobs, never having gone to film school. Mark has always been extremely generous with his knowledge and he was with me, too. I liked the important contribution I could make in sound and the ability to listen and learn from the director and actors. I wanted to be paid for using my brain. It was a quick transition. Years later, we had the good fortune to work on a show with Mary Jo Lang, who was also in costumes. I told her she should move on to sound and she soon transitioned to sound and is a foley superstar.

GARY MORGAN: It was near the end of the movie and the dog is laying on her, when she was finally won and the dog is dead, she is laying there. They wanted a shot of the real dog laying on her. So they had a veterinarian on the set, and they tranquilized the dog, like they would in surgery. It was all very safe, the veterinarian did it and the dog was completely unconscious. And they took the dog like on a stretcher and they laid Dee down and they got the dog on top of Dee. Now she is laying

Boom operator Patrushkha Mierzwa and sound mixer Mark Ulano on location with their dog who had just delivered a litter of puppies. (courtesy of Patrushkha Mierzwa).

there and they have this dog, even though he was unconscious, it kind of wiggled and groaned and kind of shook a little, and Dee wiggled!

MARGARET PINTAURO: The shoot was incredibly tough and asked a lot out of Dee Wallace and Danny. The car scenes were very difficult for the both of them. When Dee used the butt of the pistol to smash the window, it shattered the glass and she kept in character and went there and grabbed hold of my son and dragged him across the backseat of the car. It was supposed to be plastic glass, but because she hit it so hard, it

Cast and crew, including stars Dee Wallace (posing with a puppy) and Christopher Stone and sound engineers Patrushkha Mierzwa and Mark Ulano, celebrate Christmas during production. (courtesy of Patrushkha Mierzwa).

Patrushkha Mierzwa's polystyrene cup for the Cujo Christmas celebration. (courtesy of Patrushkha Mierzwa).

The blood soaked finale. (photos courtesy of Gale A. Adler).

451

smashed the real glass so there were shards of real glass everywhere. Thank God it didn't cut Danny, but I think Dee's knees were cut a little bit. After they got out of the car, the both of them came running towards me, and Dee wouldn't let anyone else touch him except for me.

JOHN PINTAURO (Danny Pintauro's father): I was on set when the window broke on the car which I didn't expect to happen. If you watch the scene carefully, Dee is hitting the car with the pistol and she breaks the plastic coating on the shank and when she hits the window again, she caught the window just right with the metal shank and that is why the window shattered. And no one expected that to happen! And she kept going on it, she didn't stop, she just kept going on with the scene and pulled Danny out of the car and kept it moving, and so that's why it worked so well! Dee was an incredible actress and a very determined actress, she didn't want to let anything stop her or deter her from finishing up that scene, so she dragged Danny out of the car and carried him to the farmhouse. And it worked out great.

Catharsis: Donna Trenton screams and smashes the glass, ushering in a rebirth.

The Pinto glass smashed to smithereens after Dee Wallace hammers it with the revolver. (courtesy of Danny and Margaret Pintauro).

GARY MORGAN: So they made a dog suit for the Labrador. It was so ridiculous! And one of the tests that we did they had the Labrador jumping around, and in the dog suit. And at one point the Labrador was thrashing around, and the dog's head comes flying off, and we have a Labrador in a St. Bernard's suit with a Labrador head! It was so funny! In the dailies, Karl Miller was so upset because we were laughing so hard at this Labrador in a dog suit, because he was really trying to sell them on that. His Labrador was so well trained, he could do anything that he wanted. Well, even if he could keep the suit on it still looked baggy. At one point they thought maybe they could use it because it looked like it was rabid and staggering around in this dog suit. They thought maybe they could use it for the staggering scenes! But it was real funny! Karl was trying to get any dog besides a St. Bernard because you can't train a St. Bernard to do things that they don't do. A Doberman attacks! He comes in and out! And that is what they were looking for – to attack! St. Bernard's are big, lumbering dogs that don't attack, they just grab on and with that massive bite the animals just succumbs, they snap its neck and they kill them. So they have to do other things to try and look like the dog was attacking. It was a challenge for Karl! And I thought everybody pulled it off. It was great!

Danny Pintauro in the makeup chair. (courtesy of Danny and Margaret Pintauro).

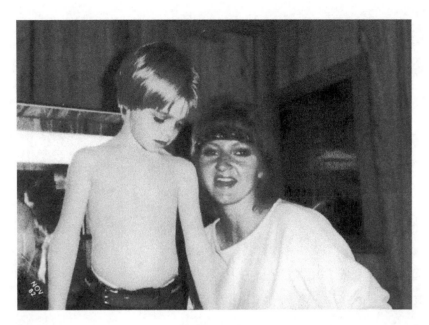

Robin Luce turns Danny Pintauro white to emphasise his dehydration. (courtesy of Danny and Margaret Pintauro).

Danny Pintauro happily smiling in between takes on the location.

"BREATHE!": Donna saves her boy and the monster makes one final appearance

Of course, being a horror film made after the massive success of *Carrie* which featured that wonderful "boo" moment right at the end of the film where Sissy Spacek's bloodied hand bolted out from underneath the rubble of a grave to grab hold of an unsuspecting Amy Irving, multiple horror movies would employ the final jump scare that evoked the message that the monster is never truly dead. Hugely popular films such as *Friday the 13ᵗʰ* (1980) and *A Nightmare on Elm Street* (1984) (both of which sparked franchises) would employ this now horror movie cliché, and *Cujo* is no exception. The malevolent dog smashes through the kitchen window of the Camber residence once last time, determined to kill the woman and her child. This frightening shock lands right at the moment where young Tad wakes up out of unconsciousness; breathing and alive in his mother's arms.

The entire sequence is shot in slow motion – bridging the three slow motion entries together: Tad racing across his bedroom floor in fear of the monster that lurks in his closet, Donna smashing through the car window to rescue Tad and screaming in a moment of pure catharsis and now this scene, with Cujo crashing back into their lives wanting to tear them to shreds, but not able to throw down the unity shared between mother and child. Donna's triumphant slaying of the monster that may very well have haunted Tad's closet is something that her husband Vic was not able to do with actions, only with words. Donna becomes the saving grace – the powerful warrior hellbent on saving her child, she transforms into the ultimate mother in motion picture history; a pure and undisputed representation of mother as protector, defender, nurturer, caretaker, primal force in keeping the child safe and alive and a response to an earthy reassurance.

Carrying her near-dead child into the Camber residence, Donna swipes the clutter on the kitchen table with it all crashing onto the floor. One noticeable item is a cruddy box of Kellogg's Corn Flakes – a trusted old brand, and not one of Vic Trenton's Sharp Cereals. Donna has entered this terrain as a middle class woman now forced into the compounds of working class trappings; her body aching and riddled with wounds, her sole purpose right here is to resurrect her dying child. She splays Tad's listless body onto the kitchen table and darts to the sink, filling her grotty hands with fresh water. She splashes it onto the boy and then breathes into his mouth. The moment is gritty and confronting – this trembling, desperate mother aching to have her son wake up and live.

In Stephen King's novel, Tad Trenton would die – he would die as a result of dehydration and exposure to the harsh elements. The closing moments of the novel would tail-end with Donna and Vic having to cope with such a horrendous loss. On top of this element would be some magic prose detailing the reality of the situation – a state commissioner of animals beheading Cujo's corpse, Donna getting treatment for rabies (something that is commonly considered worse than the condition itself) – as well as some lovingly written poetic retribution such as Cujo not ever being a "bad dog" and that it "was never his fault" and that Donna and Vic would slowly (very slowly) reunite as a couple and carefully mourn the loss of their boy. On top of this would an element of hope, with Charity Camber giving Brett a new terrier cross puppy, who is healthy and vaccinated (free from the very notion of contracting such a horrible disease).

The linkage here in this final moment of the film that brings Donna and Charity together is the fact that Donna has come into Charity's turf and fundamentally has to rescue her little boy. Charity has left her rural terrain in order to give her boy Brett a better life and a chance at happiness, away from the oppressive Joe. Stephen King's novel would discuss Charity's fear of Joe and his heavy handed nature towards their strong but still slightly sensitive sleepwalking son. Donna forces her son back to life in the movie – a decision made by producers and director Lewis Teague, as well as some dramaturgical advice from Dee Wallace herself who insisted the child survive. Stephen King would later go on the record and say that if he could go back in time and rewrite the ending of any of his books it would be "Cujo", where he would write it so Tad would live. Having Tad live works far better in filmic terms – if he was to die, there would be more to explore (Donna and Vic's grief fundamentally) and that wouldn't be a strong finale. Here in Teague's film, Donna is able to breathe life back into Tad, and as he climbs back into his mother's arms – reborn and given a second chance – Cujo leaps through the kitchen window, barking and snarling only to have Donna swiftly turn around, aim Bannerman's gun and fire.

Vic's Jaguar skids onto the Camber farm, he steps out in a panic, scrutinizes the busted and bloodied Pinto and calls out "Donna!" This is the first time Donna has had her name screamed out in a state of desperate need. For the most part, she is referred to as "Mom" or "Mommy" from Tad, but here, finally, her husband cries out her name and two things are happening in this brief final word spoken in the film: firstly, Vic most definitely needs his wife and this showcases this in trumps, secondly, Donna is validated as a human being. She is not simply somebody's wife or mother, she is a person, with feelings, ideas, vulnerabilities, flaws, compassion and a sturdy determination to protect those she loves. The final shot has Donna emerge from the Camber household, holding Tad in her arms and being reunited with Vic. This middle class family with their massive house overlooking the Maine coastline are now sweaty and stressed, ruined by the elements and stuck out on the ratty porch of "mountain people". The Trenton family's reconnection is thematically linked to previous depictions of the Camber front porch – Charity plucking chickens and re-entering the house calls out the routine and sorrowful secrecy that haunted Donna, Brett stepping out on to explore the fog chimes in on an examination of blurred dystopia (something that Vic and Donna face and something that Tad imagines as monsters in his closet), Brett carrying luggage and preparing for the trip to Connecticut evokes the notion of transition, which is something that the Trenton family all face (most notably Donna) and finally the rabid Cujo sitting upon the porch watching the overheated Pinto, growling and waiting for an opportunity to attack – a wonderfully concentrated image of fear just brimming under the surface; something that the Trentons know all too well. Inspired director Lewis Teague decides to use a freeze frame to close his masterpiece. The final shot has Donna let Tad take to his father's arms and as this image of a family reborn fades to black, composer Charles Bernstein's rousing music emerges and ushers in the closing credits as this masterfully conceived and constructed work of art comes to an end.

JOHN PINTAURO: They tried to get the dog to jump through the kitchen window, but he was having trouble doing it. They had him practicing jumping through the window and they had such a hard time doing it, so they had to do it in sections. But eventually they got the scene working, and edited it so it worked in a patchwork of sections. The dogs initially had a problem jumping through the window because the dogs didn't like doing things in front of too many people, because when they practiced it was only really the dog and the trainer. So they would get shy I guess when there was an entire crew and cameras and what not there. They also had a guy dressed in a dog suit to use as well. Gary Morgan was a great guy. I mean between Gary, the real dogs, mechanical head –

Cast and crew of *Cujo*.

I mean it all looked fantastic and turned out real good. Danny always had that amazing ability to understand what the director was trying to get. He could get into character and into the scene very easily, and he has an incredibly good memory, a memory like a trap. He had a very good recall. He would memorize the scripts because at his age during *Cujo* he could not yet read, but he would memorize his lines and everyone else's lines, and this is something that he did also on *As the World Turns*. So, from memorizing everyone else's part, that is how he would cue himself in. It's funny, one of the reasons he got the part on *Who's the Boss?* was when he was doing his lines read for his audition with Tony Danza, he corrected Tony! He said "That's not the words you were supposed to say Tony, how am I supposed to know when I come in?" You see, Tony Danza would go off script all the time, but Danny was determined to make sure each line was learned and said the way it was written on the page. Danny said to Tony "If you can't do your lines right, how do you expect me to do mine?" But just like on *Cujo*, Danny had a wonderful family unit on the set of *Who's the Boss?* – everyone on both projects were so warm and yes, it was like one big happy family.

GARY MORGAN: You can't train a dog to hurt himself at least more than once. You can trick a dog but they don't want to do something that will hurt them. If they are hurt, the dog won't trust the trainer anymore. When the dog runs and smashes against the car door – that was me. When the dogs jumps through the window – they had me jump through the window because they wanted the dog to jump through the window, and they trained the dog to run up this ramp and jump through a window. So they did it a bunch of times and eventually with no glass. Then they did it with a light screen and the dog bit it. As soon as they put the glass in, the dog ran up, stopped short and wouldn't go through the glass. Take five, he runs up, takes his cue and breaks the glass. But still didn't run through it. Dog number three around take six, the producer goes "Get the kid in the suit!" So I put the suit on and I dive through the glass. It's just

Donna Trenton (Dee Wallace) protects her son Tad (Danny Pintauro) and fires the deceased sheriff's gun at the rabid Cujo.

me breaking the glass. Then they got the dog – the real dog – to do the landing and turn around, so it looks like the dog was jumping through.

JOHN PINTAURO: Danny taped most of his lines. I would be too hard on the line running, but my wife was great, she would run through the lines with Danny. I just came for support on a couple of days of the shoot to get away from work at the time, I had a full time career as an agent but Danny's career wasn't planned, it was just happening and happened fast.

DEE WALLACE: I really remember telling Danny on set that it was all pretend and that this was all just a movie. I also had to keep reminding him that the dogs were not at all going to be hurt in anyway, because even at that very young age he was very, very concerned about the safety of the dogs. So I had to reassure him that the dogs were very, very well taken care of and completely ok. He was such a compassionate little boy, even at that very young age. He was very aware of what was going on and he understood that he had to keep a distance from the dogs on set because they had their job to do just like he did. The dogs had their own section and they had to stay away from everyone besides the trainer, because then they wouldn't do their jobs right.

Danny Pintauro behind the scenes in a jacket, protecting himself from the freezing cold during the final scene in the Camber kitchen. The water that Dee Wallace splashes over Danny in this sequence to revive him was hot, simply because the weather was freezing cold. (courtesy of Danny and Margaret Pintauro).

JOHN PINTAURO: I remember Lewis Teague but only to say "Hi, I'm Danny's father", there really was no time to get to know anyone on set.

DEE WALLACE: There would have been some time allowed for me to read the novel, but I never did, because I needed to serve the movie.

There are always some things that are very different from the book and the movie which I knew upfront. Right away Dan asked me if I thought we should kill the child in the end, which is what happens in the book, and I was violently against that. I said "There are gonna be many people who are going to come and see this movie who have not read the book, and to put them through what we're gonna put them through for two hours or so with no pay off...my God", I mean this was the 1980s and that kind of thing just didn't happen. I thought it was totally the wrong call, and in the end, Stephen King contacted us and said "Thank God you didn't kill the kid! I have never gotten as much hate mail as I did when I killed off the kid at the end of 'Cujo'!"

After the harrowing ordeal, Donna Trenton carries her damaged but alive son Tad (Danny Pintauro) to safety and back into normalcy. (courtesy of Gale A. Adler).

MARGARET PINTAURO: I eventually read the book much later. I'm glad the kid got to live in the film. And what a job Danny did. He was two years old when he started acting. He did eighty eight commercials before he started television. On *Cujo*, I never spoke to either directors on the film. I only ever spoke to Dan Blatt. And Danny knew that Dan was great. Even at that young age. Dan Blatt was just wonderful. He was absolutely lovely. He knew what he wanted and he loved Danny and that was that. Dan and I were very close. Also, Danny was about five years old during *Cujo*, so there was no teacher on set, he had not yet started school. He was great on set. My parents came down and my husband's parents came down on visit. You know, Danny did eight years on *Who's the Boss?* and then after that he decided he didn't want to be an actor anymore. He graduated from Stanford University and I had him go to school in the mornings during *Who's the Boss?* so he wouldn't miss any school and then he got into Stanford. We're very proud of him.

The National Theatre screens *Cujo* in 1983. (courtesy of Danny and Margaret Pintauro).

DANIEL HUGH KELLY: I didn't go to the premiere, because I was shooting a series. Even if I wasn't shooting *Hardcastle and McCormick* at the time, I wouldn't have gone to the premiere of *Cujo* anyway. I hate those kind of things. I hate seeing myself on the big screen, I don't do well in that environment, it is so uncomfortable. No matter how good you are, you are terrible in your eyes – you look at yourself and you think, look at that nonsense, I don't believe that, how is anyone going to believe that! I don't like the celebrity part of acting, and I don't like what it does. I rarely do publicity. I am a New York working actor and I am very fortunate to go for forty years of work, but I don't like being in the public's eye. I am very low key.

In Australia, the film played on a double at the Village drive-inn with Halloween III. (ad courtesy of Dean Brandum).

MARGARET PINTAURO: When the filming was done, my husband and I decided to have a party for the first screening of *Cujo*. We invited one hundred and ten people and we rented the whole theatre. It was terrific. We had no children come to the screening however, because it would be too emotional. I just thought the film was perfect. Absolutely fantastic. I loved it.

JOHN PINTAURO: I love the film. It comes on cable all the time and my mother used to call up from New Jersey when this would happen and say "Oh my God, *Cujo* is on TV tonight!" We would all watch it, many times. My parents and my wife's parents visited the set and that was to see Danny work.

CONRAD E. PALMISANO: The biggest thing was that the goal in the movie was to put real jeopardy between the St. Bernard and the actress. I think the movie is very, very successful in accomplishing that! It's a real thing, and it is a very, very scary movie. It's very believable and there is no special effects, there are no visual effects, no green screen, there was no satellite that came from outer space or space ship or whatever, it was just a real dog and a real mother trying to protect her child, and I think the movie is very, very successful in that light and in a realistic sense.

CHARLES BERNSTEIN: I love the shape of the film; it comes to a climax and then there's kind of a nice second climactic area when she thinks the dog is finally dead and so forth. I used silence in certain ways in that confrontation with the dog, where the tension between the notes can be felt. I have to hand it to Lewis Teague. Now, I have worked with Lewis most recently a couple years ago and talked to him a couple days ago. And Lewis just did a superb job on this thing. One thing comes to mind on some of these deaths/murder scenes when the dog kills this one and that one and eventually Dee confronts the dog – Lewis said something in the scene where I think the dog kills the deputy in the barn. There's a harp and a little *zing*! That leads into the attack. And the *zing* happens just before anything else happens on screen. And Lewis said to me, "How

468

does the music know that the attack is going to happen? I don't like that the *zing* is there." And I took a little licence to let the music know a little bit before the characters, but Lewis picked up on that, and ever since then I have been very sensitive to what does the music know? Should it know it? Should the music know that the dog is going to attack? Or should the music attack at the same time? That kind of thinking. Lewis raised throughout the movie interesting questions, so the next time you hear that little attack and you hear a little *zing* that leads into it, Lewis and I discussed that at great length. And finally we decided it's okay for the music to know a split second before the character. But in any case, the scenes like in the climactic scene with Dee and the dog, again is a great gift to the music composer! Because then we get to really, again without a bunch of loud sound effects and without a bunch of dialogue burying the music, it gets to come out and really do its job, and we just thrive on moments like that, us composers!

DEE WALLACE: *Cujo* is my best work. I am incredibly proud of it. I think it's one of the most important horror movies of the eighties and most definitely one of the best Stephen King adaptations. When Stephen King himself said that I should have been nominated for an Academy Award for my performance, that just blew me away. It was an honor to take on such a complex, dynamic, multi-layered and intelligent part. I am proud to be part of such a legacy.

The film wraps, so star, director and "dog" form a kick line to celebrate the end of an intense shoot.

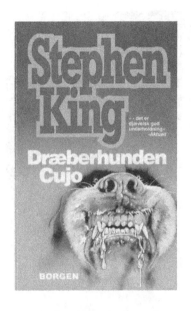

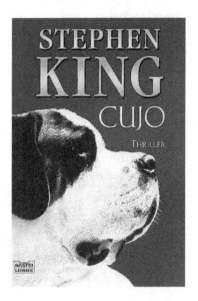

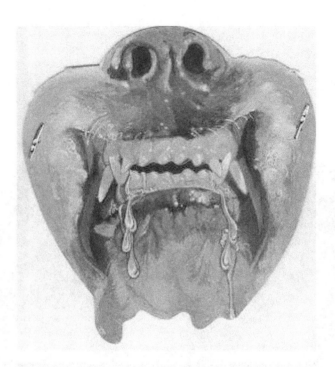

This Halloween be sure to scare them all
with this spectacular Stephen King
Halloween mask. And don't forget to pick
up the King of Horror's #1 bestseller
FOUR PAST MIDNIGHT
NOW AVAILABLE IN PAPERBACK!

Ⓢ
Signet

PRINTED IN U.S.A.

476

INDEX

479

Blair, Linda 11, 275

Blatt, Dan 21, 22, 24, 26, 27, 31, 32, 36, 51, 53, 59, 61, 62, 63, 64, 66, 79, 90, 91, 98, 102, 112, 121, 130, 131, 132, 141, 147, 156, 160, 165, 169, 190, 195, 207, 226, 227, 235, 238, 267, 297, 308, 331, 346, 348, 398, 408, 431, 466

Borgnine, Ernest 180

Bowlby, John   128

Brando, Marlon 142

Bridges, Jeff 79

Buehler, Jack 23, 48, 117, 158, 166, 298, 368, 369, 396, 397

Burstyn, Ellen 42, 441

Call of the Wild, The (book) 4

Cameron's Closet 43

Candyman 155

Carousel 181

Carpenter, John 41, 83, 272

Carr, Larry 383

Carrie 3, 63, 99, 202, 346, 457

Carrie (book) 41, 44, 99, 182, 202, 239

Carroll, Lewis 10, 266

Casablanca 136

Cat's Eye 29, 415, 416

Chained Heat 57, 58

Changeling, The 42, 62, 64, 66

Cherie, Jean 383

Christine 41, 83, 145

Christine (book) 4, 14, 272, 273

Clark, Kathie 20, 306, 328, 330, 364, 371, 372, 375, 376, 378, 380, 381, 383, 400, 409

Clark, Robert 20, 306, 308, 318, 330, 370, 372, 378, 380, 383, 400, 408, 410

Comtois, Guy J. 20, 50, 52, 84, 87, 184, 368

Corman, Roger 41, 132, 268, 300, 301, 389

Coulter, Jean 322, 330, 332, 367, 368, 370, 372, 373, 375, 376, 377, 381, 384, 385, 386, 388, 391, 392, 398, 399, 408, 410, 412

Craighead, Robert 167, 169, 170, 171, 173, 174, 175, 176, 177, 178

Cranes are Flying, The 47, 49, 56

Crawford, Joan 168

Cronenberg, David 41, 44, 420, 421

Cubby (dog) 116, 249, 277, 279, 287, 332, 333, 335, 384, 385, 386, 391, 410, 433, 434

Gordon, Keith 146
Grandey, Jerry   29, 122, 134
Gremlins 171, 173
Guc, David 54

Hanna-Barbera 69, 70, 71, 74
Hardin, Jerry 419, 422, 423, 438
Hearst, Patty 1
Heart, John X. 103
Higgins (dog) 6, 9, 261, 427
Hilkene, Michael 155, 187, 189. 252, 283, 325, 327, 416, 432
Hitchcock, Alfred 63, 64
Holstra, Judith 55, 61
Hooper, Tobe 46, 430
Howling, The 51, 113, 141, 201, 226, 245, 298, 304, 370, 443
Hudson, Rock 10

I Never Promised You A Rose Garden 66
Incredible Journey, The (1963) 109
Independence Day (1983) 121

Jacoby, Billy 106, 110, 111, 113, 118, 168, 185, 218, 219, 220, 234, 235,
    237
Jagger, Bianca   79
Jagger, Mick 66
Jason-Leigh, Jennifer 34
Jaws 94, 96, 292, 301
Jaws 2 375
Jazz Singer, The (1979) 57
Jones, Alan Roderick 134
Jones, Shirley 181

Kahn, Madeline 27
Kalatozov, Mikhail 47
Kelly, Daniel Hugh 26, 27, 54, 61, 62, 76, 77, 78, 85, 93, 95, 96, 100, 101,
    102, 104, 114, 116, 118, 119, 133, 134, 137, 142, 147, 165, 195, 201,
    206, 215, 224, 226, 230, 236, 279, 300, 329, 338, 339, 377, 396, 422,
    423, 437, 445, 467
Kelly, Nancy 129
Kincaid, Ian 114, 219. 349
King Kong (1976) 168

Miller, Karl Lewis xii, 12, 29, 34, 37, 125, 191, 241, 251, 252, 253, 254, 255, 274, 275, 282, 285, 287, 288, 289, 295, 298, 300, 307, 308, 316, 320, 323, 328, 329, 332, 333, 335, 346, 376, 383, 384, 386, 393, 409, 427, 432, 433, 434, 453, 454
Miller, Teresa Ann 37, 124, 190, 222, 246, 250, 252, 260, 261, 262, 283, 299, 319, 322, 328, 329, 332, 334, 388, 392, 415
Misery 442, 445
Misery (book) 45
Moe (dog) 248, 253, 287, 327, 328
Monty Python 171
Morgan, Gary 34, 220, 227, 228, 237, 250, 251, 261, 278, 282, 299, 318, 319, 332, 339, 346, 348, 350, 351, 352, 353, 354, 355, 356, 357, 360, 361, 364, 365, 366, 367, 376, 377, 379, 381, 388, 391, 399, 408, 410, 412, 413, 429, 434, 448, 453, 460, 462, 470
Morrow, Vic 34
Murder Inc. 61

Navy Seals 51
Neill, Ve 27, 389
Nobles, Vern 115, 196, 284, 285, 286, 331
Nono, Clare 139, 140

O'Rourke, Heather 43
O'Toole, Peter 23, 27, 414
Old Yeller 6, 8, 11, 168, 217
Oldman, Gary 90
Olsen, Merritt 73, 74

Palmisano, Conrad E. 255, 260, 300, 308, 365, 368, 392, 433, 468
Peter Pan 4, 5
Peyton Place (book) 130
Pintauro, Danny 42, 45, 49, 50, 51, 52, 53, 57, 58, 61, 63, 64, 67, 76, 77, 78, 81, 86, 96, 97, 111, 112, 114, 118, 120, 123, 124, 133, 134, 135, 136, 166, 189, 194, 195, 196, 197, 208, 210, 213, 215, 216, 237, 238, 248, 249, 266, 267, 268, 274, 277, 282, 283, 293, 297, 306, 309, 317, 320, 324, 325, 326, 327, 333, 334, 345, 346, 347, 349, 364, 365, 373, 381, 397, 399, 404, 406, 407, 408, 430, 438, 447, 449, 452, 453, 454, 455, 462, 463, 464, 465, 466, 468
Pintauro, Margaret 51, 52, 53, 63, 78, 86, 96, 123, 126, 166, 194, 213, 237, 238, 309, 327, 345, 373, 381, 408, 449, 453, 454, 455, 464, 466, 467
Pintauro, John 452, 460, 463, 464, 468
Polanksi, Roman 10

485

Stone, Christopher 51, 71, 76, 78, 79, 85, 86, 113, 170, 171, 201, 203, 208, 405, 411, 420, 421, 422, 450
Storm Fear 73
Sword and the Sorcerer, The 27, 389

Teague, Lewis 5, 10, 20, 21, 22, 23, 24, 25, 27, 28, 29, 30, 32, 41, 42, 43, 47, 49, 50, 55, 58, 59, 61, 63, 64, 66, 71, 76, 77, 79, 80, 85, 86, 87, 89, 96, 98, 99, 100, 102, 107, 109, 112, 113, 116, 121, 122, 129, 130, 133, 134, 141, 143, 146, 147, 148, 155, 156, 158, 161, 173, 174, 175, 178, 180, 182, 187, 189, 190, 195, 196, 199, 201, 206, 207, 209, 223, 226, 227, 243, 248, 252, 253, 257, 259, 265, 266, 267, 268, 271, 272, 273, 275, 277, 280, 281, 282, 283, 287, 293, 294, 297, 299, 300, 306, 313, 318, 320, 326, 327, 328, 329, 331, 344, 346, 347, 359, 366, 367, 381, 384, 396, 398, 399, 407, 409, 411, 412, 413, 414, 416, 417, 425, 429, 432, 435, 438, 445, 459, 460, 464, 468, 469, 470
Texas Chain Saw Massacre, The 105
They Only Kill Their Masters 299
Tiffany (dog) 9, 10
Travis, Neil 5, 121, 132, 155, 180, 242, 259, 399, 403, 429
Turner, Barbara 13, 34, 35, 42, 43, 44, 59, 62, 63, 64, 65, 66, 90, 91, 92, 102, 107, 114, 116, 121, 141, 158, 160, 164, 182, 201, 204, 207, 209, 210, 257, 312, 420, 429
Turning Point, The 159

Ulano, Mark 81, 120, 121, 122, 230, 231, 321, 327, 389, 390, 449, 450

Vamp 448
Vi pa Salykrakan 4

Wallace, Dee 1, 2, 11, 22, 34, 45, 51, 56, 58, 61, 67, 72, 73, 76, 77, 79, 89, 90, 91, 95, 96, 107, 108, 113, 116, 117, 119, 120, 123, 130, 132, 133, 137, 142, 143, 158, 159, 165, 169, 170, 171, 172, 173, 174, 189, 199, 201, 202, 203, 204, 206, 208, 209, 210, 224, 225, 226, 228, 248, 266, 267, 268, 274, 275, 276, 277, 278, 280, 281, 282, 283, 285, 287, 291, 293, 296, 298, 299, 304, 306, 316, 317, 318, 320, 321, 322, 324, 325, 327, 328, 331, 338, 342, 346, 347, 348, 354, 364, 365, 366, 367, 369, 370, 373, 374, 381, 383, 385, 396, 397, 398, 399, 404, 407, 409, 410, 419, 420, 422, 426, 430, 431, 434, 438, 442, 443, 445, 446, 447, 448, 449, 450, 452, 453, 459, 463, 464, 468, 469, 470
Watson, Mills 180, 187, 188, 189, 240, 241, 242, 246, 247, 255, 357
West Side Story 159
White Buffalo, The 168

Lee Gambin is a writer, author and film historian. He has written for Fangoria, Shock Till You Drop, Delirium, Scream Magazine among other horror periodicals and sites. He is the author of books "Massacred By Mother Nature: Exploring the Natural Horror Film", "We Can Be Who We Are: Movie Musicals of the 1970s" and the soon to be released "The Howling: Studies in the Horror Film". He lives in Melbourne, Australia with his dog Buddy (pictured here with another favorite killer dog movie to enjoy).

CPSIA information can be obtained
at www.ICGtesting.com
Printed in the USA
LVHW080956280220
648510LV00016B/396